The New Encyclopaedia
of Fly Fishing

The New Encyclopaedia of Fly Fishing

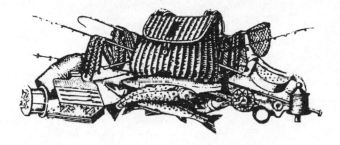

Conrad Voss Bark
and Eric Restall

ROBERT HALE • LONDON

© Conrad Voss Bark 1986
© Conrad Voss Bark and Eric Restall 1999
First edition 1986
Second edition, completely revised and reset, 1999

ISBN 0 7090 6308 3

Robert Hale Limited
Clerkenwell House
Clerkenwell Green
London EC1R 0HT

Designed by Kina Parker-Restall
Typeset in Palatino by Pitfold Design, Hindhead, Surrey
Printed in Great Britain by St Edmundsbury Press Limited and
bound by WBC Book Manufacturers Limited, Bridgend

Introduction

Unlike the making of dictionaries, which according to Johnson is dull work, we found the preparation of this revised and expanded encyclopaedia to be a most challenging and enjoyable experience, made somewhat easier by the existence of the first edition which was – and we believe is still – the first work of its kind devoted entirely to fly fishing in Great Britain. In addition to reviewing all the original entries, some of which we allowed to stand with little or no amendment, there are many new items, including for the first time information on Ireland, competitive fishing, tackle collecting, angling books, an expanded account of Welsh water, angling for the disabled and overseas fishing which has now become so very popular. Since the first edition there have been many technological developments in the realm of rod manufacture, lines, leaders, safety equipment, etc., all of which are described here. Public concern is mounting over diminishing stocks of both salmon and sea-trout, and whilst the future is bleak it is nevertheless encouraging to learn of the personal, national and international efforts being made to address a major problem which has many complex causes.

Fly fishing has a long and noble past, and we make no apology for dwelling so much on the origins of the sport, for it is only by knowing something of its history that we can begin to understand the current scene, be it on chalk streams, still water fisheries, rivers, lochs or reservoirs – all of which play an equally important role in the pastime we so cherish.

Our objective has been to provide detailed information on all aspects of fly fishing. Inevitably some decisions had to be made on a subjective basis and if, here and there, our personal preferences show through, so be it. The various entries are arranged in alphabetical order. These include descriptions of all the major rivers, lochs, lakes, still water fisheries and reservoirs and how to fish them; tackle and techniques that can be used for salmon, sea-trout, brown and rainbow trout;

fisherman's knots, casting, traditional and contemporary fly dressings; short summaries of the most significant books written about the sport and biographical notes on their authors. Longer entries offer advice on all aspects of game angling: techniques of fishing the dry fly, nymph upstream and downstream fishing, lures, dapping, etc. There are essays on the history of fly fishing and details of the major organisations and clubs connected with the sport. We have also included a Select Bibliography which provides details of publisher, significant reissues and new editions of all the major books concerned with fly fishing.

No work of this kind could have been written without the contributions and advice of many other like-minded individuals, all of whom we have sought to list in the Acknowledgements.

We welcome both comment and criticism, and suggestions for further editions, which should be addressed to us care of the publisher, Robert Hale Ltd, 45-47 Clerkenwell Green, London EC1R 0HT.

Conrad Voss Bark, Lifton, Devon
Eric Restall, Hindhead, Surrey
November 1998

Acknowledgements

No encyclopaedia of fly fishing covering every aspect of the subject in England, Wales, Scotland and Ireland would have been possible without the enormous enthusiasm and help of so many people whose names in gratitude we list below.

We thank Sandy Leventon, editor of *Trout & Salmon*, and David Barr, editor of *The Haig Guide to Salmon Fishing in Scotland*, for their contributions on the Atlantic salmon; Peter O'Reilly who knows more about fishing in Ireland than anyone we know; Professor Graham G. Shaw, chairman of the Irish Save Our Sea Trout Campaign (SOS); Dr A. G. Owen and other members of the Environment Agency; Dr Malcolm Windsor of the North Atlantic Salmon Conservation Organisation (NASCO); Dr R. G. J. Shelton of the Freshwater Fisheries Laboratory at Pitlochry; Ken Vickers for details of his research into salmon catches; Sandy Forgan of the Scottish Sea Trout campaign; to former staff members of the late National Rivers Authority and their counterparts in Ireland; the Salmon Research Agency in Mayo; Orri Vigfussson, chairman of the North Atlantic Salmon Fund whose main concern in life is to save the salmon from extinction; John Goddard who more than anyone has been responsible for our knowledge of fly life and fishing techniques; members of the Institute of Freshwater Ecology, the Salmon & Trout Association; John Parkman of the Countryside Alliance, the secretary and librarian of the Flyfishers' Club of London and Dr Shelton for information on transgenic salmon. Sandy Leventon, editor of *Trout & Salmon*, for permission to use material from an article by Dick Stephen and John Maitland on monofilaments in the issue dated May 1997.

Over the years we have learned a great deal from so many fishery owners, anglers and gillies, and would like to thank them all especially Peter Mantle of the Delphi Fishery; Kieran and Thelma Thompson of Newport House fishery in Mayo;

7

Denys Janes and Robert Starr of the Hungerford water of the Kennet; James O'Hara of Beltra, Jack and Daphne Bourke of the Test, members and gillies of the Carron beat of the Spey; Mick Lunn and Guy Robinson of the Test; Ray Hill; Donald Carr of Blagdon; Alex Behrendt and his wife, Kathleen, of Two Lakes, near Romsey; John Henderson, Dermot Wilson, Peter Rennie, Graham Swanson, James Henderson, James O'Hara, Hugh Falkus, David Jacques, Peggy Baring, Peter Borenius, P. K. George, Geoffrey Snutch, Ken Sutton, Don Thompson, Jack Thorndike, Major John Walker, Nancy Whitlock, Alick Newsom, Willie Cox, Tom Kenny of the Spey, Ron Holloway, Roy Darlington of Abbotts Barton, Lawrie Williamson of Blagdon, Oliver Kite, Donald Overfield, John Ashley-Cooper, T. C. Kingsmill Moore, Lee Wulff, Brian Clarke, Jack Heddon, Allen Edward, Charles Jardine, Charles Bingham, Gerald Hadoke, Roy Buckingham and David Pilkington of the Arundell Arms, Jean Williams, Kees Ketting, Frank Sawyer, Jack Chance, Dr J. M. Elliot of the Freshwater Biological Association, Charles Ritz, Bruce Sandison, Peter Deane and Jeremy Read of the Atlantic Salmon Trust.

To members of the Anglers' Club of New York and all our American friends who helped with the creation of this book: James M. Stewart, Herb Wellington, Colton and Carley Wagner, Craig Matthews, Nick and Mari Lyons, James Stewart and Laurie Williamson.

Fred Buller for writing the entry on pike fishing; Dr Ron Broughton for advice and the entry on grayling fishing; the unfailing courtesy and advice so freely given by Peter Cockwill; Pat O'Reilly, Environment Agency Wales and the Welsh Tourist Board for permission to use material from their publication *Fishing Wales*; John C. Branford, Director Department of Fish, Game and Wildlife Management, Sparsholt College; Orvis for technical advice and details of their bestselling flies; Martin Kendall for his encouragement and endless suggestions; Jonathan Young, editor of *The Field*; Anglers' Conservation Association for permission to quote from their leaflet 'What to Do in the Case of Pollution'; John Norris for their list of bestselling flies; Mike Tudor, Chairman, Committee for the Promotion of Angling for the Disabled; Southern Water for information on Bewl Water; John and Judith Head for bibliographical information; Northumbrian Water for details of their several fisheries; Bristol Water for information on Chew Valley, Blagdon and Barrows; Stan

Headley for permission to quote from his book, *Trout Fishing on Orkney*; Andrew Witkowski, General Manager of Farlow's for a host of things including their list of bestselling flies and for their generosity in providing the cover picture; Taff Price, Michael Evans, Jason Parker, Mike Weaver; the British Record (rod-caught) Fish Committee for permission to reproduce their game fish records; the Environment Agency, and in particular Darryl Clifton-Dey, Fisheries Officer, for information on the river Thames and on matters relating to pollution; Tony Pawson OBE and John Boon CBE for assistance with the competitive scene; David Moore, Recreation Development Manager of Anglian Water, for assistance with the Rutland, Ravensthorpe and Grafham articles; J. M. Partridge of Evans & Partridge and Bonhams for permission to use details from their auction sale records; Paul Morgan for the entry on Saltwater Flyfishing and assistance with the Bibliography; Ian Campbell of SANA and IFFA; Bob Church and Crowood Press for permission to use an extract from *Bob Church's Guide to New Fly Patterns*; Bob Church, again, for allowing us to use material from *Reservoir Trout Fishing* and *Bob Church's Guide to Trout Flies* in the preparation of the Reservoir Fishing entry; the following publishers for permission to use extracts: A & C Black for permission to quote from David Jacques' *Development of Modern Stillwater Fishing*; John Murray: William Radcliff's *Fishing From Earliest Times* and Clive Holloway: *Tunnicliffe's Countryside*.

Lastly, but of course by no means the least our thanks to our respective wives, Anne and Patricia who are both anglers, for their invaluable encouragement and help.

Abbreviations

ACA Angler's Conservation Association (formerly Angler's Co-operative Association)

AFTM American Fishing Tackle Manufacturers

APGAI Association of Professional Game Angling Instructors. *See* GAIA

ASGFM Association of Stillwater Game Fishery Managers

AST Atlantic Salmon Trust

BWO Blue Winged Olive

CEFAS Centre for Environment Fisheries and Aquaculture Science

CEFF Confederation of English Fly Fishers

CPAD Committee for the Promotion of Angling for the Disabled

DT Double taper

EA Environment Agency

EDFF English Disabled Fly Fishers

ELFA English Ladies Flyfishing Association

EYFA English Youth Flyfishing Association

F Floating

FCL Fly Fishers Classic Library

FDG Fly Dressers' Guild

FISPM Fédération Internationale de Sportive Pêche Mouche

F/S (after the line size) denotes sink tip

GAIA Game Angling Instructors Association (formerly the Association of Professional Game Angling Instructors)

GRHE Gold Ribbed Hare's Ear

HAT Handicapped Anglers Trust

HMIP Her Majesty's Inspectorate of Pollution

I Intermediate

ICES International Council for the Exploration of the Sea

IFFA International Fly Fishing Association

IHN Infectious Haematopoietic Necrosis

ISA Infectious Salmon Anaemia

ITFFA Irish Trout Fly Fishing Association

L level

NASCO North Atlantic Salmon Conservation Organisation

ND neutral density

NRA National Rivers Authority

REFFIS Register of Experienced Fly Fishing Instructors and Schools

S Sinking

SANA Scottish Anglers' National Association

SFFRG Salmon and Freshwater Fisheries Review Group

SLF Synthetic Living Fibre

ST Shooting taper

S&TA Salmon & Trout Association

STANIC Salmon & Trout Association National Instructors Certificate

TT Triangle taper

UDN Ulcerative Dermal Necrosis

VHS Viral Haemorrhagic Septicaemia

WF Weight Forward

WS&TA Welsh Salmon & Trout Association

Ace of Spades A reservoir wet fly, designed by David Collyer, popular in the 1970s and 1980s, a nice blend of matuka and black lure styles. It can be fished at all levels and is at its best during the early part of the season.

Body: black chenille
Rib: oval silver tinsel
Wing: matuka-style wing, black hen, tied down by the silver rib
Tail: black hen fibres
Overwing: dark mallard blended over the black hen
Hackle: beard-style guinea-fowl
Hook: 6 to 10, long shank

Adams The Adams, a standard American high-riding fly that makes imprints on the water only by the hackle and tail, like the Grey Wulff, had an astonishing success on the Abbotts Barton water of the Itchen in 1994 taking some 10 per cent of all fish caught on the dry fly (see *The Dry Fly: Progress Since Halford*). It suggests practically all the mayflies, olives, iron blues, blue winged olives and pale wateries. Dressings vary slightly.
Body: original muskrat or similar from rabbit or synthetics
Wings: two grizzle hackle-tips, tied in upright and slightly spread, not too close to the eye of the hook
Tail: a number of long mixed grizzly and brown hackles tied close together
Front hackle: mixed brown or grizzly
The hackles and the long tail lift the fly off the water.

Adamson, W. A. *Lake and Loch Fishing for Salmon and Sea Trout* is memorable because in it Adamson gives the description by David McNaught of the take of the 19½lb sea-trout on the dap on the Ash Island beat of Loch Maree on 25 September 1951: 'To this day I can still remember the expression on the gillie's face when he found he could not lift the net out of the water at the first attempt . . . .' The fish was taken on a Black Pennell which McNaught said was dressed 'like an inverted umbrella' on a 1/0 salmon hook, 14lb nylon, a mercerised cotton floss line and a 15-ft split-cane rod.

Aelian (AD 170-230) A Roman writer of natural history who gave the first surviving description of fly fishing. William Radcliff in *Fishing From the Earliest Times* gives the following text of the fishing in Macedonia from the Lambert translation:

> They fasten red wool round a hook and fix on to the wool two feathers which grow under a cock's wattles, and which in colour are like wax. Their rod is six feet long and their line of the same length. Then they throw their snare and the fish, maddened and excited by the colour, come straight at it, thinking by the sight to get a dainty mouthful; when, however, it opens its jaws, it is caught by the hook and enjoys a bitter repast, a captive.

Alaw Reservoir A 780-acre lowland lake on the isle of Anglesey noted for its rich wildlife and big brownies. Ideally suited to bank fishing but can be testing because of its clear water and the abundance of food, which makes the fish very selective.

Aldam, W. H. A Victorian fisherman with a sense of humour who produced a book in 1876 entitled *A Quaint Treatyse on Flees and Artyfichall Flee-Making*, based on a manuscript of a hundred years or so earlier. It contained not only the details of the tying of about 25 Derbyshire trout flies but mounted specimens of the flies themselves and of materials of which they were made. A rare and curious book much sought after by collectors; an association copy, containing a signed photograph of the author, was listed in a 1996 specialist dealer's catalogue at £1,600, and two years later, £1,750 was the asking price for a copy of the first edition. Aldam was among the first members of the Flyfishers' Club. He died in 1888.

Alder A rather dark fly, somewhat like a sedge, but with very dark black-veined wings which fold into a roof shape. Although shaped like a sedge, it is shiny, more like a stonefly. The alder frequently lands on hands and clothing and stays there for some time unless disturbed. The natural alder fly is

not often found on the water but an artificial pattern, highly praised by Charles Kingsley, and often fished wet, will take fish when alders are about. Goddard suggests this might be because the trout take it for its resemblance to an emerging mayfly nymph, or even a sedge; Harris suggests a sedge, a large heavy fly of the blue-bottle type, or even a beetle. On lakes the imitation, according to John Roberts, is best fished as a sub-surface pattern, but on rivers both the sunken and floating are effective. Taff Price takes a contrary view, for he says, 'I am one of those fishermen who has never caught a fish on the dry alder fly'. Artificial patterns are often localised – the Herefordshire Alder, the Derbyshire Alder – but the following is a reasonable compromise:

> *Body:* purple or dark brown floss silk
> *Wings:* roof-shaped; matched pair of slips taken from pheasant, grouse or partridge wings, speckled, and as dark as possible, lying flat and close to the body
> *Hackle:* black cock
> *Hook:* 12 or 10

Alexandra A wet fly designed by George M. Kelson, mostly used on lakes for trout, on rivers for sea-trout, suggesting in appearance a spawning stickleback. The fly was named Alexandra after the Danish princess who married Prince Edward of Wales, later King Edward VII, in 1863. According to some accounts it was banned in the early days because of its success.

> *Body:* flat silver tinsel from tail to head
> *Tail:* originally ibis, now generally bright scarlet floss
> *Wings:* strands of green peacock herl
> *Cheeks:* originally ibis, but now bright red or scarlet feather fibres
> *Hackle:* black hen
> *Hook:* from 6 long shank for sea-trout down to ordinary size 10 for lake trout – but the startling effect of bright green, scarlet and silver is inclined to be lost if the hook size is too small.

Allen The river Allen is in Dorset, rising near Sixpenny Handley and winding its brief way through lovely country into the Stour at Wimborne. One of the most beautiful of the chalk streams in miniature, those who have rods on the Allen try to keep it a secret. Though it is in part stocked, the wild brown trout grow large and cautious, and must be approached with due care, fine nylon and small flies. Beacon Beige, Pheasant Tail, Black Gnat are popular in sizes from 14 to 18 or 20.

Quite apart from producing wild and beautiful trout, the Allen for many years held the official record for the biggest English grayling – not up to Austrian standards, but by no means bad at 3lb 10oz – taken by Mr Iain White on 28 August 1983.

The Earl of Shaftesbury owns the upper five or six miles and allows the Bull Inn at Wimborne St Giles to let a limited number of rods to residents. Otherwise rods are difficult to come by – as indeed they are on most of the smaller southern chalk streams.

Alness   A short salmon and sea-trout river which runs into the Cromarty Firth. The Alness Angling Club lets rods, and fishing can also be had by residents of the Dunraven Hotel, Strathpeffer, and the Coul Hotel, Contin.

Amber Nymph   An imitative wet fly, almost entirely used for reservoir and southern lake fishing, first dressed at Blagdon, Somerset by the local doctor, Dr Bell, at some time in the late 1920s. It suggests a sedge pupa. Richard Walker's Chomper patterns have affinities. Dr Bell's original Amber Nymph was lightly dressed:

> *Body:* amber seal's fur
> *Back:* a strip of dark feather fibres from the head of the fly to the tail, sometimes (though not always) varnished
> *Hackle:* one or two turns only of a dark reddish hackle at the head
> *Hook:* generally 14

Seventy years later the Amber Nymph is still a favourite for bank fishing at Blagdon. Most modern dressings are too heavy and have strange additions, such as a peacock herl head. One of Dr Bell's original dressings is in the Flyfishers' Club, London.

Andrews, Ted   An artist and fly-tyer, a contributor to the *Anglers' Mail* and other journals. Ted Andrew's book, *Basic Fly Tying in Pictures*, is an excellent introduction for beginners with matched drawings and captions illustrating the tyings stage by stage.

Anglers' Club of New York, The   Originally formed in 1906 as a casting club holding fly and bait casting tournaments on one of the ponds in Central Park, New York City, The Anglers' Club is a gentleman's social club whose members are keenly interested in the sport of fly fishing.   The club is unique in that, although located at 101 Broad Street in the financial center of the city, it is not, like other clubs, used for the transaction of business or business entertaining.   The Waltonian legend over the door, 'Piscatoribus sacrum' has been so well respected over the years that a pleasant spot without any aspects of the market place has been preserved for relaxation in congenial fellowship.

The club has a substantial collection of angling and sporting literature including a considerable number of rare works. Some fifty of the club's members have authored close to two hundred books on fishing which are included in the library. The club's Bulletin, which has been published three times a year since the early 1920s, is produced exclusively for members of the club and consists of articles, anecdotes and book reviews written by members.

Several fishing outings are held each year.   A major outing is held each spring over a long weekend at a destination within driving distance of New York City, and a similar day-long outing is held in the Fall.   Smaller outings with limited attendance are held in Canada, the Bahamas and in private fishing clubs around the United States, and are well attended by both resident and non-resident members.   Lunch is served daily to members and guests, and a series of dinner programs is held.

Anglers' Conservation Association (formerly Anglers' Co-operative Association).   For over fifty years the ACA has fought 'the most successful war waged against pollution by any voluntary body in the world'.   In its very first legal action against pollution, and with a fund standing at just £200, it forced a city corporation to spend £1.8 million (£25 million in present-day terms) on a new sewerage system.   More recently the ACA negotiated compensation totalling £325,000 for an escape of flux oil which destroyed fish along the length of the river Tees.   This sum was secured on behalf of the Tees Fisheries Action Committee, representing 42 claimants hit by the disaster; the committee has stayed in being to administer the award and ensure that it is devoted to continued protection and improvement of the river.

At any one time the ACA has 35 to 40 cases on its books. Individuals, angling clubs and associations are powerless to act alone – it is only by the strength and reputation of such a body as the ACA that the fight against pollution, and the protection of our environment, can continue. Despite its many successes over half a century the ACA, a voluntary funded body, desperately requires your help; a nominal £8 (1998) by way of an annual subscription is all that it costs to become a member. The work of the ACA benefits not just the angler, but everyone who loves the countryside. Anglers' Conservation Association, Shalford Dairy, Aldermaston, Reading, Berkshire RG7 4NB.

Anglesey, Angling on *See* Alaw Reservoir.

Angling books Angling has a rich literary history, perhaps more so than any other sporting pastime, and fly fishing over the centuries has attracted many talented writers. Most of the standard works are referred to throughout the text of the *Encyclopaedia* and wherever possible we have provided in the Select Bibliography details of the publisher, date of first publication, any important reissues and new editions. Some of these titles are long out of print – rare titles eagerly sought after by the collector. There are several specialist dealers (a short list is given below) who issue catalogues at regular intervals. Another source is the angling tackle auctions, held from time to time, by Bonhams, Evans & Partridge, Angling Auctions and Mullock-Madeley, etc. Superb facsimiles are published by the Fly Fishers Classic Library, 3 North Street, Ashburton, Devon TQ13 7QL. The abbreviation FCL is used throughout our text and in the Select Bibliography to denote such an edition, where available.

Good second-hand books can be obtained from:

John & Judith Head
The Barn Book Supply
88 Crane Street, Salisbury, Wilts SP1 2QD

John Scott (Sporting Books)
Wynniatts Way, Abberley, Worcs WR6 6BZ

Wigley Books
Morewood House, Abbey Place,
Pershore WR10 1JE

Coch-y-Bonddu Books (Paul Morgan)
Machynlleth,
Mid-Wales SY20 8DJ
Bookshop offering current and out- of- print titles

See also Tackle Collecting.

Annan A good-quality salmon river in Dumfriesshire. The Newby estates have a beat above the estuary which is good for the early run. Rods are at times available from Castle Mill and Annandale Estates, and the Hallsheath Estate has many miles of fly-only water. The Red House at Newton Wamphray has three beats covering about nine miles with salmon at their best at the end of the season and sea-trout around mid-summer; large brown trout are taken on dry fly and nymph in late April and May.

Ants At times there can be a heavy fall of winged ants on rivers, which attracts the attention of trout. Dressings of artificial ants have been largely neglected. Here is Charles Cotton's:

> *Red Ant:* the dubbing of brown and red camlet [wool] well mixed, with a light grey wing
> *Black Ant:* the dubbing of the black-brown hair of a cow, some red warped in for the tag of his tail, and a dark wing

A killing fly. This is a version some 230 years later by F. M. Halford:

> *Body:* split into two parts, a thicker and longer abdomen, a smaller thorax, made up of red or black floss silk
> *Wings:* white or blue grey hackle points tied between abdomen and thorax

And to take it into the present-day, here is John Roberts's Black Ant:

> *Body:* Black tying thread built up to form an abdomen and a thorax with a waist in the middle, and then varnished
> *Wing:* Blue dun or white cock hackle-tips tied spent
> *Hackle:* black cock wound at either the waist or shoulder

APGAI The Association of Professional Game Angling Instructors now known as the Game Angling Instructors Association (GAIA). Confusingly, the original abbreviation,

APGAI, rather than GAIA, is used by qualified members.

See GAIA.

Appetiser A reservoir lure designed in 1972 by Bob Church, which might well double as a night sea-trout fly:

> *Body:* white chenille, ribbed silver tinsel
> *Wing:* large spray of white marabou herl
> *Overwing:* natural grey squirrel- tail
> *Throat hackle and tail*: a mix of dyed feather fibres – orange, green and silver
> *Hook:* 6 to 10 long shank

Said to be the first British lure to use marabou in the dressing, it is really successful when fished close to the surface film.

Arndilly Fancy An excellent salmon fly, named after the Arndilly beat of the Spey. It originated in the 1950s, but it is said to have inherited characteristics of an earlier trout pattern. There is confusion about who first dressed the Arndilly, but here is John Macdonald's version:

> *Tag:* silver oval tinsel or wire
> *Tail:* golden pheasant crest
> *Body:* yellow floss with silver tinsel overlay
> *Hackle:* bright blue wound around behind head forming a 'muff' under the wing
> *Wing:* black or dark brown fur: stoat's tail, black bear or equivalent
> *Eye:* jungle cock (or omit)
> *Head:* red lacquer or red thread

Arrow, Lough   Lough Arrow in Co. Sligo is one of Ireland's great trout fishing centres with free angling for wild brown trout; the average is 1½lb, with the occasional seven-pounder. The duck fly comes up in March and the may fly from about mid-May to mid-June. Another great attraction is fishing the drift in August and September. Avoid the dinghy sailing and surf-boarding. Good professional boatmen are available. Accommodation at the Rock View Hotel, Ballindoon, Riverstown and several other hotels in the vicinity.

Ashley-Cooper, John (1914 -1986) One of the greatest salmon fishermen of his generation. John fished more or less consistently every season and for most of the season for some fifty years, catching many thousands of salmon mostly (though not entirely) in Scottish rivers. His books *The Great Salmon Rivers of Scotland* and *A Salmon Fisher's Odyssey* are valuable guides, as is *A Ring of Wessex Water*. He was a modest man, not boastful like Kelson, for he often said that the more you fished the less you seemed to know about it. He was a member of the Wessex Water Authority, a former secretary of the Test and Itchen Fishing Association, and a director of Farlow's of Pall Mall.

Ashmere Four well-stocked lakes in Felix Lane, Shepperton, Middlesex, with a devoted following of Londoners who make up the majority of this season-ticket fishery. Both bank and boat fly fishing are available. The present owner has been running the fishery since 1964. One interesting point about Ashmere is that the fishing season is divided into two halves, 15 February to 15 July and then from 25 September to 15 December – the reason being that the water in this area heats up in mid-summer and the fishing goes off until the cooler weather arrives in September. Excellent clubroom facilities, parking, etc. Instruction available.

Association of Stillwater Game Fishery Managers (ASGFM) Formed in 1984 with the twin aims of raising standards at still water game fisheries and of ensuring that members receive full and effective recognition in dealings with the various authorities now involved in the sport. Membership ranges from the largest fisheries in the country to some of the smallest, but, large or small, all share a professional commitment to the highest standards of still water trout fishing. Association of Stillwater Game Fishery Managers, Packington Fisheries, Meriden, Coventry CV7 7HR.

Atlantic Salmon Trust Formed in 1967 to encourage and give practical assistance to the conservation of Atlantic salmon and sea-trout. It does that by providing a source of advice to government departments and fishery authorities, and to members of both Houses of Parliament, on subjects affecting the wild Atlantic salmon, so that conservation and management decisions may be taken on the basis of the best information available. With its French and North American counterparts, the Trust has obtained support from the European Union for the principles of effective salmon

conservation. It helped to inspire the formation of the North Atlantic Salmon Conservation Organisation, which regulates salmon fishing at sea, and at whose meetings the Trust is a recognised observer. The Trust also works in close harmony with the Salmon & Trout Association and with the Scottish Anglers' National Association. The Trust, a registered charity, is funded by voluntary contributions from individuals, trusts and organisations interested in salmon conservation. It receives no support from any government funds.
Director: J. B. D. Read, Moulin, Pitlochry, Perthshire PH16 5JQ.

See also North Atlantic Salmon Conservation Organisation.

Austin, R. S.   A West Country fly-dresser, R. S. Austin, became famous by his association with G. E. M. Skues who fell in love with one of Austin's creations which was originally called the Red Spinner. Skues rechristened it Tup's Indispensable – tup's because tup was the local name for a ram (some of the dubbing was taken from a ram's private parts), and indispensable because it took fish when other flies did not. It became the rage, and Austin was inundated with orders and consequently became sick of the Tup's, longing to get back to tying his other famous Devon patterns – the Blue Upright and Pheasant Tail. After his death in 1911, the fly-tying business was carried on by his daughter for many years.

See Tup's Indispensable, Pheasant Tail.

Avington   A lake fishery between the villages of Avington and Itchen Abbas, south of Winchester. It is famous for its clear water and large trout, and is the haunt of anglers hoping to catch a record fish. Avington holds the current record for a brook trout of 5lb 13oz – caught by Alan Pearson in 1981, who also had a then record rainbow of 19lb 9oz in 1977 (subsequently beaten by C. White with a 36lb 14oz catch at Dever Springs, also in Hampshire). There are three lakes of 2, 4 and 2 acres plus half a mile of Itchen carrier (the last is catch and release only); open all year. A change of management in 1997 has moved the emphasis from stocking the monsters of the past, which gave birth to the obsessive practice of fish stalking, to a more peaceful and conventional fishery where anglers can enjoy catching good average-size fish with the prospect of a double-figure specimen. Very popular, so advance booking is essential.

Avon England has five river Avons and Scotland has two (Avon comes from the Celtic *Abb, Abhain*, meaning river), but the one most fishermen think of is in the Vale of Pewsey, running through Netheravon – famous as Frank Sawyer's water – and on to Salisbury, Fordingbridge, Ringwood, and finally the sea at Christchurch. Charles Jardine recounts that his very first casting lesson was on the Avon, and his instructor was Frank Sawyer, the legendary river-keeper who revolutionised nymph fishing.

It is not difficult to fall in love with the Avon, not only because it is a beautiful river, but because it is also generous and prolific. It breeds large fish of all kinds, roach, barbel and chub as well as grayling, trout and salmon. The insect life is abundant, and bushes along the bank are sometimes covered with flies, especially during a good hatch of grannom.

The Salisbury & District Angling Club have trout water on the Avon – some of the cheapest chalkstream fishing anywhere in England – and there were limited vacancies for new members in 1998. S & DAC Membership Secretary: 29 New Zealand Avenue, Salisbury, Wilts SP2 7JX. The Piscatorial Society, more expensive, has excellent water and a fine club house. Day permits for salmon and sea-trout fishing are obtainable at the Royalty Fishery, Christchurch, but the best salmon water is held by estates, such as the Somerley Estate water at Ibsley.

Some mixed trout and coarse fishing on day tickets can be had from the Bull Hotel, Downton, and the Bat and Ball, Breamore. The upper river and tributaries are fairly closely preserved for trout.

Awe, Loch Home of the record wild brown trout. A Mr Muir is said to have landed a 39½lb brown in 1866, but that is not accepted as an official record; there is no doubt, however, about Alistair Thorne's catch there of a 19lb 10oz 6dm wild brown trout in 1993, which was the official British record until 1996 when Andrew Finlay caught a 25 lb 5oz 12dm fish there, which is currently the natural brown trout record. Awe is a very narrow loch of about twenty-two miles in length and most of the game fishing is centred around Dalmally, which has ample accommodation. Permits available from many local outlets, including Inverawe Fisheries, Taynuilt. All legal methods are allowed. Salmon and brown trout fishing is to be had on the river Awe, by Taynuilt.

Axe G. P. R. Pulman fished the Dorset-Devon **Axe** at Slimlakes Bridge, just above Axminster. (*See* Dry Fly Origins). There is a sea-trout run, but fishing is largely preserved by clubs, who do not offer permits; however it might well be worth making enquiries at the George Hotel at Axminster for trout, or the White Hart at Colyford for sea-trout. In 1982 the Axe suffered severe pollution from Seaborough down to Axminster, and many thousands of fish died. In 1997 the Environment Agency was able to report that a sustained effort by the Agency, local fisheries' organisations and local people had led to around 42 young salmon being found on just one 50-metre stretch of the river – the best figure for years.

Babingley A small, self-contained river, rising in the Hillington-Harpley area and flowing straight into the Wash seven miles to the west, that is joined on its journey by three tiny tributaries, one of which is the Congham. David Barr writes:

> The Babingley is Norfolk's nearest imitation of a chalk stream and produces a steady number of brown trout, some reaching two pounds, though the average is much less. It is also, for much of its length, the boundary of the Sandringham Estate. Mostly private, parts of its waters are in the hands of the King's Lynn Angling Club. If access were made easier, or indeed possible, this little river could easily become a host for sea-trout.

Baby Doll A reservoir lure designed by Brian Kench in 1971, and still a favourite for three reasons: it is simple to tie, has an attractive name, and attracts fish. John Goddard is of the opinion that the white Baby Doll may be taken for the larger species of the sedge pupa. The black version is known as the Undertaker. Now tied in many colours, the original was white:

Body: white nylon wool shaped like a small fish
Tail: strands of wool shredded out to look like the tail of a fish
Head: black tying silk or nylon varnished black
Hook: Long shank 6 to 10

Backing Attached to the reel spool at one end and then to the fly line at the other, its prime function is to provide extra line should a large fish run away from you. Backing also serves the purpose of building up the diameter of the spool allowing the line to be wound in larger coils thereby reducing the risk of 'memory'. Braided Dacron is the most common form of backing, with a breaking strain of 20lb for the freshwater fly-fisherman, and 30lb for salmon and salt-water angling. For most trout fishing 50 to 100 yards of backing will suffice, but salmon and salt-water requires a minimum of 150 to 200 yards. Nylon is not recommended, as it coils rather badly.

Baigent, W. Dr Baigent had a practice at Northallerton in North Yorkshire around the early 1900s and designed a fly for the Swale known as Baigent's Brown. It is what we now generally know as a variant – very little body but with long hackles that are twice as long as the hook shank.

> *Body:* yellow floss silk
> *Hackle:* large dark furnace cock, standing out well all round
> *Hook:* 10 to 16

Various explanations have been given of why these large hackles on a fly attract the trout – for they often bring up a fish which has refused a more conventional pattern – but no one can be certain of the reason. John Roberts gives another version, with black floss used for the body, peacock-herl rib and long-fibred, stiff, black cock hackles on a 14 hook, which he calls Baigent's Black.

Baigent was the author of two books, *A Book on Hackles for Fly Dressing* (privately published *c.*1941, in a small edition of some 40 copies, each containing 164 actual specimen hackles) and *Notes on the Tying of Certain Flies*, *c.*1943. Both books, which were published posthumously, are eagerly sought after and in 1998 were selling for £2,800 and £950 respectively.

Ballynahinch Lake The lower lake of a system of loughs and a river with a good reputation for salmon and grilse, fished with the fly at all times. Permission to fish the upper lake from Lisnabrucka House, Ballinafad. The lower lake has river fishing, and boats and boatmen are available. The fishing hotel overlooks the water and at one time was owned by a maharaja, better known as cricketer Ranjitsinhji who spared no expense in building footbridges, weirs and stone-built casting platforms. Contact: Ballynahinch Castle Hotel, Ballinafad, Co. Galway.

Barker, Thomas The great Izaak Walton, not himself a fly fisherman, gleaned his knowledge of flies and fly fishing for the first few editions of his *Compleat Angler* (1653), from Barker's *The Art of Angling* (1651). In fact, Barker was quite an important figure in the development of fly fishing: the first writer to give details of how to tie flies and wind hackle, notable for his emphasis on the need to find materials that would float well, and the first writer to mention the use of a reel and gaff in salmon fishing.

Barker's mayfly dressing is surprisingly modern: a chamois-leather body ribbed with black hair. He wrote well. His palmer flies . . . 'will serve all the year long, morning and evening, windie or cloudy . . .' His instructions on how to dress flies have a charming assurance:

> Now to show how to make Flies: learn to make two Flies and make all; that is the Palmer, ribbed with silver or gold, and the May Flie; these are the ground of all flies.

For salmon fishing, the reel should be able to hold a horsehair line 26 yards long, and his salmon flies, on large hooks, had to have 'six wings or four at least'. Barker's description of salmon flies suggests they might have been tied to imitate the big dragonfly but there is no certainty about this.

Barr, David Wisbech solicitor, contributor to *Country Life* and general editor of the *Haig Guide to Salmon Fishing in Scotland* (1981), and its companion, *Haig Guide to Trout Fishing in Britain* (1983). These two books marked a new approach to the concept of guide books. They contain evocative essays on the character of rivers and lakes they describe, as well as information on how they may be fished, and when and where to obtain the fishing. Highly praised at the time, if a little dated now, they remain two unique reference books.

Barrows A clear-water reservoir which straddles the A38 south-west of Bristol, and the smallest of the three Bristol Water Fisheries. The banks are steep and can sometimes be very slippery, so wading is not allowed. There are three lakes: Lake 1 is stocked with brown only, whilst Lakes 2 and 3 have rainbows. There was a limited trial in 1998 of float tubing (*see* Belly Boats) and, if successful, further dates will be arranged.

Not a large water (125 acres) but the rich fly life provides excellent sport. The 1997 season returns were 801 brown and 6,376 rainbow, with a best brown of 7lb 14oz. For recommended methods and season dates, *see* Blagdon.

Bates, H. E. (1905–1973) One of the great English novelists and short story writers, Bates was an accomplished fly fisherman; and fishing came frequently into his writing, particularly in the

character of Uncle Silas. Born at Rushden, Northamptonshire, Bates went to Kettering Grammar School, and at an early age started fishing the Nene. His writing about the countryside is probably among the most perceptive of our time; this extract is taken from *Tunnicliffe's Countryside*, chosen by Ian Niall:

> As the afternoon went on and the sun grew warmer and the voices of the girls grew drowsier under the warm-scented apple trees, and the light more vivid on the white and crimson corn-barn and the claret lily-leaves, I began to understand something of what fishing is about – why it has remained so deeply in the affections of men, why it has never become an expression of collective social snobbery, why it brings out the best and not the worst in a man's nature.

Best Fishing Stories, an anthology edited by John Moore, contains two stories by Bates.

Beacon Beige　One of the Wills family, on leave from the Somme in 1917, designed a fly called the Beige which became popular in the Dulverton area. Some thirty years later another fly dresser, Peter Deane, made improvements to the Beige and called it the Beacon Beige, after Culmstock Beacon which was near his home, then by the banks of the River Culm. The Beige and the Beacon Beige are very much West Country patterns, both admirably suggest an olive, and some say a BWO and an Iron Blue as well if you are careful. Now widely used on the Hampshire chalk streams. Here is Peter Deane's dressing of the Beacon Beige:

> *Body:* stripped peacock quill from the eye feather, with clearly defined markings so that it produces a nice ribbing effect. One has seen the quill tied over a floss base, but this is not in the original dressing.
> *Whisks:* four or five fibres from a stiff grizzle cock
> *Hackles:* grizzle, with a dark red cock wound through it. The original dressing specified a very springy Indian red game hackle, rather long in the fibre
> *Hook:* 12 to 18

Beauly　A lovely little salmon river in Invernessshire, with all the fishing open to the public. Try the Dunraven Hotel, Strathpeffer, and the Coul Hotel, Contin. The Beauly has suffered from hydro-electricity operations which have built large dams as part of a campaign for 'power from the glens' –

which generally means a loss of the spring run. Fishing is probably best from June onwards.

Beetles   Courtney Williams, Leonard West, Francis Francis and John Goddard have all said that the fly fisherman does not pay enough attention to beetles. One knows why. There are too many beetles – several hundred different families, land-bred and water-bred, and no doubt all have been, or can be, eaten by the trout (though not the water-skater, which seems immune). The best-known beetle is the Coch-y-Bondhu; another is Skues' Soldier Beetle.

Beetles fished either on or below the surface certainly do take trout, and if one considers a beetle carefully, face to face, there are certain common characteristics which, apart from size, are not too difficult to fit into a common pattern. Dr Terry of Bath and Eric Horsfall Turner have both done this successfully and produced fairly similar patterns, though Horsfall Turner's was more yellow at the rear. Putting the Terry-Horsfall Turner patterns together, (but mostly Terry, because his pattern is slightly easier), you get something like this:

Tail: a short stub of orange or of mixed orange and yellow floss
Body: rounded yellow floss over which is tied green peacock herl, twisted with yellow tying silk for strength
Hackle: a couple of turns, fairly long, of medium-red cock
Hook: from size 18 up to about 10

The beetle can be fished wet or dry, though if it is regularly fished dry more hackle may be needed to help flotation. As with most other imitation bait patterns, lead wire can be added as an underbody for still water fishing.

Behaviour   From time to time in the angling journals one reads criticisms of anglers' behaviour. Alex Behrendt made the point light heartedly but pungently in his *The Management of Angling Waters*:

It was a revelation. I had always understood that fishermen are a special breed of human: honest, law-abiding, peace-loving, helpful, generous-minded, self-critical, unselfish, modest and kind. Then I had to deal with some of them and found that they are just like everyone else – some good, some not so good. Some of them are not the least ashamed of cheating if the opportunity arises. What can you think when you find a tin of maggots underneath the seat of a boat in a trout fishery with the rule 'fly only'? Or when you see a man casting and with every cast the sunlight catches the brilliant flash of a fly spoon? Then there is the fellow who sneaks to his car before he comes to weigh in the fish. Should you . . . look into his creel to admire his catch you would find that the chap could not count to five, the correct bag limit. There are seven trout in his creel.

Behrendt and other fishery managers know that when a group of people work or play, certain codes of behaviour must be observed; yet the problem of making rules also raises the spectre of enforcement. A former keeper at Blagdon, Donald Carr, had a list of the worst offences:

Playing transistor radios
Parking cars close to the water's edge
Peeing in or near the water
Unhooking small trout by tearing out the hook and tossing them back into the water with a splash
Cruelty in other ways: letting trout suffocate in the air or flapping about in a boat or on the bank
Net stakes: a habit of coarse fishermen, who are used to staking out a swim, and do the same with landing nets on a reservoir
Keep nets: in use to hold trout until the end of the day when the big ones will be kept and the others returned
Bunching: when one bank angler catches a fish the others on either side draw in close and cast over his water
Walking close behind other anglers and risking a fly hitting one's face on their back cast

Behrendt, Alex A pioneer of lake fishing, Behrendt established the first major lake fishery in England at Two Lakes, in Hampshire, in 1951. Behrendt had originally envisaged a carp farm at Two Lakes, but, finding that the English do not eat carp as the Germans do, he turned it into a trout fishery. He quickly established a reputation for the skill of its management, the size and quality of its trout, and the beautiful landscaping of the lakes and the surroundings.

By 1980 the two lakes that Behrendt had started had become seven. For many years Behrendt's *The Management of Angling Waters*, with sketches by his wife Katherine, was the standard work on lake fisheries. Behrendt is now (1998) retired; the fishery he founded is in other hands and is now operated as a syndicated water.

Bell, Dr H. A. (1888–1974) Although he never wrote a word about fishing and shunned publicity, Dr Bell of Blagdon had the greatest formative influence of any man on the development of reservoir fishing in the first half of this century.

Howard Alexander Bell served in the First World War and after his return to civilian life opened a practice in Sussex, but from 1920 onwards he fished Blagdon whenever he could. In 1935 he was able to buy a practice at Wrington, and a few years later opened a surgery at Blagdon village, as close as he could get to his beloved lake.

In those days Blagdon was fished with spinners or with traditional sea-trout and low-water salmon flies. Fly fishing was carried out from boats and bank during the evening rise. Daytime fishing with the fly was thought to be of little use. Bell had read Skues and, following his example, used a marrow spoon to spoon out the trout he caught (one of his friends said, 'He would scoop out his grandmother if he thought there was anything in her'). The stomach contents of the Blagdon trout were a revelation. There was nothing there but small larvae and pupae, among them the pupae of the famous black midge.

Bell realised that the natural food of the trout bore no relation at all to the Jock Scotts, the Mallards and the Peter Rosses which were being fished by his friends. He was a good fly dresser and began to tie patterns that imitated and suggested these food insects. Success came at once. Fishing during the day, often in bright sunlight, he would come back with a limit of eight trout, many of which he gave to his patients. His friend, Alick Newsom, described his methods:

A typical cast would be a Worm Fly on the tail, a Grenadier on the first dropper, and a Buzzer on the top dropper. The flies were not leaded. They were quite small. He fished from the bank, using a standard 1X gut cast and cast out as far as was comfortable. He made no attempt to go for distance but let the flies sink slowly, waiting for some time, but judging the time so that the tail fly did not get snagged on the bottom. He used the knot at the end of his greased silk line as a bite indicator. When the flies were fully sunk he would gather them in slowly. He had a pear-shaped landing net attached to a cord slung over his shoulder. He liked to fish over sunk ditches and holes and moved slowly along the bank, searching for weed beds. During the Second World War, for example, a German bomb had exploded just off the north shore

and he often fished the crater because of the good growth of weed. He was a shy man and liked to fish alone and when he became so successful he hated anyone writing about him.

Bell's reputation grew and was perhaps even increased by his reluctance to have anything written about him. There was a legend that he put a magic oil on his flies, which was why he always caught more than anyone else. Willie Cox of Bristol, who knew Bell well and was influenced by him, said that people would watch him fishing through binoculars to see what he did.

Bell's success in fishing imitative patterns was widely followed, and copies of his flies began to be tied commercially by Veals of Old Market Street, Bristol. Gradually the idea of using what one writer in the *Fishing Gazette* called 'imitation bait' began to spread. Many of Bell's flies are now traditional patterns and include the Blagdon Buzzer, the Grenadier and the Amber Nymph. Some of his patterns are in the museum of the Flyfishers' Club in London.

Belly Boats, or **Float Tubes** An inflatable tube covered with a protective outer layer which may include a seat for the angler as well as storage pockets. Very popular in the States for still water fishing and increasingly being seen here on the larger reservoirs. The lower profile is preferred by many anglers as it is believed there is less chance of spooking feeding fish than when fishing from a boat.

Beltra Badger A salmon fly first tied by Martin Maguire of Newport, Co. Mayo for Lough Beltra. It is now a favourite on many loughs and rivers, including the Delphi. Tied on 2 to 10 singles, doubles, or even small tubes.

Tag: silver tinsel and yellow floss
Tail: golden pheasant topping
Body: flat silver tinsel
Rib: oval silver tinsel
Hackle: lemon yellow
Throat: bright blue tinsel
Wing: badger hair with a few fibres of red bucktail, with a topping over
Head: black

Beltra, Lough A great game fishing lough in Co. Mayo, holding trout, sea-trout and salmon. Visitors are inclined to fall in love with Lough Beltra, not only for the fishing, but also for the wild beauty of the surroundings and the distant mountains. Traditional small salmon flies fished on the drift, three flies to a cast, will bring up quite a few small brownies and then the sudden surge of a big fish, often close to the boat. Booking for boats and boatmen, and excellent accommodation, is available at the Newport House Hotel, Newport, Co. Mayo.

Berners, Dame Juliana A lady generally believed to be the author or editor of the first English textbook on fishing, including fly fishing – *The Treatyse of Fysshynge Wyth an Angle*, published in 1496 from St Albans Abbey. Her name has been spelt in different ways but she is accepted as being what one historian called an illustrious female of noble birth who was the prioress of the nunnery of Sopwell, near St Albans.

One did not need to be a misogynist to have slight doubts about the Dame but it was not until an amateur historian and fly fisherman, Jack Heddon, began probing into the Westminster Abbey's records in the 1970s that doubt matured. William Caxton, the first English printer, set up a press near the Abbey in 1476. Heddon found that Westminster Abbey's own researchers, looking for the site of Caxton's Press, found that it was close to a large house called St Albans which filled most of the present grass-covered area to the east of the Chapter House, where we now have the statue of King George V. Heddon was able to point out that the colophon (publisher's imprint) on *The Treatyse* – 'apud villa sancti Albani' – meant 'near St Albans House' and not the City or Abbey of St Albans. In other words *The Treatyse* was published from the large house called St Albans which adjoined Caxton's Press.

In some ways it is a pity to have lost the Dame. She has been with us for so many years. Heddon's evidence, however, seems to put the matter beyond doubt – though one problem solved does create another: if the Dame didn't write the *Treatyse*, who did? (*Source*: Jack Heddon, private ms, 1983.)

Bewl Water Acclaimed by many anglers as the most scenic fishery in the south east, Bewl Water was first opened for fly fishing in 1978.   It has 770 acres of water, 650 of which are available for fly fishing. Some 50 miles from central London and one mile south off the A21 London to Hastings road, it is operated by Southern Water. Its irregular shape means there is always somewhere to fish, whatever the wind direction, and, with a generous stocking policy of 42,000 rainbow plus 5,000 brown trout per annum, there is an abundance of fish for the taking. The reservoir record for rainbow stands at 16lb 6oz and that for the heaviest brown at 12lb 11oz.

There is a tackle shop on site, and a qualified instructor is available. Boat and bank fishing with wading in most areas. The season (1998) runs from 21 March to 30 November (catch and kill from 3 April to 31 October; outside these dates brown trout must be returned). Fishing is restricted to artificial flies, or lures, tied with traditional materials.

The Country Landowners' Association have provided a specially equipped Wheelyboat, developed with the aid of the Handicapped Anglers Trust, for the use of handicapped anglers. The Bewl Bridge Fly Fishers' Club maintain a register of members willing to accompany a handicapped angler in the boat.

Bibio An Irish lough fly, first tied by Major Charles Roberts of the Burrishoole fishery, Newport, Co. Mayo, in the late 1950s. The story goes that when asked to give it a name, as the fly was having some success, he said that he would call it the Bibio, because he had seen the word somewhere and had taken a fancy to it (no doubt he later remembered that the word came from *Bibio johannis*, the St Mark's fly). The Bibio is widely used on English reservoirs. The dressing is:

> *Body:* black seal fur, or similar, in three sections – black at the head and tail with a hot orange fur visible in the middle of the shank
> *Rib:* fine oval silver wire
> *Hackle:* black cock from head to tail; not too crowded and with a slightly longer black cock at the head
> *Tying:* black thread
> *Hook:* 14 - 8

Bingham, Charles Author, regular contributor to all the game fishing magazines, chairman and a founding member of REFFIS, Charles Bingham took up fishing at an early age and in 1976 established a game fishing school on Dartmoor with his wife. His first book, *Salmon and Sea Trout Fishing* was published in 1988 and was followed by *The Game Fishing Year*, *The River Test, Chalk Stream Salmon and Trout Fishing, Trout,*

Salmon and Sea Trout Fishing, Salmon Fishing on Small Rivers, Sea Trout – how to catch them and *Freshwater Fishing for Beginners,* with Tony Allen in 1998. His main interests are salmon fishing on the fly, sea-trout fishing at night when alone, chalk stream fishing for trout, and ornithology.

Black Gnat A convenient description of several hundred varieties of small black flies. Most belong to the order *Diptera,* which includes the housefly, but some do not, and are midge or reed smuts. The simplest dressing for a Black Gnat is almost certainly Roger Woolley's:

> *Body:* black quill or black silk
> *Hackle:* black cock
> *Hook:* 16,18 or 20

If one feels there should be wings, as some do, then two small pale blue or off-white hackle points can be added, splayed out on either side of the body, but kept short. This is, some think, more effective than putting wings along the back, as Halford did.

Entomologists and anglers do not see eye to eye on black gnats, and nor do some of the best fly fishers either. J. W. Hills, in *A Summer on the Test,* said:

> The species which inhabits the Test is called *Bibio johannis,* and appears, as its name implies, at midsummer, on St John's Day. It has a larger cousin, the hawthorn fly, *Bibio marci,* which comes out at the end of April, and is at its height during the second or third week of May. It is not, I think, common on the Test; but it is the common black gnat of Devonshire, where the trout take it greedily and refuse anything else, and the black gnat season is the best for heavy baskets. I have done well with it on the Otter.

'Black Palmer' Pseudonym of the author (now unknown) of *Scottish Loch Fishing* (1882), one of the first books to emphasise the effectiveness of fishing Scottish lochs with a team of wet flies. The flies were, in general, fairly large patterns: March Brown, Mallard and Claret, Teal and Silver, tied to gut, fished on the drift with long rods – the type of fishing popular among Scottish angling clubs in competitions.

Also, of course, the name of a popular floating or wet fly, representative of a number of insects, midges, beetles and sedges.

Black Lure One of the earliest reservoir lures, which has been altered and added to by many fly dressers over more than half a century.   Some of the changes have made it look prettier or more distinguished but none have made much improvement to it so far as catching fish are concerned.   This was Willie Cox's dressing at Blagdon some sixty years ago which must be getting back fairly close to the original:

Body: black wool, fairly thick
Rib: silver tinsel
Wings: two, sometimes four, black cock saddle hackles, extending well past the bend of the hook and curving outwards so that when the lure is retrieved the hackles move slightly together, giving the impression of life
Hackle: black cock
Hook: long shank 6 or 8

In most cases the overall length of the fly is almost twice that of the hook.

Black and Peacock Spider A wonderful pattern for imitative fishing, particularly on still waters, the Black and Peacock has been a favourite now for over half a century. The surprising thing about this fly is that it came into being by accident. One day in the 1930s T. C. Ivens was fishing a winged Alder artificial on a reservoir without success. He looked at it, wondering what was wrong, thought it was rather overdressed, and cut off the wings. Almost at once the wingless Alder began to take trout. There was no need to alter the body dressing, only the name, so it became what a wingless Alder looks like – a black and peacock fly:

Body: bronze peacock herl
Head hackle: relatively long soft-fibre black hen, two turns only
Hook: 12 and 14 are the most usual, but larger sometimes

Reservoir fishermen sometimes use lead wire or lead foil under the dressing to make it sink more quickly, but this must be a matter of taste. The unleaded fly is often taken while sinking slowly through the water without other movement. It was one of Ivens' deceiver patterns and possibly the most popular. According to John Roberts few patterns have caught trout so consistently. Incidentally, cutting the wings off a Butcher will improve this fly's effectiveness too, according to an article by Robin Lemon in *West Country Fly Fishing*.

Black Pennell   Another invaluable still water wet fly, one of a series designed some hundred years ago by H. Cholmondely-Pennell for lake and sea-trout fishing. In the thicker and larger sizes the Pennells are very useful for the dap.

Body: black floss silk
Rib: silver tinsel
Tail: golden pheasant tippet
Hackle: black cock, rather long in the hackle. For wet-fly fishing dress sparsely, for the dap thickly
Hook: a matter of choice, the most usual being 10 or 8 standard sizes

Black Spider   A most useful, if not the most useful, of upstream wet flies; and a favourite of W. C. Stewart who wrote about fishing on the Scottish Borders in his book *The Practical Angler* (1857), in which he emphasised the importance of fishing the wet fly upstream. This was one of his favourite flies, lightly dressed, with a mobile hackle:

Body: brown silk
Hackle: greeny-black feather from a starling's neck
Hook: 14 - 16

Black spiders do well in fast water, riffles and eddies, in fact the kind of water you often get on the Tweed and its tributaries.

Blae and Black   A pretty useful little fly, originally an Irish pattern, widely used for lake trout. It has a number of variations – Blae and Silver, Blae and Gold and so on – but, as with the Pennell, the black is the most popular:

Body: black seal's fur or black wool
Hackle: black hen (but if only cock fibres are available, then tie the cock hackle fairly short) as a beard hackle
Wings: matched slips of coot lying low on the body
Tail: golden pheasant tippet
Hook: 12 - 14 for lake trout, larger for migratory trout

A silver tinsel rib may be added. The Blae and Silver has an all-silver body with blue dun hackle but the coot wings remain.

Blagdon Boil   A turmoil of surface water caused by big trout attacking shoals of small fry. Brian Clarke gave a vivid description of a boil in his introduction to *West Country Fly Fishing*. The phenomenon is most likely to occur at Blagdon in August when the sticklebacks are breeding. The big trout come in and herd them into the shallows, especially at dusk when the water 'boils' with attacking trout and leaping sticklebacks.

Blagdon Buzzer   An artificial fly designed in the 1920s by Dr H. A. Bell to imitate the large midge pupae:

Body: fine black wool tapered from a thin point by the bend of the hook to a larger body by the thorax, ending with a slight hump behind the eye of the hook
Rib: four or five turns of fine flat silver tinsel
Head: a tiny fluff of white wool or silk just behind the eye of the hook, over the back of the hump of the thorax

Bell's dressing is very delicate and fine. It might be as well to add that the true 'buzzers' are the winged midges which, when flying over the lake in vast numbers, create a buzzing sound caused by the rapid movements of their wings. The Blagdon Buzzer artificial represents the midge pupa and is fished sink and draw fairly close to the surface, sometimes almost motionless in the surface film.

Blagdon Lake   'I don't know of any angler who fishes Blagdon who fails to feel passionate about the place.' Charles Jardine, *Trout & Salmon*.

Blagdon is the oldest of the three reservoirs operated by Bristol Water Fisheries and covers some 440 acres, and was stocked and opened for fly fishing in 1904. It has inspired much literature, including books and articles by H. T. Sheringham, Plunket Greene and Bernard Venables, and it was here that the first imitative lake patterns were tied by Dr H. A. Bell during the 1920s and 1930s.

Nestling close to the steep northern face of the Mendips, it is an idyllic setting for superb trout fishing. Nearly all of the banks are easily accessible. Rowing boats, to which anglers may attach their own electric motors, are available. One boat, adapted to take a wheelchair, is provided for disabled anglers. The 1997 returns were 2,448 brown (slightly more than the larger Chew Valley Lake) and 16,082 rainbow with a best rainbow of 7lb 10oz. Stocking plans for 1998 allow for 29,000 fish with good numbers of bigger fish between 3 and 5lb.

Recommended methods (also apply to Chew and Barrows):

Imitative patterns for much of the season, but in the early weeks sinking lines and bright lures, such as nobblers, chenilles, tadpoles and boobies. Leaded or gold head nymphs and damsels perform well in the shallower areas. In the months of May, June, and July there is usually an abundance of food available – flies, corixa, daphnia and pin fry. A floating line with small nymphs fished slowly is then the successful method in most areas, and Hare's Ear nymph, Pheasant Tail nymph, Buzzers, Damsel fly and Corixa are suggested. With rising fish dry flies and emergers work well: Shipman's Buzzer, Bob's Bits, raiders, and hoppers in red, orange or claret. In late summer and autumn fish come closer to the shores often feeding on the prolific shoals of fry. The best flies are usually: Appetisers, Baby Dolls and floating fry, but many fish can still be taken on the usual nymphs and gold heads.

Season dates (1998) 26 March to 29 November.

Blue Charm   A traditional fully-dressed salmon fly, dating back to the 1800s, which is still popular today for low-water fishing, especially in small sizes:

Body: black floss or wool ribbed with three or four turns of fine flat silver tinsel
Tail: golden pheasant crest, up-turning to meet the wing
Wings: two matching strips of dark mallard flanked as cheeks by thinner strips of light mallard or teal
Hackle: blue-dyed hen tied at the throat as a beard hackle

Peter O'Reilly, in *Trout and Salmon Flies of Ireland* tells of an Icelandic gillie who banned the Blue Charm from his fly box because he considered it too deadly.

Blue Dun   An artificial fly that suggests various olive duns. The original dressing was by Walton's friend Charles Cotton in 1676. Cotton's dubbing for his Blue Dun were combings of the blue under-fur from the neck of a black greyhound. Those who do not have access to black greyhounds will find the following dressing not an unreasonable substitute:

Body: yellow silk dubbed with mole or dark blue rabbit fur
Wings: starling or cock slips
Hackle: pale or medium blue cock
Hook: 14 - 16

In darker shades it might do well for an Iron Blue.

Blue Quill *See* Blue Upright.

Blue Upright Originally a Devon pattern, the Blue Upright has a twin brother, the Blue Quill. This dressing is by Austin of Tiverton:

> *Body:* undyed peacock herl, stripped and taken from the eye feather of a peacock's tail
> *Hackle:* steely blue gamecock, wound on at the head or from head to shoulder
> *Whisks:* several strands of the same hackle
> *Hook:* 14 - 16

The quill body is probably the most useful, but if no quill is available dark rabbit mixed with mole fur can be used as dubbing. The Blue Upright is generally used when olives are about. If the hackle is a little darker it can well stand in for BWO or an Iron Blue. A very versatile fly.

Blue-Winged Olive Known for short as the BWO, the natural blue-winged olive (*Ephemeralla ignita*) is a largish olive which floats downstream with its larger than usual wings cocked a little forward – with a little practice, not all that difficult to recognise. On chalk streams they seem to hatch mostly at spinner time, in the evening, but in many spate rivers they are up during the day.

There are problems about the BWO; everyone has tied life-like artificials, yet for some reason the trout may only take them occasionally and at some times not at all. Many fishermen have given up exact imitation and simply offer a Beacon Beige, Red Quill, Pheasant Tail or Blue Upright when the BWO are hatching.

For purists there are good dressings to be had from Halford, West and others. One of the more attractive is David Jacques':

> *Body:* yellow ostrich herl covered with olive coloured plastic, well-stretched
> *Wings:* two pairs from the wing feathers of a coot
> *Whisks:* blue dun
> *Tying silk:* hot orange
> *Hook:* 14

Jacques had grounds for believing that Skues' faith in the value of an Orange Quill during the hatch of BWO cannot be sustained, and that it is only of value when the spent is on the

water. This belief seems to be confirmed by Goddard's underwater photographs in *The Trout and the Fly*, which show that the spent has a distinct orange tone which might well match up with the Orange Quill.

Interestingly enough, the experimental pattern of the BWO tied by Dr J. C. Mottram, probably around the year 1910 or earlier, was a forerunner of the principle incorporated by Peter Deane in his Shadow Mayfly in 1950. These odd-looking shadow flies can be effective. This is Mottram's dressing:

> *Body:* none
> *Hackles:* grey cock hackled from head to tail
> *Whisks:* grey cock
> *Wings:* two grey hackle points, set upright
> *Hook:* 14 or 16

Boat Fishing There are two kinds of boat fishing. One, the competitive kind has developed comparatively recently. Teams representing clubs or nations fish one of the big lakes or reservoirs, such as Corrib or Rutland, with fixed rules and against the clock. There are team and individual prizes for the largest fish and the biggest total catch. In some ways it is similar to competition fishing on rivers for coarse fish.

The other kind, generally known on the big lochs as fishing the drift, is a most casual kind of fishing. One or two rods share a boat, generally (though not always) with a local boatman-cum-gillie at the oars to give advice and direct the boat to the most likely spots where the boat is then allowed to drift. The drift must be controlled and must not be too fast or too slow.

Ordinary trout rods are used, preferably longer rather than shorter (9 or 10ft is about right), with a floating line and a nylon cast with three flies. The flies are part of the magic, for they don't represent anything in particular, only moving insects of some indefinable kind.

One of the great exponents of fishing the drift was an Irish judge, T. C. Kingsmill Moore, who designed flies for the drift which are now used world wide. Bumbles he called them, and this is the Claret Bumble:

> *Tail:* a few cocky strands of golden pheasant tippet
> *Body:* medium claret seal's fur or similar, ribbed oval gold
> *Body hackles:* claret dyed cock mixed with black cock
> *Shoulder hackle:* blue jay

He doesn't give the hook size, for that depends on whether one is after trout or salmon (and this dressing has taken many of both over the years).

With the wind behind him the fisherman casts a reasonable distance ahead, and as the flies fall he brings the Bumble back towards him, bubbling and flickering over the water, the other two flies following just below the surface (nor does it matter much what these are – a Peter Ross, a Green Peter, a Hairy Mary, whatever takes his fancy). When the fish is hooked the fisherman brings the line back behind the boat, so that the boatman can net it, avoiding the front of the boat which might well overrun the fish.

Another way of fishing the drift is dapping, and for that you will need a longer rod. At the end of the usual line is attached another twenty or thirty feet of a lighter line terminating with a yard or so of nylon with a bushy fly at the end of that. The wind carries the fly ahead of the boat and the fly is dapped on the surface of the water. When a fish rises to it, the strike is delayed until the fish takes and turns down before the hook is set.

Yet another way is to tail a heavy lure deep down behind the drift of the boat. There are times when a big fish takes very deep indeed, especially the big *ferox* of the Irish loughs.

Finally treat the gillie-boatman with respect and affection and make sure he is happier and better off at the end of the day than he was when the partnership began.

See Reservoir Fishing

Booby No one seems to know if the Booby, which was invented by Gordon Fraser, is a nymph, a lure, or even a fly in the accepted sense, but there is no denying its success, particularly in the deep water found in reservoirs. It is usually fished on a fast-sinking line, though the prominent polystyrene balls, or eyes, make it very buoyant, so that it floats up from the leader (which should be kept very short – 3ft at the most). Bright colours seem to feature in most patterns, though there is a black version. The Booby is banned on most small still waters, and very understandably where a policy of catch and release is in force, because there is a tendency for the trout to take it deep, making release difficult without damaging the fish.

Borgie The River Borgie is a mere seven miles long, running into Torrisdale Bay on the north coast of Caithness; however those seven miles provide some fine fly fishing. Spinning and worming are forbidden. Strutt and Parker let rods, and the Bridge Hotel at Skerray provides accommodation. There are three main beats, with two rods on a beat, reached by a forestry road which runs almost the whole length of the river. New pools have been made in recent years and a hatchery built. Like all Highland salmon rivers it needs the right height of water to fish well.

Bourne Remember this line in the famous speech by Hamlet? '. . . The undiscovered country from whose bourn, no traveller returns . . . .' Bourn or bourne means frontier, in most cases a frontier river. *Bartholomew's Gazetteer* lists 19 bournes from Borne End to Bournemouth, but the only one that matters to a fly fisherman is Plunket Greene's Bourne, a miniature chalk stream tributary of the Test immortalised in *Where the Bright Waters Meet*, first published in 1924 and still in print.

It is possible to get a rod from time to time on this water near Hurstborne Priors; enquire locally. It is not stocked, or was not until recently, and provides some of the most delicate and difficult fishing imaginable. In memory of Plunket Greene, fish a winged iron blue, size 16. *See also* Chalkstream fishing.

There is another Bourne, a small tributary of the Salisbury Avon. Inclined to dry up in the upper reaches in a hot summer because of abstraction it is, therefore, known as a winter-bourne.

Brenig Acknowledged to be the premier fly-only fishery in Wales, Llyn Brenig is a 920-acre reservoir, one of four in the Dee valley, surrounded by heather-clad slopes and spruce forests. Can be very exposed during windy weather, due to its altitude, and is at its best from late May onwards. With its modern visitor centre and a fleet of 22 boats, Brenig is a popular venue for national and international tournaments.   It offers native brown trout and rainbows which are stocked on a regular basis. Wheelyboats are available for disabled anglers. Fly fishing courses there are run by world champion caster Hywel Morgan.

Bridges, Anthony *Bridge's Modern Salmon Fishing* – now out of print, though copies are available from specialist book dealers – is an invaluable reference book. It deals with methods of fly fishing, bait fishing and spinning for salmon and has chapters on tackle and casting, as well as useful tables on the calculation of fish weights from body measurements and comparisons of the Pennell and Redditch hook sizes. Bridges' advice on strategy and tactics is as useful now as it ever was and in many ways a good deal more valuable and clear than that in several later books on the salmon.

Bridgett, R. C. A Scottish schoolmaster, angling correspondent of the *Glasgow Herald*, author of several fishing books in the 1920s on trout-fishing in Scotland, including *Loch Fishing in Theory and Practice* and *Dry Fly Fishing, By Loch and Stream* and *Tight Lines*. All useful books, but slightly schoolmasterish prose. He writes:

> My chief purpose is to make known the virtues of the dry fly to Scottish anglers and others, whose great privilege it is to fish streams of cheerful flow; to show them how to take trout with the fly both from the sparkling currents and the placid pools, not only in spring, but also in the height of summer, not under cover of darkness but in the happier sunlight.

Brora A kindred river to the Helmsdale in Sutherland. Like the Helmsdale, it is fly only, and big tubes are invariably used. Rods are not easily obtained. For information try the tackle shop in Fountain Square, Brora.

Buchan, John (1875–1940) A great fly fisherman, John Buchan wrote one of the best of all poaching stories, *John MacNab*, as well as many romantic adventure stories featuring Richard Hannay: *The Thirty Nine Steps, Greenmantle, The Three Hostages* and others. He was for many years an MP and, as Lord Tweedsmuir, Governor-General of Canada.

Bucknall, Geoffrey Blagdon, Chew and other reservoirs feature in Geoffrey Bucknall's *Fly Fishing Tactics on Still Water*. He deals with boat and bank fishing, buzzers, sedge flies and olives, floating and sunk line tactics, and, though the rods he recommended are now out of date, the tactics are not.

Bugs and Balls The addition of silver, copper or black balls to nymphs for fishing close to the riverbed. Bugs are said to have been invented in the 1980s to answer the problem of getting a fly onto the bottom. Richard Walker devised the Mead Mill specially for deep-lying grayling on the Test, also the Angora Grub and the Green Rabbit. (*Source*: John Roberts, author of *The Grayling Angler*, writing in *Trout & Salmon*, October 1997).

Buller, Frederick Fred is the archetypal all-round angler, best known for his classic books on the pike, *Pike, The Domesday Book of Mammoth Pike* and *Pike and the Pike Angler,* but his interests, and expertise, are much wider, for he is also an accomplished journalist, naturalist and angling historian. *Successful Angling*, with Richard Walker, Fred J. Taylor and Hugh Falkus, was his first venture in joint authorship. That was followed by *Freshwater Angling*, which he wrote with Hugh Falkus, and it was an immediate success. A second and enlarged edition came out in 1988, and, with a series of reprints, total sales to date approach 60,000 copies.

Fred is a member of the Flyfishers' Club and managing director of the gun-making firm Frederick Beesley. He has fished throughout the British Isles, Russia, Poland, Italy, China, Canada and the West Indies; but today he prefers trout and sea-trout fishing in the west of Ireland and fly fishing for salmon in Scotland. He writes historical articles for *The American Flyfisher, Journal of the American Museum of Flyfishing,* and *The Flyfishers' Journal.*

Bumble Flies A Derbyshire pattern of trout fly, used by Halford and revived and redesigned by the Irish judge T. C. Kingsmill Moore. In his book *A Man May Fish* Kingsmill Moore wrote:

> The Bumbles are general patterns for loch fishing which suggest surface life without any attempt at imitation. They must be translucent, have a certain amount of gleam, gentle contrasts, and must suggest the movement of insects caught in the surface film or blown by the wind. On Irish lochs they are generally fished on the drift.

There are several tyings of different coloured Bumbles but the Claret Bumble is one of the most popular:

Body: medium claret seal's fur ribbed oval gold tinsel
Body hackles from head to tail: a mix of claret and black cock

Shoulder hackle: blue jay
Tail: four strands of golden pheasant tippet
Hook: 12 - 8

A Golden Olive Bumble is based on the Invicta Fly and there are several more variations – *see* Kingsmill Moore's book, one of the best ever written about Irish fishing, for more dressings.

Burrishoole Fishery Two loughs (Furnace and Feeagh) in Co. Mayo, both fished fly from a boat with an experienced boatman at the oars. The fishery is highly organised and hosts the research centre of the official Salmon Research Agency. The lower lough, Furnace, is close to the sea and gets a reasonable run of grilse and sea-trout (reasonable, that is, under present conditions). Bait fishing is not allowed, only the fly (generally size 8 and 10 singles for salmon; and 10, or even 12, for sea-trout). Furnace is a beautiful lough, and it was here that the Green Peter was first popularised as a salmon fly. The companion lough, Feeagh, is further inland and has a wild beauty all its own; Peter O'Reilly wrote that 'Feeagh casts a spell on you the moment it comes into view.' Contact for both loughs can be made via the Salmon Research Agency, Newport, Co. Mayo. Bookings can also be made for the fishing for guests staying at the Newport House Hotel, Newport, Co. Mayo.

Butcher An admirable wet fly for lake and river fishing which was designed at least 160 years ago. Courtney Williams wrote:

> The Butcher is said to have been invented by a Mr Jewhurst of Tunbridge Wells, Kent, in association with a Mr Moon, a butcher of that town. Originally known as 'Moon's Fly' it received its present name about 1838, probably on account of its connection with the 'purveyor of meat' mentioned above and possibly also because of its colouring, the red tag suggesting raw beef and the wings the traditional blue apron of a butcher.

Whatever its origins it is a remarkably effective fly, and even more effective according to Robin Lemon (*West Country Fly Fishing*) as a still water fly if the wings are taken off, as T. C. Ivens did with the Alder. The standard dressing is:

Body: flat silver tinsel, sometimes ribbed with fine silver wire
Tail: originally red ibis, now more often red or scarlet floss
Beard hackle: black hen or cock

Wings: two matching slips of the blue-black feathers from a mallard drake's wing, excluding those with white tips
Hook: for delicate work on clear-water lakes down to 14, but up to 10 or 8 for night sea-trout fishing
Variations: the Bloody Butcher has the same dressing but a scarlet hackle. The Kingfisher Butcher has a gold body, orange hackle and fibres from a kingfisher's wing as a tail.

Buzzer Another name for a *chironomid,* a long-legged, gnat-like insect with a humped thorax, a long abdomen, and wings that are often slightly shorter than the body. The angler's name for them is derived either from their habit of buzzing around over the water surface or possibly because in a large swarm they do make a faint buzzing sound. *See* Midge.

C

Caddis The larva of the caddis or sedge fly, the best known of some 200 species being those that live in small tubes on the river bed which they construct from grains of sand, wood, plants or other tiny pieces of detritus. When the larva is fully developed it seals up the case and turns into a pupa which remains in the cocoon and inactive for some time – perhaps weeks, perhaps months, depending on conditions and on the species. When ready, it bites open the case and rises through the water to hatch, either from the surface or from a stick or rush on which it climbs until ready to change. Trout feed on the pupae rising to the surface, on the freshly-emerged fly, and on the female flies returning to the water to lay their eggs.

(*Sources include*: J. R. Harris, Martin Moseley, John Goddard and David Jacques).

Caenis Lake fishermen will sometimes find dozens of tiny white flies on their coats and hats towards sunset. They are known by a number of names – *Caenis*, White Midge, Anglers' Curse or White Broadwing – and belong to the *Caenis* species, are the smallest of all the *ephemeroptera*. Their wings are broad and very white, they have long tails and a stumpy body. They hatch in enormous numbers. Goddard's Last Hope is a useful fly when the curse is on the water, but the hatch is often so numerous that one artificial in the midst of millions of the natural insect does not always stand much chance. Some anglers give up, and when the trout are cruising round the lake souping up *Caenis*, will fish a large lure.

Camel At the picturesque little port of Padstow in North Cornwall holidaymakers who enjoy watching the fishing boats come into the small stone-walled harbour may not know that this is the estuary of the river Camel, a small river with a good run of sea-trout and some salmon. Tickets to fish the Camel for trout and sea-trout can be had from fishing associations at

Wadebridge, Liskeard and Bodmin. Ask at the tackle shops –
there is a good one at Homeleigh, Launceston Garden Centre.

Caperer One of the many sedges with hairy, roof-shaped
wings. These are so similar to each other that unless you are an
entomologist, you may not be able to decide whether you are
looking at a caperer, a cinnamon sedge, or half a dozen others
of a very large family of flies. The natural fly is reddish or
cinnamon in colour and widespread, and one reason it is so
popular is that the name is easily remembered. William
Lunn's Caperer is a very good artificial:

> *Abdomen:* strands from a dark turkey tail twisted on crimson silk
> *Mid-abdomen:* two swan feathers, dyed yellow, to form a band
> halfway along the body
> *Thorax:* more strands of dark turkey, as on the abdomen
> *Wings:* coot or landrail substitute dyed chocolate brown and tied
> roof-shape close to the body
> *Hackle:* red and black cock tied in front of the wings
> *Hook:* 12 or 14 are usual, larger if bigger sedges are moving

The best, certainly the most evocative, advice about fishing the
caperer is given by J. W. Hills in *A Summer on the Test*:

> On days when the river is as burnished metal, when the thinnest
> gut looks like a blind-cord, when you reduce your flies smaller
> and smaller but still the insolent trout disregard your almost
> invisible badger smuts and houghton rubies; why then, reel in and
> knot on your biggest caperer. Do not be afraid. Never mind that
> not one of the real insects is to be seen; never mind that the trout
> are obviously taking spinners; never mind that so heavy a fly falls
> with a sickening thump on the polished stillness of the water;
> never mind that to your eye as you stoop and blink anxiously
> along the glittering surface this great fly seems as unpalatable as
> an autumn leaf or the feather of a cock turkey; never mind all that,
> for you may be sure it will not have floated far before a trout will
> have gulped it, if there be a trout within reach. And then, oh my
> brother, oh my erring brother, do not behave as I always do and
> strike too soon.

Carey A small Devon river, a tributary of the Tamar, with
wild brown trout of between ¼ to ½lb that gives excellent
upstream fishing. There are occasional deep pools, good
shallow runs and riffles, and nice picnic places in spring on
banks lined with wild daffodils. All the Devon flies do well,

and a dry Coachman, Blue Upright and Pheasant Tail are among the best. The Arundell Arms at Lifton has water.

Careysville Fishery   Probably the best known fishery on the Cork Blackwater river, consisting of 1¾ miles of double bank fishing for fly or bait, depending on the height of the water. It takes four rods in February and March, three from April to July, and two rods in August and September. There is a fishing hut where lunch is served every day, and accommodation is available at Careysville House. February is said to be the most productive month for spring salmon. One often hears arguments along the whole length of the Blackwater about the various methods of fishing for salmon, but if there is one method more effective than others, says one of the experienced Blackwater fishermen, it is the fly. There are several good hotels that cater for fishermen: The Careysville Fishery, Fermoy, Co. Cork; the Blackwater Lodge Hotel, Upper Ballyduff, Co. Waterford; Ghillie Cottage, Kilbarry Stud, Fermoy, Co. Cork; and the Ballyvolane House, Castlelyons, Co. Cork.

Carter Platts, W.   For many years angling editor of the *Yorkshire Post* and author of *Modern Trout Fishing*. Platts had strong views:

> To the liberal-minded angler there can be no more objection to fishing the maggot as a hook bait, than to the same use of the worm. It is the prodigal use of ground bait, to which the maggot fisher is often addicted, that is the bone of bitter contention between him and the fly fisher. From the ethical point of view alone, ground-baiting for trout is abhorrent to the soul of the fly fisher; he places it on the same level as throwing down a handful of corn to attract a covey of partridges and then blazing into the brown.

Cassley   The Sutherland river made famous by Edward Grey (Viscount Grey of Fallodon), who fished the Rosehall beat for many years around the end of the century and left a vivid account of what it is like in his classic, *Fly Fishing*. Beats on Grey's water can be obtained through the Achness House Hotel, Rosehall.

Casting 'The pleasure of a really good cast is almost orgasmic,' Peter Hinton-Green, *Ndeke Tales*, from *The Angler's Quotation Book.*

See diagram opposite.

Casts *See* Leaders.

Catch and Release 'These fish are too valuable to be caught only once,' said Lee Wulff. He pioneered catch and release in the 1930s, and it became necessary on many American rivers during the following twenty or thirty years, to avoid the stock of wild trout being wiped out. Fly fishing in America is virtually free fishing in a number of areas; all that is needed is a state licence to fish, which costs twenty or thirty dollars for a whole season. In most cases there were no restrictions on the size of fish that could be taken and no catch limits. Consequently, an unlimited number of fishermen were taking home as many trout as they could carry, for sale or for the freezer – no river could stand that kind of pressure for long.

The various chapters (branches) of a conservation society, Trout Unlimited, brought pressure to bear on the state authorities who then declared a number of rivers or sections of rivers to be no-kill areas. This meant barbless hooks had to be used and all trout caught had to be immediately released. The restrictions were successful. Adequate stocks of wild fish were restored.

Many anglers now practise catch and release from habit, or on principle, whether or not they are fishing a no-kill area. It is said that on public water on a famous river, such as the Beaverkill in the Catskills, trout may well have been caught and released 14 or 15 times. They become more difficult to deceive, and fishermen pride themselves on taking the most difficult and wary fish.

Some exponents of catch and release still net their fish or pick them out of the water by hand before releasing them, but the most favoured method is to use barbless hooks and release them under water without handling the trout at all.

No-handling is becoming more popular as scientific evidence has suggested that handling and netting both cause damage which might shorten the fish's life or inhibit growth. Catch and release has been practised on a number of British fisheries, but abandoned because of the damage caused to trout by handling. Nevertheless, it is gaining favour and has

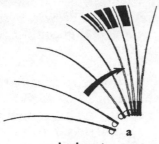

back cast

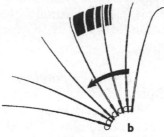

forward cast

Casting. The task of the fisherman is to activate the spring of the rod, and it is the rod, not the fisherman, which casts the fly.

Figure A shows the rod lifting the line off the water for the overhead cast, and the dark areas show where the maximum power is applied. *Figure B* shows the forward cast. The rod is moved forward with the increase in power in the darkened area, where the final power stroke or 'flick' of the rod is applied.

Casting faults are: too much wrist action, application of power stroke too soon or too late, jerky movements, reaching forward on the forward cast in an attempt to 'throw' the fly, gripping the rod too fiercely.

Line velocity can be improved by the use of the free hand hauling on the line either on the back cast alone – the single haul – or on both back and forward casts – the double haul.

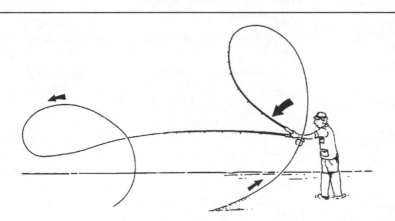

The roll cast

The Roll Cast in a sense a natural flip of the line which has many uses, being part of the action of a Spey cast (see p. 227). This shows the overhead roll cast in which the loop of line is brought behind the angler and then a power stroke of the rod sends it rolling out again. Not easy to show on paper and needs practice and a good teacher, preferably a fully qualified professional.

even spread to salmon and sea-trout waters. A simple device is now available, consisting of a slotted tube which is run down the leader to the fly for easy removal without netting or handling.

Cefn Mably   A complex of five spring-fed lakes between Newport and Cardiff, situated off junction 28 on the M4. It is open all year and is stocked with rainbow and brown trout with an average minimum of 2¼lb. Double-figure fish are also stocked and the record catch is an 18lb rainbow. The 6½-acre Lodge Lake is fly only and has a reputation for large fish. Facilities for the disabled.

Chalkstream fishing   Much of the chalkstream fishing in southern England is in private ownership, controlled by local associations or syndicates making it difficult for the angler seeking a day's fishing. There are however, a number of organisations offering this facility, with or without a qualified guide and/or instructor.

Strutt & Parker have access to some thirty miles of first-class fishing on the Test and carriers, together with two of the main tributaries, the Anton and Dever. Fishing can be arranged on a daily basis, and the services of a gillie or instructor can be provided if required.

Strutt & Parker Sporting, 37 Davies Street, London W1Y 2SP.

Orvis owns and manages stretches of water on the rivers Test and Itchen. Undoubtedly the best-known is the Ginger Beer beat at Kimbridge, which is just downstream from Halford's favourite water and is noted for its free-rising fish – in recent years there have been catches of a 9lb 4oz brown and a 10lb 8oz rainbow. Timsbury, beats 5 and 6, are renowned for a prolific mayfly season and excellent evening rises. Their Itchen water at Abbotts Worthy is considered to be among the best wild brown trout stream fishing in the country. Orvis also run fly fishing courses on the Test in Hampshire, in Yorkshire, Wales (sea-trout) and Devon (game fishing).

Orvis, Vermont House, Unit 4A, North Way, Andover, Hants SP10 5RW.

Famous Fishing (in association with Sage) provides guided chalkstream fishing on eighteen different chalkstreams in the south of England. Many of their beats have connections which appeal to those interested in fly fishing history. A good example is the stretch of the Hampshire Bourne described in

Plunket Greene's classic *Where the Bright Waters Meet*. A speciality of theirs is a week-long trip with fishing on a different river for wild brown trout each day.

Famous Fishing, Greystones, Teffont Evias, Salisbury, Wiltshire SP3 5RG.

Fishing Breaks have daily rods on all the major southern chalkstreams – including the Parsonage beat on the Test between Stockbridge and Romsey; Bullington Manor on the Dever, an upper arm of the Test; Newton Stacey, which marks the junction of the Test and Dever; Compton Estate, which is halfway between Stockbridge and Romsey; Itchen Stoke and Gaters Mill on the Itchen; Wrackleford, north-west of Dorchester, on the Frome; Sydling Brook and the Piddle, two tributaries of the Frome, and part of the Compton Chamberlayne Estate on the Nadder.

Fishing Breaks Ltd, 23 Compton Terrace, London N1 2UN.

Roxton Bailey Robinson, 25 High Street, Hungerford, Berkshire RG17 0NF, have daily rods on the Test, Nadder and Wylye.

Chess   A small trout stream rising near Chesham in Buckinghamshire and flowing into the Colne near Rickmansworth. (It was reported at one time that rainbow trout were breeding on the Chess). Latimer Park Lakes, a well-run and well-stocked fishery, has both lake and river fishing. It is stocked daily with triploid rainbows to 14lb and browns to 10lb, which are reared on site. The fishery is fed by spring water from the river Chess.

Chetham, James   A seventeenth-century fisherman who came from Smedley near Manchester. Author of *The Angler's Vade Mecum* (1681), which owes a good deal to Cotton and Barker, he produced some interesting patterns of flies for spate rivers (stoney rivers he called them) and was the first angling writer, as far as is known, who used a starling's quill feather for winging – an improvement on the mallard used by Barker and Cotton. He was meticulous in giving his dressings:

> Little Blue Dun. Made of Down of a Mouse for Body and Head, dub'd with sad Ash-coloured silk; Wings of the sad-coloured Feather of a Sheepstare's Quill. Note that the Feather got from the Quills or Pens of Sheepstares Wings, Throstle Wings, Fieldfare Wings, are generally better (the first 2 especially) to use for Dub-fly Wings than those got from a wild Mallard or Drake.

Sheepstare is the old name for a starling. Sad means dark-coloured.

Chetham also had a good dressing of the Black Gnat, probably derived from Cotton and Barker:

> Black Midge or Gnat: Made of the Down of a Mole, Dub'd with Black Silk, Wings of the light grey feather of a Sheepstare's Quill.

The dressing is a basic one and has survived to this day. G. E. M. Skues has something like it, and Halford certainly had similar dressings to many of Chetham's. Chetham's Blue Dun is an improvement on Cotton's, though all these old writers used dubbing which we would find difficulty in getting nowadays – such as hair from black greyhounds and old foxes:

> Blue Dun. Made of the Down of a Water-mouse and the Blewish dun of an Old Fox mixt together, Dub'd with sad Ash-coloured Silk; Wings of the Feather of a Sheepstare Quill.

In all his patterns Chetham was most concerned to imitate the natural insect as closely as possible, and in the second edition of his book (1689) made a point of saying 'the fly is always to be on the very surface or top of the water'.

Chew The River Chew in North Somerset near Pensford is coloured and slow-flowing but holds a reasonable stock of wild brown trout. They are frequently wormed but will certainly take the nymph put to a bulging fish under the willows. Several fishing clubs have water, and a good place is Bond's Bridge at Chew Magna.

Chew Valley Lake With some 1,200 acres Chew, ten miles south of Bristol, is by far the largest of the three reservoirs managed by Bristol Water Fisheries. Situated in the heart of the Chew Valley, the lake is surrounded by unspoilt meadow and woods, making it a perfect setting for a day's fishing. Opened in 1956, and considered at that time to be one of Europe's finest fisheries, it is today ranked among the top four in Britain.

More often than not the trout are moving actively on the surface and provide fishing of a high standard. The policy (1998) is to stock 42,000 takeable fish throughout the season with the addition of larger fish of 3 to 5lb. The 1997 season returns were 1,518 brown and 22,908 rainbow, with a best brown of 10lb.

There is some seven miles of bank fishing, with Woodford Bank, North Shore, Wick Green and Nunnery Point being the most popular areas. There is a fleet of 30 motor boats, and extra boats can be arranged for larger competitions; two motor boats are available for use by wheelchair anglers, who must be accompanied by an able-bodied person.

Chew has its own resident professional fly fishing guide, John Horsey, a respected writer and contributor to *Stillwater Trout, Trout & Salmon* and *Trout Fisherman* magazines. Chew tends to be heavily booked during the prime fishing months, so prior booking is recommended.

For recommended methods and season dates *see* Blagdon Lake.

Chironomid *See* Midge.

Cholmondeley-Pennell, H. (1837-1915)   An Inspector of Sea Fisheries for a number of years in the 1870s, Cholmondeley-Pennell was a great all-round fisherman, and his publications include *The Modern Practical Angler, The Sporting Fish of Great Britain* and *Improvements of Fishing Tackle and Fish Hooks.* He also edited the Badminton Library book, *Fishing.* Today he is probably best remembered for the Pennell series of flies.

Church, Bob   A noted Midland tackle dealer, and an international fly fisher with two world championship gold, one silver and one bronze medals to his credit. Bob Church was among the pioneers of deep lure fishing on reservoirs and has a reputation as an innovative fly-tyer.   For over 26 years he has been a regular contributor to the angling press, including *Angling Times, Trout Fisherman* and *Practical Gamefishing,* and has written numerous books on fly fishing. His first, *Reservoir Trout Fishing* (with Colin Dyson), was an immediate success and reprinted several times.   Other titles include *Imitations of the Trout's World* (with Peter Gathercole), *Stillwater Trout* (with Charles Jardine), *Flyfishing for Trout* (with Peter Gathercole), *Bob Church's Guide to Trout Flies* and *Bob Church's Guide to New Fly Patterns.*

Clarke, (James) Brian   A professonal journalist, later an industrial communications specialist, Clarke has been absorbed all his life by what he once wrote of as 'the loveliness of light and water and trees and birds, and the separated, drowned-

music mystery of fishes.' A prolific writer on angling and other subjects, and a regular broadcaster and photographer, he is author of *The Pursuit of Stillwater Trout* which helped to rehabilitate the art of imitative fishing on lakes. In 1980, with John Goddard, he published *The Trout and the Fly*, a detailed study of the trout described by Richard Walker as 'likely to prove to be the most important contribution to the literature of trout fishing this century.' Both books ran to several printings and translations. Clarke writes on fishing for *The Times*, and formerly did so for the *Sunday Times*.

Coachman A most useful general pattern fly which takes fish on rivers and lakes, fished wet or dry, for most of the season. What it represents is uncertain, possibly a beetle or one of the dipterans. The origin of the Coachman is obscure. It is often attributed to Tom Bosworth, coachman to the Prince Regent and the young Queen Victoria. Since the Prince Regent and his father were said to be interested in fly fishing, it could be so; however, Salter's *Angling Guide* (1814) says, 'There is a fly used very much at Watford in Herts called Harding's Fly or the Coachman' (the river would probably be the Colne, which must then have been a fine trout stream). Whether Mr Harding or Mr Bosworth first tied the Coachman, or whether both tied a Coachman, remains unresolved. The standard pattern is:

> *Body:* green peacock herl twisted in with the tying silk
> *Wings:* two slips of white feather, swan or goose – upright for the dry fly, sloping back for the wet
> *Hackle:* medium red cock
> *Hook:* sizes vary according to how the fly is to be fished, from size 16 for a dry fly on a clear stream to 8 or 6, sometimes weighted, for still water and sea-trout wet-fly fishing.

The white wing has great advantage, for it can easily be seen – by the fish when fished wet, by the angler when fished dry. The Coachman, with variations, appears on many rivers world wide. In America, there is a Royal Coachman with a purple body, gold twist and a fluff of peacock herl at the tail.

Cockwill, Peter This amiable Cornishman, with his fly fishing feet firmly planted in the small streams, moved to Surrey in the late 1960s, just as still water fishing was developing. A master of still water angling, and responsible for many of today's fly patterns and fishing techniques, Peter Cockwill has written extensively for several fishing magazines and is the author of *Introduction to Fly Tying, Big Trout Fishing* and *Trout From Small Stillwaters*.

By profession a water chemist, Peter worked in local government for twenty-two years before leaving to set up his own game fishing shop in Surrey which has import agencies for the major American manufacturers. Well known for his record catches, he had the first ever 20lb rainbow in the UK, and has held many fishery records. He has an enviable record in major competitions, having twice won the UK Small Fisheries Championship and competed five times in the European Open (coming first on one occasion and being placed on the other four). He was a member of Bob Church's team which won the English final of the Benson & Hedges championship.

Peter has fished all around the world and hosts parties of anglers to Alaska every year. A qualified instructor, he operates a syndicate trout fishery, sits on many fishery committees and is in great demand as a club speaker.

Coch-y-Bondhu A trout fly that imitates a Welsh beetle. Courtney Williams gives this dressing as standard:

> *Body:* two or three strands of copper-coloured peacock herl twisted together with the tying silk for strength, with two turns of flat gold tinsel as a tag
> *Hackle:* Coch-y-Bondhu, that is to say a cock feather with a black centre and a red list (red border)
> *Hook:* 14 - 12

The Cochy is a good general beetle pattern and is not dissimilar to others, such as Dr Terry's and Horsfall Turner's.

Collyer, David J. A regular column on fly-dressing in *Trout Fisherman* magazine gave David Collyer a reputation as one of the most inventive fly-dressers of the 1970s and 1980s. He is the author of the two-volume work *Fly-Dressing* which gives details of the tying of a considerable number of patterns from chalkstream dry flies to salmon flies, tubes to traditional feather wings.

Colquhoun, John Author of several angling books, including *The Moor and the Loch* (1840) which gives two fly patterns for

lake fishing that were quite possibly the forerunners of the Mallard and Claret and the Teal and Red. The first had a dark mallard wing and a brown mohair body, the second a teal wing with claret mohair.

Competitive Fly Fishing   There is a marked dichotomy of opinion between anglers who subscribe to that 'solitary vice' and those who indulge in competitive fishing – though of course, one does not have to be enjoyed at the expense of the other. Whatever your view, there is no denying the popularity of competitive fly fishing, which has its origins (both at national and international level) in Scotland – the oldest recorded major event anywhere in the world was staged at Loch Leven more than a hundred years ago and this same event is still fished as the Scottish National Trout Fly Fishing Championship. Today competitions, ranging from the relatively new small still water events to the international championships attract anglers in their hundreds of thousands. The variety and form of competition is enormous and encompasses dry, wet, bank and boat fishing, fly-tying and casting, for the able-bodied and disabled, inter-services, juniors, men and women.

The first international match between England and Scotland was in 1928, and the competition was extended to include Wales and Ireland in 1932. Today over twenty countries participate in European and World Championships.

One of the most prestigious national competitions, for club teams, was that sponsored by Benson & Hedges from its inception in 1982 to 1997, and by the House of Hardy from 1998.

The several national and international bodies involved in the organisation of competitive fly fishing are given below:

World and European:
Fédération Internationale de Sportive Pêche Mouche. General Secretary: James Ferguson, 6 The Strand, Rye, East Sussex TN31 7D

Home Internationals:
International Fly Fishing Association. Hon. Sec. Ian Campbell, Cruachan, 16 Marindin Park, Glenfarg, Perth & Kinross PH2 9NQ

England:
Confederation of English Fly Fishers (CEFF). Hon. Sec. John

Boon CBE, Romach, Ross Road, Newent, Glos GL18 1BE
English Disabled Fly Fishers. Derek Lucas, 50 Hazelwood
Road, South Wigston, Leics LE18 4LS. Associate member
CEFF
English Ladies Flyfishing Association. Wendy Miller, 40
West End, Whittlesey, Peterborough PE7 1LS. Associate
member CEFF
English Youth Flyfishing Association. Mike Watts, 66
Northampton Road, Kettering, Northants NN15 7JX.
Associate member CEFF

Ireland:
Irish Trout Fly Fishing Association. Austin Murray, 47
Ginnell Terrace, Mullingar, Co. Westmeath

Scotland:
Scottish Anglers National Association (SANA).
Hon. Sec. Ian Campbell, Cruachan, 16 Marindin Park,
Glenfarg, Perth & Kinross PH2 9NQ. International
Secretary Dr Neil McCarry, 57 Galbraith Avenue, Milngavie,
Glasgow G62 6LZ.

Wales:
Welsh Salmon & Trout Angling Association. Moc Morgan
OBE. Swyn Teifi, Pontrhydfendigaid, Ystrad Meurig, Dyfed
SY25 6RF

Conn, Lough   Lough Conn in Co. Mayo has a great reputation
as a fine brown trout fishery, and there is a moderate run of
salmon as well. It is a big lough of some 14,000 acres, nine
miles long and two to four miles wide. Visitors should check
whether there are fishing competitions on certain days, as
these may well take over all the boats and available boatmen.
The brown trout fishing is free, and this is very much a free-
taking lough for those who fish the drift in front of the boat.
Salmon are generally taken by deep trolling, but there are
times when one will take flies fished on the drift. Fishing
holidays can be organised by Healey's Hotel, Pontoon, Mayo;
Cong Gateway, Lackafinna, Cong, Mayo; and the Pontoon
Bridge Hotel, Foxford, Mayo.

Connemara Black   A fly for all seasons. In Ireland it is a
popular fly for trout, sea-trout and in large sizes for salmon. In
England mainly used for fishing the large reservoirs for
stocked rainbows. A very versatile fly:

Body: black seal's fur or similar
Wings: bronze mallard
Hackle: black cock with blue jay at the throat
Tail: golden pheasant topping
Tag: orange floss
Rib: oval silver tinsel, fine
Hook: 14 - 8

Conon There is a Conon in Skye, but the main salmon river of that name is in Ross and Cromarty, coming down from Loch Luichart over the great cascades of the Falls of Conon and out into the Cromarty Firth. The Fairburn Estate has water, and so have Cononbridge Hotel and Strathgarve Lodge Hotel.

Conway Now spelt on the maps in true Welsh style as the Conwy, this river rises on Mignient and flows down through Fairy Glen and over the spectacular Conwy Falls before settling down to a gentler pace below Betws-y-Coed, where it is a salmon and a noted sea-trout (sewin) river. Above Conwy Falls there is some wonderful wild brown trout fishing to be had – small fish maybe, but a real challenge to one's casting and angling skills. Day tickets are available from fishing associations in Betws-y-Coed. The best advice on the choice of fly patterns is always local advice: each sewin river is different, and the local anglers know which sizes and patterns work best at different times in the season. Night fishing for sewin usually begins in June and continues until September.

Corixa A stillwater beetle, varying in size, often known as the water boatman, or lesser water boatman, but not to be confused with those gyrating surface insects which are water skaters. The *Corixidae* have oar-like back legs which they use to shoot up to the surface fast for a drop of air and return to their weed bed, jiggling about a good deal both ways. Some entomologist-anglers say trout do not eat *corixa*, some, including Goddard, say they do. It may depend on the species or on the trout. The Chomper flies designed by Richard Walker may suggest *corixa*, and Goddard and many others have devised patterns. This one is fairly standard:

Body: white floss silk, nicely rounded, over fine lead wire
Rib: fine silver wire
Wing cases: a bunch of dark mallard fibres tied fore and aft
Beard hackle: a few fibres of grouse
Hook: 10 - 12

Corrib, Lough   Lough Corrib in Co. Mayo must be among one of the world's greatest game fisheries. It stretches in a great crescent around Connemara from Galway City for over 30 miles. The season starts with the fly for trout in late March, generally the duck fly, and the big mayfly time is in May, lasting for nearly a month. There are some salmon and pike and *ferox* trout, which are generally taken by trolling. Fishing is free, plenty of boats, boatmen and tackle shops are to be found in angling centres such as Oughterard. Accommodation is available at the Boat Inn, The Square, Oughterard; the Corrib Wave Guest House, Portacarron, Oughterard; the Lake Hotel, Oughterard; Lakeland Town and Country Homes, Oughterard; and Knockferry Lodge, Knockferry, Roscahill, Co. Galway.

Corrib, River   The river drains Lough Corrib, its tributaries include the Mask and Carra, and it flows into Galway Bay. The river is only 5½ miles long but is regarded as one of Ireland's top salmon fisheries, and from the anglers' point of view is divided into four sections. The first reaches from Friars Cut at the lough to the Weir. The next fishery down is the Weir or Galway fishery, which everyone applies for; the third step down is the New beat; and the final stretch is reserved for local anglers. Spinning, shrimp or fly are generally used, as are tubes or size 4 trebles. The angler must use leaders of from 15 to 20lb; body waders and a wading staff are essential, and one must be able to cast a long line. Accommodation at the Ardilaun House Hotel, Taylors Hill, Co. Galway.

Costa   The third and least well-known of the Yorkshire trout streams (the other two being the Driffield and the Foston becks), this is a well-loved little river, quite narrow, that provides some excellent trout fishing. Its origins are at Keld Head, Pickering, in North Yorkshire. Due to careful maintenance by the Pickering Club, it is once again regaining some of its former glory. The Costa was always a favourite of that great angling writer Eric Horsfall Turner, who on most days in the years before his death could be found stalking the butter-yellow trout of this little chalk stream.

Costelloe and Fermoyle Fisheries   comprise in the upper reaches, Clogher, Carrick, Fermoyle, Rusheen, Muckinagh and Schoolhouse loughs, while the lower section has Glenicmurrin Lough, the most famous of them all. The river and lakes get a small run of spring salmon from March onwards, and of grilse from May onwards. If there is a sea-trout run, that would be best from mid-June through July to September. Permits and accommodation from the Manager, Costelloe and Fermoyle Fisheries, Bridge Cottage, Costelloe, Co. Galway.

Cotton, Charles (1630 – 1687) Translator, poet, fisherman, country squire, friend of Izaak Walton, and author of the second part of *The Compleat Angler* in the fifth edition (1676). One of the best books about him is *Charles Cotton and His River* by Gerald G. P. Heywood, whose research into the Peak District, the river Dove, Charles Cotton's house at Beresford Dale and the Fishing House is unrivalled.

Cotton learned his fishing as a boy, when he fished the Dove as it ran through the grounds of Beresford Hall, his father's house. He is believed to have studied at Cambridge, and in 1658 he inherited the estates of Beresford and Bentley on the Staffordshire-Derbyshire borders. But it was not until he was over 40 that he wrote the famous addition to Walton's *Compleat Angler*.

The dressings of 65 flies given by Cotton, many of them with some variations, are in use today. He recommended casting a fly across the river, or else up and down, according to the wind. The rod was a flexible 17ft with a tapered horsehair line some 3ft longer. Cotton's list of flies and instructions for dressings are given in Lawrie's *Reference Book of English Trout Flies*.

Currane, Lough Visitors come from many parts of Europe and even further afield for Currane's spring salmon run and also for the big sea-trout, though both have declined in recent years. The early season salmon are taken by trolling as a rule but many are nevertheless inclined to take the fly. For the salmon a double-handed rod, a 16lb leader and standard fly patterns on sizes 4, 6, and 8 are recommended. The fishing is free. There are about four or five hotels listed in the official tourist guide but the one most anglers seem to prefer is the Butler Arms Hotel, Waterville, Co Kerry.

Curse For the Angler's Curse, *see Caenis*.

Cutcliffe, H. C. A surgeon whose home was at South Molton, Devon. While on active service as a doctor in India Cutcliffe

wrote a book about fishing the Mole and Bray in Devon. His book, *The Art of Trout Fishing on Rapid Streams* (1863), is notable for the elaborate details which he gives on fly-tying in the Devon style. He advocated the use of hackle flies fished upstream either on or just below the surface of the water.

D

Daddy Longlegs   The Crane fly, a terrestrial, is avidly taken by trout when blown onto the water during August. Sometimes the trout will attempt to drown the bigger struggling flies before eating them, which means a strike on the second rise or when the fly line moves. There are a number of Daddy patterns, here is Richard Walker's:

Body: Veniard plastic mayfly
Wings: light ginger hackle points, tied spent (badger as an alternative)
Legs: six long strands of black horsehair or nylon knotted and tied to lie backwards along the body
Hackle: a collar of light red cock, six turns
Hook: up eyed 10 or 12

The Parachute Daddy by Peter Deane is an interesting illusion fly:

Body: white nylon floss with the end projecting upwards behind the eye
Hackle: dark brown cock with fibres, ½" to ¾" long (13–18mm), tied parachute-style round the projecting end of the white floss, leaving a flare of white floss visible overall
Tail: half a dozen fibres of dark brown cock, tied rather long
Hook: 10 or 12 long-shank

The upstanding white floss over the hackle gives this fly good visibility at a distance. Walker and Deane's patterns can be fished inert in or on the surface, occasionally twitched, sometimes moved on a long draw, like a wake fly.

Damselfly   A smaller cousin of the dragonfly, the damselfly is more popular with lake fishermen because when plenty are about the trout feed well on the nymph, and the artificial nymph is smaller and more easily handled than imitations of the big dragon nymph. Most of the adult damsels are a vivid

blue but the nymphs are darker, almost olive-green, sometimes slightly yellow. Trout leap at the egg-laying adults but the nymph is the favourite. One of the best designs is Peter Lapsley's:

Tying silk: brown, buff or yellow
Underbody: 10 to 14 turns of fine wire under the thorax (optional)
Tail: three cock pheasant tail feather fibre points, tied short
Abdomen: pale green seal fur, ribbed with fine oval gold tinsel
Thorax: pale green seal fur
Wing cases: brown feather fibre
Legs: one turn of grey partridge, clipped short on the top by the wing case
Hook: 8–10 long-shank

An interesting point about the damselfly nymph is that it may well give an impression of a free-swimming sedge pupa in addition to what it is intended to represent, as can be seen in the illustration drawn from life by C. F. Walker in his *Lake Flies and Their Imitation*. Standard patterns of the damselfly are not infrequently taken when there are sedge hatching but not a damsel in sight. The damsel, therefore, might well be in business as a general pattern of underwater insects, representing at least two of the most popular ones.

The natural nymph swims with a pronounced wiggle, a movement captured in Peter Gathercole's dressing for the Damsel Wiggle Nymph from *Bob Church's Guide to New Fly Patterns*, an admirable book which introduces 400 brand new flies using modern materials:

Tying silk: Olive pre-waxed
Tail: Marabou dyed olive
Rib: Fine gold wire
Body: Medium-olive SLF
Hackle: Grey partridge dyed olive
Wing-cases: Olive feather fibre
Head: Very small lead eyes with a clear varnish tying off
Hook: Long-shank, size 10; either a specific angled pattern or a hook bent with pliers

Peter Gathercole says, 'Points to consider in producing an effective imitation of the damselfly nymph are colour, slimness of profile, and mobility. The Damselfly Wiggle Nymph fulfils all three, not least mobility'.

Peter Lapsley points out that one can easily distinguish

between a dragonfly and a damselfly. The damselfly fold its wings over its body when at rest, the dragonfly leaves them wide open and flat, at right angles to the body.

Dapping   *See* Boat Fishing

Dark Watchet   A trout fly of the northern streams, invaluable on rivers like the Wharfe in Yorkshire. It may suggest a nymph or a drowned iron blue, for it is almost invariably fished wet, upstream. The Dark Watchet is a puzzling fly for the fly-dresser because there are several patterns, some more hackled than winged, similar to the Bloas.
    This may be a compromise:

Body: two or three turns of bright scarlet silk showing at the tail, the rest dubbed lightly with mole fur
Wings: dark coot or blackbird, lying well back
Hackle and whisks: dark blue cock
Head: scarlet silk
Hook: 14 or 16

It is of interest that on rivers like the Wharfe the flies – iron blues and olives – invariably hatch quickly and rarely ride the stream, as the flies do on the chalk streams. The dry fly is therefore of much less importance. If the trout are seen rising they may well be just taking nymph, which, on these stony rivers, move fast. A Dark Watchet cast just above the rise and pulled in fast will generally provoke a take if the fish is still in position. Otherwise the Watchet can be fished inert on the drift, just below the surface.

Dart   Among the loveliest of Devon rivers, the Dart is one of many streams that rise among the great peat beds of Dartmoor. In the upper reaches it begins by being two streams, the East and West Dart, which provide delicate and exciting fly fishing as they wind their way through pools and rapids, high granite boulders, bright swathes of cotton grass and heather. They gradually fall from the bleak heights of the moor towards Dartmeet, where they join and become the Dart.
    The two upper rivers, Duchy of Cornwall water, provide some of the cheapest wild brown trout fishing in England. Permits to fish the water at only a few pounds can be had from inns like the Forrest Inn at Hexworthy and the Arundell Arms at Lifton, and at some village shops and post offices. The wild brown trout rise well to a dry fly fished in the

pockets of water between the rocks, in the long glides in the curl of the water under the banks. In the early season there are good hatches of March Brown and Large Dark Olive, followed later by the Olive Upright, the Blue-Winged Olive and the August Dun. Popular artificials include the Hare's Ear, Pheasant Tail and Coachman. There are good articles on fishing the Dart by Mike Weaver and Charles Bingham in *West Country Fly Fishing*. David Barr writes:

> Below Dartmeet the Dart reveals its true potential as a real salmon river, though in times of low water there are not many pools that remain fly-fishable. There is exciting fishing down to Newbridge, but the best of the Dart is to be found through Holne Chase down to Buckfastleigh, where pool is followed by pool, each one capable of holding salmon and sea trout. The Chase Pool at Holne Chase is a classic salmon pool with a low water taking-place close to its head and another lower down that is equally effective in six inches of floodwater. As has happened to nearly every river, the spring run for which the Dart was once renowned has diminished, but with rain in March and April there should be still fine fish to be caught. Between the weir at Totnes and Buckfastleigh, the local association controls most of the fishing. Above Buckfastleigh the water is almost entirely fly only – rightly so, because at the right level there is no more perfect fly water.

Davy, Sir Humphrey (1778–1829) As well as being a chemist, physicist, President of the Royal Society in 1820 and inventor of the miners' safety lamp, Penzance-born Davy was a devoted and lifelong fly fisherman who wrote happily of fishing the Colne and the Wandle, among other rivers. His description of a mayfly hatch on the Colne is frequently quoted as an example of fishing the floating fly: 'Now I shall throw the drake a foot above him. It floats down and he has taken it'. Davy's mayfly dressing – he tied his own – was almost as good as anything we have today:

Wings: mallard feathers dyed yellow
Body: monkey fur dyed yellow
Legs: olive mohair

He wrote a book on fishing, *Salmonia* (1828), which showed a remarkable knowledge of insect life, well in advance of his time. It was written as a conversation between several fishermen rather on the lines of Walton's book but, unfortunately, without Walton's charm. It is, however, still

worth reading. For example:

> For my health I thank God and my ancestors: and though I do not expect like our arch patriarch Walton to number ninety years and upwards, yet I hope, as long as I can enjoy in a vernal day the warmth and light of the sunbeams, still to haunt the streams – following the example of our late venerable friend, the president of the Royal Academy, Benjamin West, in company with whom, when he was an octogenarian, I have thrown the fly, caught trout, and enjoyed a delightful day angling and social amusement, in the shady green meadows by the bright clear streams of the Wandle.

Deane, Peter (1917 - 1998) Invalided out of the army in 1943 after contracting polio whilst on leave, Peter Deane set up a fly-tying business in Devon and quickly established a reputation for quality and invention. His great successes include the Shadow Mayfly, Parachute Daddy Longlegs and the Beacon Beige. In spite of being confined to a wheelchair for the rest of his life he was able to fish many rivers and was also a keen ornithologist.

Dee The Aberdeenshire Dee, about 80 miles long, rises in the Cairngorms and flows into the sea at Aberdeen on Scotland's east coast. It is one of the most attractive of salmon rivers and a great favourite of the royal family – their holiday home is on its banks at Balmoral. The river is notable for its spring fishing and, on this, good advice is given by John Ashley-Cooper in *A Salmon Fisher's Odyssey*:

> The river provides the most attractive fly water and it seems a shame to use anything else in it. Most people would say that small fly fishing with a floating line (as popularised by Mr A. H. E. Wood of Cairnton in the 1920s) is the most attractive method. Though no one would deny its merits I am not sure that I altogether agree. I do find that fishing a medium-size fly on a floating line with a sinking tip is a most enjoyable and effective method at a time when many fishermen are falling back on bait. If the water is cold I am only too glad to use a sunk line with a biggish fly . . . . Few people realise how deadly a sunk fly can be in the hands of a skilled performer.

Bell Ingram of Edinburgh and Strutt & Parker of London and Edinburgh are agents for some of the best beats but one may have to wait a long time. Just above Balmoral are the Invercauld Estate waters which are very productive and are let

on a weekly basis by the estate office at Braemar. The Invercauld Arms Hotel also has water for guests. Philip Green's *New Angles on Salmon Fishing* has invaluable advice on the Dee.

Dee (Welsh) The Dee rises in the Aran mountains and flows through Bala (the largest natural lake in Wales), Corwen, Llangollen, Overton and finally Chester. The stretch upriver from Llangollen, together with several of the Dee's tributaries, is best for the trout angler. The upper water is swift-flowing and offers excellent fishing. In 1990 anglers from around the world came to fish for grayling (two-pounders are common) on the river Dee in the World Fly Fishing Championships. Inexpensive day tickets are available on most stretches of the river.

Delphi Badger A delightful little tube fly, very takeable in many fisheries quite apart from Delphi:

> *Tying silk:* red
> *Body:* ½" plastic tube
> *Dressing:* an untidy bunch of badger hair tied all round the tube
> *Head:* red

That's all there is to it – very simple, but spring salmon and grilse like it, and so do sea-trout if there are any.

Delphi Fishery (Bundorragha River) The river is not very long, about a mile and a half, but has a great reputation. It drains two loughs, Finlough and Doo, and the river and these two loughs constitute the renowned Delphi fishery which has greater-than-average takes from salmon and still some from sea-trout. Fishing is fly only, and a popular fly is the Delphi Badger. Accommodation for fishermen is available at the Delphi Lodge, Leennane, Co. Galway, which has its own rod-room and tackle shop. Self-catering cottages are also available locally.

Delphi Silver A sea-trout fly named after the famous Delphi fishery but its use has spread widely, even to the Faroes:

> *Body:* in two parts, flat silver tinsel
> *Tying silk:* black
> *Hackle:* black cock tied to divide the body between the two parts of silver and a larger black hackle at the head

Tail: two very small jungle cock eyes tied back to back
Hook: 8 to 12

Derwent (Derbyshire) *See under* Wye (Derbyshire).

Derwent (Yorkshire) Sometimes this limestone stream gives the impression of a chalk stream, and its trout are free-rising. There is some excellent fly fishing near Scarborough on the Derwent Angling Club water. Tickets for this long stretch of about eight miles can be obtained from tackle dealers or at the Hackness Grange Hotel at Hackness, where one can also enjoy feeding tame rainbows in the hotel lake. Nymph fishing on the Derwent is restricted, and most trout are taken on the dry fly – Greenwell, Blue Quill and Pheasant Tail.

Deveron A good salmon and sea-trout river some fifty miles long in north-east Scotland; it enters the sea at Banff. Bell Ingram of Edinburgh are agents for some of the best of the private fishing, but beats are not easily come by. Tickets for association water can be obtained from tackle dealers at Huntley. John Ashley-Cooper records that the biggest Deveron fish weighed 61lb, caught in October 1924, by Mrs Morrison on the Wood O'Shaws pool in the Mount Blairy water. Taken on a 1½ inch fly – it is the biggest fish ever caught on a fly in Britain. He writes that the fish was not weighed until the day after it was caught, so its true weight might have rivalled Mrs Ballantyne's 64-pounder from the Tay.

Disabled, Angling for From small beginnings there are now, and not before time, facilities throughout the country for the visually impaired and physically disabled person to enjoy fly fishing.

England: HRH The Prince of Wales launched the first of many Wheelyboats in 1985 and the Handicapped Anglers Trust: Boating for the Disabled, a registered charity, began its work of promotion and distribution. These boats have become a familiar sight on inland waters throughout the UK from Cornwall to Caithness, offering the freedom of the water to countless disabled adults and children. The boat was specially designed and is purpose-built with a bow ramp which lowers onto the shore to allow easy access by wheelchairs. Once on board, the flat, level and unobstructed deck makes manoeuvring wheelchairs a simple matter. Built of double skinned aluminium, the Wheelyboat is extraordinary stable and with its foam-filled bottom, is virtually unsinkable. The boat measures 12' x 5' and can be propelled by oars or an outboard motor.

Although first promoted for handicapped fly-fishermen, the boat has become a boon to the disabled of all ages whose lives are enriched by the joys of water-borne activities. As well as angling these can include bird-watching, photography, painting, environmental studies, family picnics or simply the delights of going out in a small boat.

All the boats in use, and there are are some seventy of them, have been generously sponsored by water authorities, angling clubs, industry, local authorities and private individuals. In 1996 the National Lottery Sports Fund agreed a grant towards the cost of another ten Wheelyboats. The Salmon and Trout and Country Landowners' Associations, the British Field Sports Society, the Lloyds Bank Charitable Trust and Action Research have all been particularly supportive.

HAT Director (1998): Brian Dunn, Taigh Na Iasgair, Russell Close, Little Chalfont, Bucks HP6 6RE.

The English Disabled Fly Fishers Association was formed in 1980 to promote competitive fly fishing for the disabled but now covers all aspects of the sport. The organisation is run by a committee of ten disabled people and is supported by the House of Commons and Commoners Fly Fishers and the Sports Council. It is an associate member of the Confederation of Fly Fishers and of the Salmon & Trout Association.

Membership secretary (1998): John Redfern, 81 Gladys Road, Smethwick, West Midlands B67 5AN

Scotland: In 1971 an angling instructor experimented with teaching fly fishing to blind persons, and such was the interest that very soon disabled persons were being included. A Committee for the Promotion of Angling for the Disabled (CPAD) was established, and in the late 1970s it became a standing committee of the Scottish Sports Association for the Disabled (SSAD); in 1998 it became affiliated to the Scottish Anglers National Association (SANA). It was involved in the creation of a special boat-seat that allows a disabled angler to fish from any boat. It organised the first national fly fishing championship for disabled anglers in 1979, and the first international match against England, Wales and Ireland in 1980, and in 1982 it published the *Facilities Guide for Disabled Anglers in Scotland.* Since those early days the Scottish Sports

Council has been actively involved with CPAD in promoting angling for disabled and handicapped people in Scotland. The work of the CPAD is recognised throughout the British Isles and they will assist any body interested in fly fishing for people with a disability.

There are now many Scottish waters suitable for the independent wheelchair-user who may fish for salmon, sea-trout and brown trout. In the case of boat fishing an able-bodied companion is necessary, and assistance is forthcoming from most local angling associations, who maintain a register of volunteers.

CPAD Chairman (1998): Mike Tudor, Lomondside Cottage, The Loan, Falkland, Fife KY15 7BD.

SSAD Administrator (1998), Mrs Margaret MacPhee, Fife Institute of P&RE, Viewfield Road, Glenrothes, Fife KY6 2RB.

Ireland: The Irish Fly Fishing Association covers the whole of Ireland, organises the annual Irish Disabled Fly Fishing Championship and selects a team to represent Ireland at the Disabled International. The Ulster section holds a monthly competition at Tildarg Fishery, near Ballyclare. It has two electric powered Wheelyboats at Tildarg and one Wheelyboat at the Park Lake Fishery, Dungannon.

Hon. Secretary (1998): E. J. Black, 6 Old Park Drive, Ballymena BT42 1BG.

Wales: Fishing for the disabled in the Principality is in the capable hands of the Welsh Salmon and Trout Angling Association which has its own dedicated team coaches for the disabled. The Environment Agency Wales, Welsh Water, WSTAA and individual angling clubs are exceptionally supportive of disabled anglers, enabling them to compete on a par with the able-bodied. Many fisheries now have purpose-built casting platforms in addition to Wheelyboats.

Hon. Secretary (1998): Moc Morgan OBE, Swyn Teifi, Pontrhydfendigaid, Aberystwth, Dyfed SY25 6EF.

Don Aberdeenshire is noted for its rivers, and the Don is one of the most attractive. The Grant Arms Hotel at Moneymusk has good salmon water. The trout fishing can be excellent, and some big fish are taken, as the Don is a limestone stream and very fertile. Take March Brown, Dark Olives and Iron Blues with you, but the best fly for Don trout is said to be Baigent's Brown, a large variant.

Dovedale Famous for its association with Charles Cotton and Izaak Walton, the river Dove at Dovedale, a National Trust beauty spot, is now the haunt of picnickers, paddlers and campers. This makes fishing difficult, and at holiday times impossible without a long walk upstream. Above and below Dovedale there is some excellent private syndicate fishing. Visiting Americans on a Walton-Cotton pilgrimage can stay at the Izaak Walton Hotel at Dovedale which can provide fishing. The Izaak Walton museum is at Shallowford Cottage in Stafford.

The Dove is a limstone stream with a good head of wild brown trout of ½ to 1lb with a few larger fish from time to time. It has a good growth of weed and some nice hatches of olives, especially the blue-winged olive, and sedges. The river is fairly shallow, and the fish take fright quickly and are inclined to desert those areas frequented by the holiday crowds.

Dovey (Dyfi) The sea-trout – sewin in Wales – start to run the Dovey (as the English still think of it, in spite of the Ordnance Survey) by June. There are salmon, but the Dovey is really a sea-trout river, and, as in most of Wales, there is a good deal of worming. Permits for association water can be had from most tackle shops and hotels, but one should be careful about crowds on the pools during the height of the run. Night, early morning and late evening are best. Local flies with unlikely names are popular, and it is best to try local patterns first. The best areas are around Machynlleth, Llanbrynmair and Dinas Mawddwy, where the Brigands Inn has water.

Driffield Beck A beautiful chalk stream in east Yorkshire, which provides some of the best, though highly preserved, fly fishing that can be found anywhere in England. Donald Overfield says it is equal to the Test:

> The twin feeders of the Driffield Beck have their sources at the Kirkburn and the Elmswell springs due north of the market town of Driffield. They then flow southwards to join together at Poundsworth, the site of the Driffield Angling Club's superb headquarters and head-keeper's house, from where they flow directly south through water meadows, eventually joining the river Hull.
>
> The Driffield Angler's Club formed in 1833 is the second oldest flyfishing club in the country, the oldest being the Houghton on the Test. The Club controls approximately twelve miles of pure

chalkstream from the twin springs to the village of Wansford, from which point the stream is owned by the Golden Hill Club and then West Beck Preservation Society. Midway down the Driffield Anglers' water the stream has a natural barrier in the form of a mill race, and above the race the fishing is brown trout only, while below the barrier the water contains brown trout, stocked rainbows and tremendous shoals of grayling. No day tickets issued and the water is closely controlled.

Driffield Dun An excellent Yorkshire fly; always fished upstream, similar in many ways to Border spiders:

Body: lead-coloured fur, mole or mole mixed with rabbit, ribbed with yellow silk, dressed sparse
Hackle: four or five turns of dun cock hackles, ginger or honey dun will do
Whisks: a few fibres of the same
Hook: 14 - 16

Dry Fly, Origins The first fisherman to attempt to create a dry fly was a Cromwellian soldier, Robert Venables (1662). He tied a hackle fly, turned it upside down so that the point of the hook lay upwards and then clipped the hackle on the top of the shank so that the remaining hackles would give the impression of wings. It was in a sense a forerunner of some of our own techniques, but was too complex to be popular.

In those days they were not called dry flies but floaters and, various fishermen made great efforts to tie flies that floated as long as possible. New designs came from the first serious entomological studies of John Taverner (*Certaine Experiments Concerning Fish and Fruite*, 1600), William Lawson (*Comments on John Denny's Secrets of Angling,* 1617, 1621), Charles Cotton (1630–1687), Thomas Barker (*The Art of Angling*, 1651) and James Chetham (*An Angler's Vade Mecum*, 1681). In the 1700s came the Bowlkers, father and son, who fished floating flies, generally the olives, that would stay on top of the water where the natural flies 'sported in their thousands'. The Bowlkers were among the first to tie big salmon flies in which small beads were used to create eyes on the heads of the flies, a device which twentieth-century reservoir trout anglers were to re-invent with great enthusiasm.

It is interesting that many of the new developments in fly and tackle design came not from the chalk streams in the south but from the provinces, the Midlands, the limestone rivers of

Derbyshire like the Dove, and W. C. Stewart and James Baillie on the Scottish Borders. Stewart was emphatic about the need to fish the fly upstream '. . . the great error of fly fishing as usually practised is that the angler fishes downstream whereas he should fish up . . . .' Stewart's book, *The Practical Angler*, first published in 1857 has been reprinted many times, most recently in 1996 by FCL. The first book exclusively devoted to fly fishing was George Scotcher's *The Fly Fisher's Legacy* (1810). Alfred Ronalds' *The Fly-Fisher's Entomology* (1836), created a greater understanding and knowledge of insects and George Pulman of Axminster, in his *Vade Mecum of Fly Fishing for Trout* (1841), was the first to use the words 'dry fly' – although this simply meant a fly that he had taken out of his box to replace a fly that had become soaked.

Two gillies and tackle dealers may have been the first around the 1840s to tie true dry flies. They were James Ogden of Gloucestershire (*Ogden on Fly Tying*, 1879) and David Foster of the Derbyshire Dove (*The Scientific Angler*, published posthumously by his sons in 1882 from Foster's notebooks going back to some time in the 1840s). Ogden also claimed that he tied the first dry flies in 1840, but there is no certainty about this, and both men knew each other. Foster is generally credited with the first dry fly, because of the detailed way he described the dressing in his notebooks. Here, briefly, is his description:

> The hackle for the legs must be tied ample and full to assist flotation . . . and the wings must be full and erect or cock up as the saying is . . . so as to admit the fly to be comparatively dry for some little time, when, becoming saturated, a few backwards and forwards whisks of the line and rod should be given before delivery of the cast again . . . .

So, somewhere around the 1840s to the 1860s, the dry fly as we have come to know it was invented and recorded in the notebooks and shop talk of tackle dealers and gillies in the provinces. It then spread to the fishing and country magazines, and from them to the chalkstreams, where Marryat and Halford created rigid codes in the belief that they had discovered the acme of unchanging perfection in designing and fishing the dry fly. The belief did not last; a revolutionary change in dry fly design was on its way. It came from a book by E. W. Harding (*The Fly Fisher and the Trout's Point of View*, 1931), who was one of the first to use an observation tank, and

found to his astonishment that a trout looking towards the surface from below did not see the floating fly at all but imprints and sparkles of light. The trout, said Harding, lived in a kind of Looking-Glass world where everything became curiouser and curiouser the more it was explored. The findings were confirmed by John Goddard, and in America by Vincent Marinaro. It was as though for each generation there had to be new flies that came and went into and out of fashion.

Duck Fly There are times – generally in the spring and especially on the big Irish loughs – when midges hatch in enormous numbers, and it is then that an imitation of a midge comes into its own. Why it is called the Duck Fly is not known for certain though it has been suggested that ducklings, before they are strong enough to dive for weed, eat small black flies, probably midge pupae, floating on the surface.

The most usual dressing is the Black Duck Fly. This is J. R. Harris's:

> *Body:* black floss silk, thickened near the shoulder
> *Wings:* two dun or cream cock-hackle points, tied sloping backwards
> *Hackle:* a few turns of rusty black cock tied in front of the wings
> *Hook:* 12–16

The Olive Duck Fly (large olive midge) is of similar design with a pale-green or apple-green body ribbed with thin gold wire.

Dunkeld A fly for all seasons, for salmon as well as trout. Originally tied at Dunkeld on the Tay, it is now frequently used in still water fishing:

> *Body:* gold tinsel, sometimes ribbed with gold wire as well
> *Tag:* golden pheasant crest, upturned to meet the wing
> *Cheeks:* jungle cock
> *Hackle:* beard hackle of hot-orange feather fibres
> *Hook:* almost any size but small stickleback size for lake trout; for salmon not much larger than a 6, because mallard fibre is short and one must try to get a reasonable balance between the mallard wing and the golden crest coming up to meet it

Bob Church's Guide to New Fly Patterns has a double-page spread of 16 colour photographs demonstrating, step-by-step, the tying of this popular wet fly.

Dunne, J. W. (*d.* 1949) Dunne was a passionate and inventive fly fisherman, and his book, *Sunshine and the Dry Fly*, introduced white painted hooks with a dubbing of rayon floss (cellulite) which, when oiled, became translucent. The wings were made from silks blended to mathematical formulae. The flies were successful but never became popular because of the difficulty of obtaining the right materials for tying them. Quite apart from his invention, the book remains fascinating to read for his enthusiasms and interpretation of the pleasures of fishing:

> Fly fishing stands almost in a class of its own. For the lore of nature which a fly fisherman may enlist to his advantage covers an area a hundred times greater and a thousand fold richer than are those which lie open to, for example, the votaries of bait and minnow. And indeed it may almost be said that in no sport in the world, with the possible exception of big game shooting, does knowledge, as opposed to mere physical dexterity, prove so fascinating in acquirement, or reap so delightfully satisfactory reward.

Durnford, Richard (1843–1934) A sporting clergyman, the Rev. Richard Durnford of Chilbolton, Hampshire fished the upper Test and the Anton from 1809 to 1819. His *Fishing Diary*, published in 1911, gives some fascinating vignettes of sporting life in Regency days.

Eden   There are four Eden rivers, but the best known is the one that rises on Black Fell Moss and flows by Appleby, Kirkby Stephen and Carlisle into the Solway Firth.   And a fine river it is, with a run of sea-trout and salmon at times as well as some good stocks of wild brown trout.   The sea-trout run from June onwards.   The salmon can be sparse. Bracken Bank Lodge at Lazonby has water.

Two other Cumbrian rivers, the Eden and Calder have good runs of sea-trout and the Sella Park Hotel at Calderbridge has water, some with day tickets, but, as on the Border Esk, there is a good deal of local bait fishing.

Arthur Ransome fished the Eden and paid tribute to a great Eden fisherman, William Nelson, in *Rod and Line*. Nelson fished the river between Wild Boar Fell and Armathwaite and by the rapid glide under the Castle Rock at Appleby; he was also a good grayling fisherman and 'a great hand at creeper-fishing, for which he had invented some ingenious artificial insects, and few could beat him in the use of the minnow'. Ransome said that Nelson's book, *Fishing in Eden* (1922), will be read by Eden fishermen as long as the river runs – a specialist book dealer may be able to provide a copy.

Edmonds and Lee Harfield H. Edmonds and Norman N. Lee, close friends and fishing companions, published a book privately at Bradford in 1916 (a facsimile was published in 1980) with the long but precise title of *Brook and River Trouting, A Manual of North Country Methods*. This is possibly the greatest book on North Country fishing ever written, or certainly among the top two or three. In 1996 a specialist dealer was quoting £ 4,750 for a copy of the de luxe edition which contains samples of the actual silks and materials used in the dressings of North Country flies and of flies themselves, all beautifully tied and framed, of which only 50 copies were issued. The ordinary first edition sells for about £145 and the

1980 facsimile, published by Orange Partridge Press of Ilkley, for about £75.

The 36 flies include the Waterhen Bloa, Snipe and Purple, Partridge and Orange and the winged and hackled tyings of the Dark Watchet. It is noticeable how small and delicate these flies are, most of them tied on very small – 16 and 18 – hooks. Edmonds and Lee emphasised the method of fishing upstream with a short line, casting frequently to a rise or to likely places, by no means a matter of chuck and chance it:

> . . . though the dry fly purist may shrug his shoulders at the remark, it is not too much to say that if he were transformed from the pellucid waters of the Chalk stream to some rapid broken river of the North, and were to endeavour to fish the wet fly, it would be some considerable time before he achieved any great success. Whereas the man who had thoroughly mastered the art of wet fly upstream would be able quickly to adapt himself to the conditions and surroundings of the home of the dry fly.

Ebble A small chalk stream that rises near Tisbury in Wiltshire and flows into the Hampshire Avon below Salisbury, providing very delicate fishing:

> A nice little brook, often weedy and sometimes overhung, and like most of the little chalk streams exclusive, with long waiting lists to get a rod. Enquiries around Odstock and Coombe Bissett might produce something.

England Ladies Flyfishing Association Formed in 1989, the aim of ELFA is to promote the sport of flyfishing for and by ladies. The results of their annual national championship determine the team that will represent England in the international the following year. Since 1989 the team has competed in ten internationals and has won eight gold medals. Charles Jardine is team manager (1998).

Wendy Miller, as well as being secretary and treasurer, is also team captain (1998).

Membership details from Wendy Miller, 40 West End, Whittlesey, Peterborough PE7 1LS. *See also* Competitive Fly Fishing.

Environment Agency for England and Wales This was created by the Environment Act of 1995 and took up its duties the following year. It combines the functions previously carried out by the National Rivers Authority (NRA), the Inspectorate of Pollution (HMIP) and several other bodies. It is one of the world's most powerful environmental regulators with responsibility to protect air, land and water through education, prevention and enforcement. Its responsibilities include the protection of natural water resources; flood warning and defence; fisheries, recreation, conservation and navigation; regulation of waste and industrial processes; water quality and pollution prevention. There are three statutory committees in each of the Agency's regions: the Regional Fisheries Advisory Committee, Regional Flood Defence Committee and the Regional Environment Protection Committee. Among several of the Agency's publications *An Action Plan for Fisheries* will be of interest to anglers. Copies are available at the following regional offices:

Anglian: Kingfisher House, Goldhay Way, Orton Goldhay, Peterborough PE2 5ZR

Midlands: Sapphire East, 550 Streetsbrook Road, Solihull B91 1QT

North East: Rivers House, 21 Park Square South, Leeds LS1 2QG

North West: Richard Fairclough House, Knutsford Road, Warrington WA4 1HG

Southern: Guildbourne House, Chatsworth Road, Worthing, West Sussex BN11 1LD

South West: Manley House, Kestrel Way, Exeter EX2 7QL

Thames: Kings Meadow House, Kings Meadow Road, Reading RG1 8DQ

Welsh: Rivers House, Plas-yr-Afon, St Mellons Business Park, St Mellons, Cardiff CF3 0LT

The head office – at Rio House, Waterside Drive, Aztec West, Almonsbury, Bristol BS32 4UD – is responsible for overall policy and relations with national bodies including the government.

Eriff A good salmon river quite close to the Delphi Fishery in Co. Galway. Both empty into Killary harbour, and both share the beauty of this part of the world. Owned by the Central Fishery Board, the river is well organised with clearly marked beats. Accommodation for fishermen is at Aasleagh Lodge, Leenane, Co. Galway.

Esk (Border)   Comparatively short, yet one of the most prolific sea-trout rivers in Britain. The Esk and its tributaries form part of the border between England and Scotland before the main Esk enters the Solway Firth north of Carlisle. At one time the Border Esk was spoilt by extensive worming, especially ledgering, but there are now some controls over bait fishing in certain places. Nevertheless, visitors should find out in advance if the rods they are offered are on fly-only waters. Flies are standard Teal Blue and Silver (the Falkus Medicine), Peter Ross, Black Pennell and Mallard and Claret. There are one or two local patterns, one the Whaup and Yellow, tied with a yellow silk body and a curlew (whaup) wing. In low-water conditions, very small flies are used, down to 12s and 14s. Most of the fishing takes place at night but the smaller sea-trout (herling) can often be taken during the day on a small dry fly or a 14 or 16 wet fly. The Esk and Liddle Fishing Association has water to let at Canonbie.

Esk (Cumbrian) This is Hugh Falkus's river, a moorland stream that rises near Scafell and flows into the sea at Ravenglass. In recent years the river is said to have suffered from increased acidity. The sea-trout, when there, run large. The Pennington Arms at Ravenglass may be able to arrange fishing.

Esk (North and South) Two delightful salmon rivers, the North Esk and South Esk are on the east coast of Scotland, coming into the sea at or near Montrose. Dalhousie and Gannoch Estates and Brechin, Montrose and Kirriemuir angling clubs are able to provide fishing. The spring and autumn runs of both salmon and sea-trout are best. John Ashley-Copper considers that the best beats on the North Esk lie immediately below Morphie dyke, on the lowest two miles of the river above the tide, and gives good advice about the fishing.

Esk (Yorkshire) A splendid river, not more than fifty miles long, which has seen better days. It runs into the sea at Whitby on the Yorkshire coast, and the best of the fly fishing was from Glaisdale to Ruswarp. David Barr writes:

It is a modern fishing tragedy that this attractive river, flowing through unspoilt moorland gorges and deep valleys, has deteriorated so much (in 1984) that it can scarcely be rated any

longer as a quality sea trout and salmon river. There is good dry fly fishing for trout.

Evans, Michael Hugh Michael Evans was brought up on the river Darenth, a natural chalk stream, in Westerham, Kent and commenced trout fishing at an early age; he was just eight when he caught his first salmon on the Tweed. He is sole proprietor of Michael Evans & Co, which specialises in the development of game angling products, including the Speymaster and Arrowhead range of rods and fly lines. Secretary of the Association of Professional Game Angling Instructors (APGAI), Michael is an international game angling instructor, guide, lecturer and demonstrator. Writer and presenter of three best-selling videos, *Basic Fly Casting*, *Distance Casting* and the *Double Haul and Spey Casting*. Michael is also a regular contributor to several fly fishing magazines. His excellent *Fly Fisher's Guide* is now in its second edition.

Speaking philosophically Michael says, 'Fishing is a lot like life . . . a mixture of hope and expectation, encouraged by triumph and trampled on by disappointment'.

Exe Rising on Exmoor, the river Exe turns south, runs past Dulverton and Tiverton, and into the sea at Exmouth. There is a good run of salmon but, surprisingly enough for a Devon river, very few sea-trout. Private water is often open to the public (see *West Country Fly Fishing*), and the Carnarvon Arms Hotel, near Dulverton, has some fine salmon water on the Exe as well as good trout water on the Barle and Haddeo. The Fisherman's Cot Hotel at Bickleigh also provides salmon rods and the South West Water office at Exeter has some salmon water just above the town.

The Exe has a number of small tributaries which provide good wild trout fishing. Fishing hotels include the Tarr Steps and, at Simonsbath, the Exmoor Forest.

The Culm, one of the Exe tributaries, is a particularly delightful clear water stream for which permits can be obtained from the tackle shop next to the post office at Uffculme.

Falkus, Hugh Actor, naturalist, film director, Spitfire pilot during the Battle of Britain, Hugh Falkus's wildlife films received international acclaim and reached audiences worldwide. His books include *Freshwater Fishing* (with Fred Buller) which was a bestseller, *Sea Trout Fishing* and *Salmon Fishing*. All three are elaborate productions, lavishly illustrated with photographs and line drawings, and have the Falkus hallmark of the closest attention to the most minute detail: how to tie knots, how to cast, the tackle to use, the best rods, the strength of nylon, the best flies, strategy, tactics – all the many things a beginner needs to have explained. He died in 1996, aged 78. His last book, *The Salmon and Sea Trout Fisher's Handbook*, completed by his friend Malcolm Greenhalgh, was published in 1998.

Farlow's of Pall Mall   The firm was founded in 1840 by Charles Farlow 'to supply the Angling Brotherhood of the Nobility, Gentry and Public at large'. Its original premises, at 221 The Strand were modest compared to the grand shop we know today in Pall Mall. From the outset the founder's insistence on the highest standards of quality and service quickly earned him a reputation which has continued for over a hundred and fifty years. Farlow was proud of his merchandise: 'all my rods are manufactured on the premises, under my own superintendence . . . made as they ought to be; differing materially from the slop-rubbish vended by certain persons professing to be makers, and which are sold to mislead and take in unwary purchasers, instead of taking out wary fish'.

With the retirement of Mrs Farlow in 1960 the last link with the family was severed. In 1964 the business moved to its present site at 5 Pall Mall, having by this time bought Walker Bampton of Alnwick, who had been making rods under the Farlow name. A year later Farlow's amalgamated with

Sharpe's of Aberdeen, famous throughout the trade for their impregnated rods and complete range of nets, gaffs and tailers.

Farlow's several shops in Pall Mall house London's largest selection of fishing tackle, shooting accessories and country clothing. Today Farlow's knowledgeable and friendly staff welcome customers from all walks of life and from all over the world, and for those unable to visit, it operates a superb mail order service.

In 1998 Farlow's became a wholly-owned subsidiary of another equally famous name in angling, the House of Hardy.

Farlow's Magazine A quarterly colour magazine, published by Farlow's Ltd, 5 Pall Mall, London SW1Y 5NP, which has a reputation for its excellent articles and regular reviews of the latest tackle.

Farson, Negley (1890–1960) A foreign correspondent of the *Chicgao Daily News* in the 1920s and 1930s, Farson travelled the world for his newspaper but always took his fly rod with him. The publication of his fishing adventures in *Going Fishing* was highly praised and was one of the few fishing books this century to reach the best-seller lists. In America, Arnold Gingrich said *Going Fishing* contained some of the grandest reading in all angling literature, and it was warmly greeted over here by many writers and fishermen, including H. E. Bates, Colin Wilcox and Jack Hargreaves. The book was reprinted several times and a beautiful edition, illustrated by C. F. Tunnicliffe, appeared in 1981. In the foreword to this edition Hugh Falkus wrote:

> I first read *Going Fishing* in 1943, when as a prisoner of war, I was serving a term of solitary confinement following an escape attempt, and a friendly guard smuggled the book into my cell. For a couple of months it was my only literature, so I can claim to have read it pretty thoroughly! But Negley Farson proved more than a solace, he was a revelation. Of all the fishing books I have read, his was the best. It still is.

Fernworthy Reservoir Containing brown trout only, natural and stocked, this natural 76-acre South West Water fishery near Chagford, north Devon, is set on the edge of Dartmoor. Conditions can be bleak at the beginning of the season, but as soon as the weather starts to warm up excellent fishing is to be had in some very pretty surroundings. Bank-only fishing with limited disabled access. Open May to October. Small dark wet flies such as Blae and Black, Black and Peacock, Bibio, and Black Pennell seem to work well here throughout the season. Later in the year try Daddies and the dry Black Gnat.

Field, The   First published in January 1853, *The Field* was initially more of a general weekly newspaper, covering Parliament and London social life as well as country sports. Over the years the political and social reports declined, and successive editors concentrated more and more on hunting, shooting, fishing and farming.

One of the first writers on fishing in *The Field* was Francis Francis in the late 1850s, and others who followed him included William Senior, F. M. Halford, G. E. M. Skues, John Bickerdyke (the pen-name of C. H. Cook), H. T. Sheringham, H. D. Turing. After many years as the angling correspondent William Senior became the editor, and he encouraged Halford and Marryat to write of their experiences with the floating fly at Ramsbury on the Kennet and later on the Itchen and Test.

The Field has led many campaigns on country matters, fighting for clean rivers, against corruption and misleading advertisements about fishing lets, and was one of the first papers to take the lead in investigating reports about the Loch Ness Monster – made difficult at one time by a practical joker who, among other things, used a hippopotamus's foot to make strange footmarks on the muddy shore. *The Field* was not deceived.

In recent years *The Field* has been notable for distinguished essays on fishing by Dabchick, (the pen-name of Wilson Stephens, who was editor from 1951 to 1977). His successor, Derek Bingham, also a fisherman, was succeeded by Simon Courtauld in 1984, who in turn was succeeded by Julie Spencer. Since 1991 the editor has been Jonathan Young, a member of the Flyfishers' Club. Current fishing writers include Max Hastings, Chapman Pincher, Jeremy Paxman, Tom Fort, Keith Elliott and Charles Rangeley-Wilson.

Findhorn   A fast spate river in Moray and Nairn, not all that far from Speyside, with some spectacular rapids and falls at Dulsie Bridge. The Cawdor Estate office at Cawdor has good beats on the middle river, where fishing can be very good indeed in the right height of water. Even in low water there

will be fish ready to take in the throat of the pools if one puts on a small dark fly over them and lets it play. The Cawdor water includes the famous Quilichan pool which is reached by an open bucket bridge. On the upper river, fishing is available from the Freeburn Hotel at Tomatin.

Floatants   A dressing applied to a dry fly to help it to float on the surface of the water. One of the most popular brands comes as a paste which is liquefied by rubbing between the fingers before being applied sparingly to the hackle, body and tail of the dry fly – too much and the fly will sink. The aerosol type is sprayed directly onto the fly and allowed to dry. The third form comes in a bottle into which the fly is dipped and then dried by false casting half a dozen times. Another version, in crystal powder form, is claimed to be more versatile than paste or liquid, for it will also dry and recondition a soaked fly.

Float Tubes   *See* Belly Boats.

Fluorocarbon   The new 'wonder' tippet material which looks set to replace both nylon and copolymer in the same way these materials superseded gut. For information on its many qualities *see* Leaders.

Fly Dressers' Guild   Formed in 1997 to promote and cultivate the art of fly-dressing, today the guild has over 60 branches and 3,000 members in the UK, as well as over 450 overseas members. The Guild publishes a quarterly magazine, *Flydresser,* and membership is open to anyone with an interest in the subject.

Membership secretary (1998): Pat C. Kerley, 8 Tidworth Road, Porton, Salisbury, Wiltshire SP4 0NG.

Fly Dressings   Reference works on fly patterns for trout fishing are Courtney Williams' *A Dictionary of Trout Flies; The Illustrated Dictionary of Trout Flies* by John Roberts and *The Handbook of Fly Tying* by Peter Gathercole.

For lake and reservoir fishermen, the dressings of some forty of the most popular flies are contained in *Stillwater Flies: How and When to Fish Them,* edited by John Goddard. More recent is *Bob Church's Guide to Trout Flies,* which has some 400 patterns of dry and wet flies, nymphs and lures and dressing materials.

A sequel, *Bob Church's Guide to New Fly Patterns*, introduces 400 brand new flies making use of modern materials that have revolutionised the art of fly-tying.

The basic skills of how to dress flies are shown stage by stage in colour photographs in *Flytying Techniques* by Jacqueline Wakeford. Another excellent book is *The Flytier's Manual* by Mike Dawes, which describes the essential equipment needed for fly tying, has 200 colour photographs of flies and over 300 line illustrations demonstrating the sequence of tying. Jacqueline Wakeford's *Flytying Tools and Materials* deals with the subject of tools and the treatment of natural fly-tying materials in great depth. Illustrated with more than 220 colour photographs taken by Jacqueline's husband David Hawker, it gives the beginner and intermediate fly tyer a reference for the natural coloration and appearance of hackles and winging materials, both feather and fur. Tying threads, hooks, tinsels, artificial materials for bodies and wings, ways to make flies sink or float, dyeing, curing and preserving feathers, hair and fur are also dealt with in this book. A correspondent writes:

> There was a sudden outburst of inventiveness among the design of reservoir lures from about the mid-1960s onwards, much of it based on American influence, the Nobbler patterns of the 1980s derive from the lead-headed American jig. Many American lures were directly imported without any alteration in the dressings, such as the Muddler Minnow and the Popper Bug.
>
> Artificial flies for river trout were inclined to move away from direct imitation towards impressionism, such as the Shadow Mayflies designed by Peter Deane. Halford's list of 33 dry flies for the chalk streams declined in influence, many skilled dry fly men using a mere one or two patterns – Lunn's for the spinners and a Beacon Beige for the duns.
>
> Salmon flies were considerably simplified with the growing popularity of hairwings on singles, doubles, trebles and tubes. The influence of Esmond Drury trebles appeared to increase, that of Waddington to decline. The Munro Killer and the Torridge Special, two black hairwings, illustrated the trend towards simplicity.

Flyfishers' Club   A social club for fly fishermen based at 69 Brook Street, London W1Y 2ER, and founded in 1884 'for the social intercourse of gentlemen interested in the art of fly fishing'. Many famous fly fishermen have been members in

past years, including Skues and Halford, and the present membership includes many well-known names in the fishing world. The club library, containing some 2,500 fishing books, is the most comprehensive in Europe. During the year there are many social events, lunches, rummage sales and an annual dinner. The club secretary is Commander T. H. Boycott OBE RN.

Fly Fishing and Fly Tying   A magazine for the progressive game angler and fly tyer, edited by Mark Bowler and published eight times a year by Rolling River Publications Ltd, Aberfeldy Road, Kenmore, Perthshire PH15 2HF.

Fly Patterns   The most popular fly patterns vary from year to year, but on rivers they tend to be fairly constant, one pattern possibly becoming a little more fashionable than another (most likely because of more frequent mentions in fishery reports one year) but then falling back to a previous level in a year or so's time. Reservoir flies and lures change far more rapidly; some of the most popular patterns of the 1970s are now rarely seen. Most 'new' flies are simply a variation on an existing pattern, often using materials which were not available at the time the original was tied.

The best-selling salmon flies are now hairwing tubes. The fully dressed doubles and singles are still in demand though the dressings are generally simpler than they were when first published, largely because so many of the exotic feathers used in the dressings are no longer obtainable.

The following list of best-selling flies for 1987 was prepared from information kindly supplied by Farlow's of Pall Mall, Orvis and John Norris of Perth:

Freshwater Flies
Dry Flies: sizes 14 to 16
Adams, Black Gnat, Blue Winged Olive, Beacon Beige, Gold Ribbed Hare's Ear, Lunn's Particular, Olive Dun, Sherry Spinner, Tup's Indispensable, Greenwell's Glory, Pheasant Tail, Grey Wulff.

Wet Flies: sizes 10 to 14
Black Pennell, Bibio, Butcher, Dunkeld, Connemara Black, Invicta, Peter Ross, Soldier Palmer, Partridge and Orange, Mallard and Claret, Black Spider, Black and Peacock Spider.

Nymphs: sizes 10 to 14
Superglue Black Buzzer, Suspender Buzzer, Emergers, Montana, Shrimp, Gold Ribbed Hare's Ear, Damsel, Pheasant Tail, various Gold Heads.

Sedges: sizes 10 to 12
G & H Sedge, Cinnamon Sedge, Murrough Sedge, Alder, Richard Walker's Sedge, Deer Hair Sedge, Red Sedge.

Mayflies: sizes 8 to 12
Grey Wulff, French Partridge, Shadow, Silhouette, Daddy Longlegs, Yellow Spent, Grey Drake, Yellow Drake.

Reservoir Lures: sizes 8 to 10
Booby, Cat's Whisker, Sinfoli's Fry, Muddler, Minnow, Appetiser, Viva, Orange Nobbler.

Salmon Tube Flies (brass) : sizes ½ to 2"
Comet, Tadpole, Garry Dog, Stoat's Tail, Tosh, Francis, Willie Gunn, Thunder & Lightning.

Salmon Flies (singles) : sizes 4 to 1/0
Copper Shrimp, Thunder & Lightning, Munro Killer, Comally.

Salmon Flies (doubles): sizes 2 to 12
Yellow Shrimp, Tosh, Garry Dog, Stoat's Tail, Hairy Mary, Willie Gunn, Silver Stoat's Tail, Ally's Shrimp, Blue Charm.

Salmon Flies (trebles): sizes 2 to 12
Ally's Shrimp, General Practioner, Stoat's Tail, Garry Dog, Collie Dog, Silver Doctor, Munro Killer, Blue Charm, Silver Stoat's Tail.

Saltwater Flies
Bonefish: sizes 4 to 8
Gotcha, Pink Flash, Gold Charlie, Chilli Pepper, Forgetful, Bonefish Special, Bitter Amber, Epoxy Mini Puff.

Tarpon: sizes 2 to 3/0
Glo Bad Crab, Black Death, Red & White Whistler, Deceivers, Cockroach.

Permit: sizes 4 to 6
Deer Hair Shrimp, McCrab, Ultra Shrimp.

Popular flies are discussed, and illustrated in colour, in *Trout and Salmon Flies* edited by Douglas Sutherland and Jack Chance. *See also Bob Church's Guide to Trout Flies*, 'The

Magnificent Seven', Pat O'Reilly's personal choice in his *Matching the Hatch*; and two books by Taff Price: *Tying and Fishing the Nymph* and *Tying and Fishing the Sedge*.

Fore-and-Aft Fly   A type of fly dressing, still sometimes used, in which there is a larger hackle at the tail than at the head, with the body dubbed in between the two. This tilts the fly forward on the water which is said to give it an appearance more similar to the position of the natural fly when riding the stream. David Jacques used the fore-and-aft dressing for his mayfly patterns. John Roberts attributes this dressing to use on the Piscatorial Society's waters on the Kennet by Horace Brown in the early 1900s.

Foston Beck   Like the Driffield Beck, another of the great Yorkshire chalk streams, the Foston Beck is an excellent wild brown trout water. In *The Haig Guide to Trout Fishing in Britain* David Barr, who was secretary of the Foston Fishing Club for ten years, recalls one September day in 1959 when he took eight trout weighing fifteen pounds, all on the upstream nymph.
David Overfield writes:

> Foston has its origin in the chalk springs of the Yorkshire Wolds that surface in the area of the village of Kilham and then flow directly south. The stream widens into fishable proportions at Bracy Bridge, at which point it is reminiscent of the Itchen, from where it flows down through the tiny village of Lowthorpe, its speed of progress slowing as it approached the village of Foston, some six miles in all. The water is controlled by the Foston Fishing Club. Day tickets are not issued.

Fowey   A good Cornish sea-trout river with a long and picturesque estuary leading to the sea at the port of Fowey (pronounced Foy). Some big sea-trout come in quite early, in March or April. The National Trust at Lanhydrock is a good place to enquire about day permits on association water, but beware of holiday weekends and bait fishermen. Like most Cornish rivers, the Fowey is well bushed, and in many places a fly is impossible.

Francis, Francis (1822–1886)   Angling editor of *The Field* for over 30 years from 1854, Francis Francis was born Francis Morgan but changed his surname to Francis to comply with a relative's will under which he inherited property. He published many articles and books on fishing and was one of the first to advocate the use of the dry fly. His best known publication, *A Book on Angling*, was published in 1867 and ran to several editions; a revised edition, edited by James Waltham, was published in 1983 as *Classic Salmon Flies: The Francis Francis Collection*. There is a memorial to him in Winchester Cathedral.

Freshwater Fisheries Laboratory, Scotland Its main task is to provide scientific advice to the relevant departments of the Scottish Office on all aspects of the biology of migratory and freshwater fishes in Scotland. Work on salmon and sea-trout forms the bulk of the research. Much of the work is carried out in liaison with members and staff of the District Salmon Fishery Boards, the Scottish Environment Protection Agency and independent research trusts and foundations. Laboratory staff also contribute to the activities of the International Council for the Exploration of the Sea (ICES) and the North Atlantic Salmon Conservation Organisation (NASCO). The laboratory is also a major research contractor for external customers.

The Freshwater Fisheries Laboratory, Faskally, Pitlochry, Perthshire PH16 5LB.

See also Pollution.

Frome This lovely river rises in the hills above Dorchester, where it is a chalk stream with excellent trout fishing. Its several tributaries merge and flow through Dorchester, thence eastwards through former water meadows, and therefore at times through two or more channels. Aylmer Tryon wrote:

> Below Wool the river deepens as it winds its serpentine way to Wareham, named after an ancient weir and salmon trap which virtually destroyed the entire salmon run until litigation at the end of the nineteenth century at last allowed rods to fish for salmon with some hope of success. The Frome flows into the sea at Poole Harbour, a short distance below Wareham, near the mouth of its sister river, the Piddle, which is similar in most respects but smaller.
>
> The Frome fly fishing for salmon is difficult and often discouraging because most fish lie in the deep bends under the banks which often overhang, so the majority of the fish are caught

on baits and until a few years ago on prawns. However, in recent years the Wessex Water Authority restricted the netting, while the Frome and Piddle Association introduced a voluntary ban on prawns in the spring months with the object of restoring the spring run, and this is showing signs of at last having some effect.

Fly fishing in the Frome in March when the season opens is perhaps more likely to succeed with large weighted tube flies fished deep. But as the water warms in May and June Shrimp flies and Hairy Marys, size 6 or 8, fished fast and stripped up under the near bank with an inshore bend may well produce an enormous rise or even a huge fish which in such a small river seems to have added proportions – often with disastrous results. There is a good grannom hatch in March and early April; in some years plenty of mayfly in late May and early June: in July a good rise of BWO; and in summer evenings sedges are popular with fish and fishermen. The record Frome salmon weighed 42½lb, caught in 1929. A sea-trout weighing 22½lb, taken in 1946 on a prawn, was for many years a record catch. S. R. Lanigan caught a 4lb 3oz grayling in 1989 which is the official British record.

Much of the Frome is estate water. The Woolbridge Manor Hotel, near Wareham, has rods. Advance booking is necessary.

G

GAIA The Game Angling Instructors Association (formerly the Association of Professional Game Angling Instructors). Founded in 1969 by Lt-Col. Esmond Drury, Arthur Oglesby, Jack Martin and several other leading anglers of the time who recognised the need for setting a standard of professionalism for game angling instructors – a standard now accepted world-wide. Members (APGAI) are required to pass detailed examinations qualifying them to teach in one or more of the three disciplines – salmon, trout and sea-trout as well as fly dressing.

The Association now has members both in the United Kingdom and abroad, many of whom are well-known figures, offering a range of tuition from private casting lessons to full residential courses.

As Secretary Michael Evans says rather forcibly, 'Any instructor who does not hold the STANIC (Salmon & Trout Association National Instructors Certificate) and preferably the APGAI qualification in the relevant discipline as well, is at best a well-meaning amateur and at worst a liability. A good fisher does not necessarily make a good teacher, as it is far harder to break a bad habit than it is to learn properly in the first place.'

Secretary (1998): Michael Evans, Little Saxby's Farm, Cowden, Nr Edenbridge, Kent TN8 7DX.

See also STANIC *and* REFFIS.

Garry Dog Considered by Peter O'Reilly to be one of the most useful dressings of modern times for river fishing for salmon, though its origins date back to the mid-1880s. It became a popular dressing for the tubes of the 1950s. It is tied on tubes of aluminium, plastic, bronze or copper, depending on how deep you want it to sink, and that also determines the size, which can be anything from ½" to 3".

Body: black floss silk
Tag: yellow floss
Rib: oval or flat silver tinsel
Wing: two bunches of red and two of yellow bucktail, or similar (for example dyed squirrel), tied in varied bunches round the tube
Hackle: a collar bunch of bright blue guinea fowl, or similar, tied at the head, fanning out on either side under the hook
Head: black

Gathercole, Peter He is considered to be one of this country's leading fly-dressers and acknowledged as an accomplished natural history photographer whose pictures have appeared in a number of books by other authors. Gathercole contributes regularly to the angling press both in Britain and overseas. *Imitations of the Trout's World*, which he wrote with Bob Church, was highly praised, as was his most recent work, *The Handbook of Fly Tying*.

'Ghost Wing' Flies When a winged artificial fly comes into the trout's visual 'window' (the area of the water surface through which the trout can see out into the world above), a curious development takes place. Looked at from below the water surface, the wings appear to leave the body of the fly and then return as it comes closer to the centre of the window. This was first seen by Colonel E. W. Harding using an observation tank, later by John Goddard with an underwater camera and by Vincent Marinaro in America.

See Dry Fly, Origins.

Gilbert, H. A. An invaluable reference book for the Wye, *The Tale of a Wye Fisherman* contains a picture of the biggest rod-caught Wye salmon, weighing 59½lb, together with records of five other Wye fish over 50lb. It also has Miss Doreen Davey's account of how she caught the 59lb springer at Cowpond in 1923:

> At about 5.30 pm having lost all hope and fully expecting another blank day I hooked a fish on a small minnow I had put on for a change. The fish swam about and did more or less what he liked ... At about 7 o'clock he got quite cross and we could see how big he was, and my father's chauffeur, John Hellis, lit a fire on the bank so we could see to gaff him. Other people came up and brought candles.

The end came with almost dramatic suddenness. The fish was steered in and in a mixture of splash and spray the faithful John Hellis with the gaff, and Charlie Donald with his hands as much round the tail of the fish as he could get them, managed to haul him out of the water. The fish was landed at 7.55 pm after being hooked at 5.40 pm . . . .

I have had dozens of nice letters of congratulation from friends and from complete strangers. Among the strangers some have sent poetry and one proposes that I should marry him. However, this is another 'catch' and I am not rising.

Ginger Quill   A variation of the Orange Quill and the Red Quill which is said to be most useful when spinners are on the water. The dressing is similar, a peacock body and ginger cock hackle and whisks – the quill can be left undyed but most fishermen prefer it dyed black.

Gnats *See* Midge

Gobage   French for a trout's rise, meaning 'mouthing', from which derives the slang 'Shut your gob'.

Goddard, John   Goddard, who was born in London in 1925, served as a paratrooper in World War II and for a time afterwards was head of the tackle firm E. F. Goddard & Co. – is described as 'an international master of fly fishing'. His latest book, *John Goddard's Trout Fishing Techniques* contains a foreword by one of America's leading fly fishermen, Lefty Kreh, who writes:

> . . . without any doubt, John Goddard is the best trout fisherman with whom I have spent time on the water . . .

Goddard's other books include *Trout Fly Recognition*, which was hailed at once as a major work, comparable to those of Ronalds and Halford. Three years later came the companion volume, *Trout Flies of Still Water*. He has also written *Big Fish From Saltwater, The Superflies of Stillwater, The Trout and the Fly* (with Brian Clarke – another significant work), *Stillwater Flies, Fly Fishing For Trout* (also with Brian Clarke), *John Goddard's Waterside Guide* and *Trout Flies of Britain and Europe*.

A Fellow of the Royal Entomological Society, Goddard has specialised in dressing imitative flies for rivers and stillwaters. Some are famous, like the Goddard Caddis (or G & H Sedge), whilst others have been retired as being too complex or too difficult to tie. He has specialised in matching the hatch through the brilliant use of underwater photography. The underwater camera captured for the first time the appearance of the natural fly, the flare of the fly's wings as it approaches the trout's 'window', how floating nylon looks from below, the flash of a line, the brilliant glow of a spinner's wings in the sunset, and many other original views which have been reproduced in his books.

Gold Ribbed Hare's Ear   Sometimes called Hare's Ear, or GRHE; a chalk stream variant of a much older trout fly known in the West Country as a Hare's Fleck. The Fleck has a body dubbing of hare's fur, dun hackle and whisks, and starling wings, the dubbing kept in place by gold wire and is a useful pattern when olive duns are hatching. The chalk stream pattern is sometimes tied without wings or hackle to suggest an emerging nymph, and is fished in the surface film. In America and a number of other countries rabbit fur is frequently substituted for hare's fur and has become a standard emerger pattern. There are no standard patterns of the GRHE these days, as there are so many variations in the dressing. This is a common and effective emerger:

> *Body:* medium-coloured hair from a hare's ear (taken from the base of the ear) or dun-coloured rabbit's fur
> *Whisks:* a few short fur fibres
> *Rib:* fine gold wire or thin gold tinsel
> *Thorax:* thicker dubbing of fur, covered over the back with dark feather fibres from a hen or cock pheasant to suggest the wing cases
> *Legs:* strands of fur picked out with the dubbing needle
> *Hooks:* 14, 15 or 16 to suggest the emerging olive, larger to suggest various stillwater insects. A damsel fly larvae will need an 8 long-shank, weighted

Grafham Water   One of the UK's top fisheries noted for its quality fishing and spectacular brown trout. This 1,600-acre reservoir, which has been designated as a Site of Special Scientific Interest, includes a large nature reserve on the western side which is jointly run by Anglian Water and the Wildlife Trust and also offers watersport facilities. For much of the season boat fishing (there is a fleet of 50 power boats available for hire) gives a higher catch rate than bank fishing.

A superb new fishing lodge is under construction with completion expected for the 1999 season.

Grafham produces a fast growth rate of fish from the opening of the season until late summer, and it is stocked regularly (at least 2,000 brown and 75,000 rainbow trout a year). It was here that Bob Church, Dick Shrive, and other regulars, fishing from boats, experimented with deep sunk lures, lead lines and drift control rudders in the mid 1970s. Another pattern of fishing was developed by Arthur Cove of Wellingborough who fished a large Pheasant Tail nymph on 8 or 10 long-shank hooks on a floating line. Towards autumn, the trout feed avidly on coarse fish, and on most evenings there is a good midge rise.

Local advice for boat fishing: in bright sunlight, fish the headlands not the bays; the natural banks go off because the fish move out into deeper water. Start fishing with a fast-sink line, because it saves time when you want to ascertain what depth the fish are at. When fishing the windward shore start your engine first, leave it in neutral, then pull up the anchor. For the bank angler: if you are fishing the dam when the water is flat calm, try a golden lure made from ripple flash on an intermediate line. Many anglers change to shooting heads around May to June, as the fish move further out from the bank.

Fishery records: brown trout (fly) 17lb 2oz (1994) and rainbow 13lb 13oz (1992).

Grannom (*Brachycentrus subnubilus*)   A charming little sedge fly which appears on many rivers in the spring, sometimes in vast numbers, covering the bushes for miles.   Almost everything that needs to be said about it was contained in *Fisherman's Fly* by David Jacques:

> . . . how can I fail to feel affection for this gentle insect in whose delectable company I have passed so many hours? From its very birth I watched it, clumsily and awkwardly engage in tumbling games with its brothers and sisters; then, through its infancy and maturity, nestling in its case, harming no other living creature, but waiting patiently and trustingly for the victuals on which its life depends to be brought to its threshold; to its breath-taking metamorphosis from an aquatic animal to a fairy-like creature of the air and, finally, to its lonely death in obscurity . . . .

Jacques bred grannom in his home and lived with them, watching their every move for hours at a time. They opened a new world for him and his comments make fascinating reading.

There have been many tyings of the grannom – it is the greentail fly of the fifteenth-century writers – but this is probably the easiest if not the best:

> *Body:* dark hare's ear dubbed on green tying silk with a tiny ball of light green wool at the tail
> *Wings:* two slips from the wing feather of a hen pheasant, tied roof-shape and sloping well back close to the hook
> *Hackle:* in front of the wings, rusty dun cock
> *Hook:* 14

Gray, L. R. N. Lindsay Gray was better known under his pen-name, Lemon Gray. An outspoken fisherman in the 1950s and 1960s, he ran a private house, Devon Lodge, as a fishing hotel with water on the Torridge. He recounted his experiences in *Torridge Fishery.* Maurice Wiggin, then fishing correspondent of the *Sunday Times*, wrote a foreword:

> . . . He [Gray] is a prickly outspoken privateer clean out of his age, the horror of bureaucrats, the scourge of committees. An exhausting, uncompromising, cruelly effective tutor, a first rate fly fisherman and fly dresser, a staunch friend . . . .

Gray had a great deal to say about fishing and fishing hotels. When he had guests at Devon Lodge whom he did not like, he would ask them to leave. If they asked why, he would say that if they stayed on he would have to tell them, and, as he was a kindly man, he did not like to be rude.

Grayling Ron Broughton writes: A cousin of the *Salmonidae* – sharing the adipose fin and the extended territory throughout northern Europe, Asia and North America – the grayling is well known for its feeding on the fly life of rivers and still waters. It has two main sub-divisions. The European grayling (*Thymallus thymallus*), is found from the north in Scandinavia and European Russia to as far south as the limestone rivers of northern Italy and Yugoslavia. The Arctic grayling (*Thymallus articus*) is located east of the Urals across Asia, and in Canada and in a small and diminishing number of places in the USA, such as the Big Hole river. Grayling are not found in either Japan or Ireland. It is now believed that the European grayling

came from around the Danube, survived in small pockets throughout the Ice Age and migrated across Europe to England and Wales into the east-flowing rivers which then included the Severn, the Welsh Dee and the Ribble. Further territorial expansion was by man's efforts, the first transference being into the Test in 1816 and the most recent, into the Cheshire Gowy in 1994.

Mature in three years, with a growth as rapid as the rainbow trout's, it will live a further six or more years at a slower rate of growth. The official British record (rod-caught) grayling is 4lb 3oz, taken by S. R. Lanigan in 1989 from the river Frome.

Grayling do not seek food only from the bed of the river, but will rise to the fly on the surface or just below it with a persistence and particularity as to choice of fly that can put stocked trout to shame. It will rise to the fly, both natural and artificial, throughout the winter as well as the warmer months. Thus the grayling angler, if he delights in trying to 'match the hatch', has to have a greater knowledge of river fly life than is needed during the trout season, which requires him to be aware of the various stone flies that hatch from late autumn to early spring.

Until the end of the nineteenth century trout and grayling were considered to be complementary in angling literature, until the Freshwater Fishes Act of 1878 officially separated them according to which side of the coldest month they spawned, and reclassified the grayling as a freshwater or coarse fish. It has needed the formation of the Grayling Society in 1977 to re-educate anglers as to its indubitable virtues as a game fish.

Recommended reading: *Grayling*, R. V. Righyni; *Grayling: The Fourth Game Fish*, R. B. Broughton; *The Grayling Angler*, John Roberts.

Grayling Society   Founded in 1977, the society aims to promote a proper appreciation of the sporting qualities of the grayling, to collect and record information about it, and to provide members with information and advice by means of a newsletter and a bi-monthly journal. Founder member and first chairman, Dr R. B. Broughton is now President. General secretary: Steve Skuce, 7 Oaktree Way, Little Sandhurst, Camberley, Surrey GU17 8QS.

Green, E. Garrow   A frequent contributor to *The Fishing Gazette* between 1900 and 1930, Garrow Green wrote under the pen-name of Black Hackle about fishing in Ireland, where he had served as an Army officer, and in Devon, where he lived. His book on Dartmoor fishing, *Trout Fishing in Brooks*, which contains excellent advice, was published in the 1920s.

Green Peter   An Irish loch fly used in various sizes for brown trout, sea-trout and grilse. Peter O'Reilly says he regards it as the number one lough fly that can be fished throughout the whole season, either wet or dry. A Green Peter is really a green sedge, and this is the wet fly dressing:

> *Body:* green fur ribbed with fine gold tinsel
> *Hackle:* red game
> *Tying:* thread, brown or green
> *Hook:* 12–8

There are several variations.

Greenwell's Glory   A famous trout fly tied by James Wright of Sprouston on Tweed to the design of Canon Greenwell of Durham in May 1854. Wright named the fly at a celebration dinner, probably in the nearby town of Kelso. It is a little difficult to be certain what the Greenwell's Glory was intended to represent – probably one of the larger olives.

> *Body:* yellow silk
> *Wing:* inside feather of a blackbird's wing
> *Hackle:* coch-y-bondhu
> *Hook:* 14 - 16

The wings of the original are upright, not sloping, though the wet fly dressing now has sloping wings. The fly is mostly tied with tail whisks of the same colour as the hackle and a fine gold rib is added, but neither were in the original dressing.

Grenadier   An imitation bait for lake and reservoir fishing designed by Dr Bell of Blagdon in the 1920s and 1930s, the Grenadier suggests a small red larva or midge. It was originally tied unweighted:

> *Body:* red silk
> *Rib:* fine gold tinsel
> *Head hackle:* one or two turns of partridge, the fibres short
> *Hook:* 14

Dr Bell always fished his patterns very slowly, allowing them to sink quite a way down, then bringing them in gradually. He generally had three flies on the same cast, the Grenadier in the middle or on the point.

Grey Duster A very useful general-purpose trout fly which probably suggests a dun but will take fish when sedge are on the water. Courtney Williams found it effective during a hatch of the big mayfly on both the Inny and the Test. The standard dressing does not seem to have whisks, but they can be added:

> *Body:* light-coloured rabbit or hare's fur, slightly blue
> *Hackle:* well-marked badger with black centre and white list
> *Tying silk:* brown
> *Hook:* usually 14 or 12

Grey, Edward (1862-1933) Sir Edward Grey, Viscount Grey of Fallodon, is best known to fishermen as the author of *Fly Fishing*, first published in 1899 and still in print. In the wider field of public affairs he was one of Britain's most distinguished statesmen and held the office of Foreign Secretary from 1905 to 1916. Grey was a sensitive and evocative writer on country matters and for some time had a small cottage on the Itchen. He fished the Rosehall water of the Cassley, the Lochy, Spean and Tweed. His advice on both salmon and trout fishing was admirable. The best edition of his book is the one which he revised in 1930, with line drawings by Daglish. It was this edition, with its delightful graphics by Arthur Rackham, which was chosen by FCL for the facsimile they published in 1972 and reprinted in 1997. Here is Grey's description of fishing in the Highlands:

> The pure act of breathing at such times seems glorious. People talk of being a child of nature, and moments such as these are times when it is possible to feel so; to know the full joy of animal life – to desire nothing beyond. There are times when I have stood still for joy of it all, on my way through the wild freedom of a Highland moor, and felt the wind, and looked upon the mountains and water and light and sky, till I felt conscious only of the strength of a mighty current of life, which swept away all consciousness of self, and made me a part of all that I beheld.

Grey Wulff *See* Mayfly.

Grouse and Green   A useful wet fly for lake and river trout, better known in the north of England than the south. The grouse hackle can be long or short. If the colour of the body wool or floss is changed, the fly then becomes Grouse and Orange or Grouse and Purple, etc. The green body is the most popular:

Body: apple green wool or floss
Rib: fine gold or silver wire
Tail: a few golden pheasant tippet fibres, quite short
Hackle: grouse breast or rump

Gut Fine gut casts (leaders) were made in fairly short lengths from silkworms, the lengths knotted together to create a taper. Gut casts were in common use until after World War II when they were replaced by nylon.

H

Hairy Mary A hairwing salmon fly, especially liked and well used on many Scottish rivers, tied in 1960 by John Redpath, owner of a fishing tackle shop in Inverness. It is also known as the Irish Hairy Mary. The following is one of many dressings:

> *Tag:* gold tinsel
> *Tail:* topping
> *Body:* black floss or wool
> *Ribbing:* oval gold tinsel
> *Throat:* bright blue hackle tied as a collar before the wing is tied
> *Wing:* a bunch, sometimes small in low water, of reddish brown hair
> *Hook:* varies from 8s to 5/0 for fishing in Norway

Halford, Frederic M. (1844-1914) A great angler-entomologist who was highly praised during his life and frequently criticised afterwards, sometimes by those who had never read his works. Halford's achievements are admirably summarised by Donald Overfield in *Famous Flies and Their Originators*.

Halford came from a wealthy Midlands family and began worming in a pond near his home almost as soon as he could walk. When he was seven the family moved to London, where he continued to fish in the Serpentine and the Thames, and also in the sea at Eastbourne.

In 1868, when Halford was 24, a friend offered him a day's trout fishing on the Wandle. He knew little or nothing about fly fishing and followed the advice of the members of the syndicate on the Wandle to cast a dry fly upstream to the rising fish. Fascinated, he then gave up sea and coarse fishing to concentrate on the fly. In 1877 he became a member of the Houghton Club on the river Test, which had about 17 miles of some of the best trout water in Hampshire.

In 1879, by chance, Halford met a retired army officer, G. S. Marryat, who had the reputation, according to Sir Edward

Grey, of being 'the best trout fisherman in England'. Marryat was able to give Halford good advice on flies and fly tying. They became friends, and the next year Halford took rooms at Bossington Mill on the Test with the intention of studying, with Marryat's help, the natural flies of the river and their matching artificials.

> ... throughout our work [Halford wrote] we never departed from the determination we had mutually arrived at, to reduce to writing the results of any experiments, and consider them, carefully, together, and where possible verify them. ...

Nothing so comprehensive had been undertaken since the work of Ronalds which had resulted in the publication of *The Fly Fisher's Entomology* 44 years earlier, in 1836. This time two leisured and wealthy men could concentrate together on the study of insect life about them and select, prepare or invent the appropriate matching artificials.

After six years' intensive work came the result, Halford's *Floating Flies and How to Dress Them* (1886). We do not know why Marryat refused to have his name given as the joint author, but there is little doubt that he had equal if not the major share in the preparation of the book. What was the reservation on Marryat's part? It is impossible to say, although the two men were very different – Marryat was never a purist to the extent that Halford was. Whatever the reason, Halford was now set to become the leader of the dry fly movement, which eventually triumphed over all others so far as the Hampshire streams were concerned. The main point about the dry fly was simply that it was the most efficient way of taking trout which were feeding on duns and spinners.

Halford's works now followed fairly rapidly: in 1889 *Dry Fly Fishing in Theory and Practice*; in 1895 *Making a Fishery*; in 1897 *Dry Fly Entomology*; in 1903 his life story, *An Angler's Autobiography*; in 1910 *The Modern Development of the Dry Fly*; and in 1913, *The Dry Fly Man's Handbook*.

Halford's instructions on how to fish the dry fly were precise:

> Dry-fly fishing is presenting to the rising fish the best possible imitation of the insect on which he is feeding in its natural position. To analyse this further, it is necessary, firstly to find a fish feeding on the winged insect; secondly, to present to him a good imitation of this insect, both as to size, and colour; thirdly, to present it to him in its natural position or floating on the surface

of the water with its wings up, or what we technically term 'cocked'; fourthly, to put the fly lightly on the water, so that it floats accurately over him without drag; and fifthly, to take care that all these conditions have been fulfilled before the fish has seen the angler or the reflection of his rod.

Great men – and Halford was a great man – have faults. His was to imagine that the dry fly had superseded all other methods of fly fishing, an understandable enthusiasm, but one which ultimately led to egotism and intolerance, a lack of humour, and a rigid code from which no deviation was permissible. An unpublished story about Halford is worth recording. It was told by Toby O'Brien, a civil servant, about his uncle Tommy White who was a great athlete and a great fly fisherman at Blagdon in the early days. White was invited by Halford to fish the Test with him some time around 1910. Toby O'Brien continued:

Tommy was thrilled. There he was, fishing with the great man. Halford put on a delicious little fly and cast it perfectly. The trout took no notice: Tommy followed Halford and put up a bushy monster that had no relationship whatever to the flies on the water, cast it to the trout, and the trout took it at once. Tommy was not asked again.

See also *An Angler's Autobiography*, with previously unpublished material and a new Preface by John Halford, FCL, 1998.

Halford's Flies In some sense it is a misnomer to think of Halford's flies, for many of the flies listed by Halford were Marryat's and some such as the Coachman, were traditional. Halford's first list of 100 flies for the chalk streams was later reduced to a more manageable 33, though today it is doubtful if any good chalk stream fisherman uses more than a dozen. Probably the best known, still in general use, are the Rough Olive, Medium Olive, Iron Blue, Blue Quill, Blue Dun, Red Quill, Red Spinner, Ginger Quill, Wickham, Blue Winged Olive, Grannom, Alder, Black Gnat, Silver Sedges, and several different mayflies (Green Drakes) and mayfly spinners (Spent Gnats). There is a well-known story about why Halford deleted the Gold Ribbed Hare's Ear from his list: it was because he could not decide what natural fly it was supposed to represent.

Half Stone   A Devon trout fly, fished wet or dry, almost always upstream:

Body: yellow silk with a pinch of mole fur on the shoulder by the hackle
Whisks: strands of blue cock
Hackle: four or five turns of blue cock
Hook: 12-14

Hall, John Inglis   Author of *Fishing a Highland Stream*, with a foreword by Sir Geoffrey Cox, who called it a minor classic. It expresses one man's love for a small river, the Truim, in the Central Highlands, and has the most charming opening sentence that any fishing book can possibly have:

As in marriage, so in fishing; one's choice is made by accident. One opens the door of a room and there, for better or worse, the lady sits. One can see a river from a train, a car, one halts to stretch one's legs, and is lost.

Halladale   A salmon river in Caithness flowing north into the sea at Melvich. A river of great charm winding through wild valleys in empty mountainous country, it is a spate river, as are all its neighbours in Caithness and Sutherland – Thurso, Helmsdale, Naver – all approached by twisting single-track roads where you are just as likely to meet deer as men. Midsummer is the time to expect low water, and fishing will then be very dour, but a day or so's rain will make all the difference, and fish will be on the move in no time. Small flies on a sink-tip line are favoured, except in spates, when big heavy tubes and sinking lines are needed.

The Forsinard Hotel has beats on the Halladale and the Melvich Hotel at the mouth can also arrange fishing.

Hanningfield Trout Fishery   This 600-acre reservoir, near Chelmsford in Essex, run by Essex Water, has seen several record rainbow trout (resident) catches: two of 16lb in 1995, 18lb 9oz in 1995, and a British record 24lb 1oz 4 dm by John Hammond on a Goldhead Hare's Ear Nymph in June 1998. In the 1997 season there were 55 double-figure fish caught, the heaviest being 17lb 14oz. A vast supply of natural food, plankton and daphnia, combined with a reduction in the stocks of coarse fish are possible explanations for these giant fish.

Boat (rowing and motor) and bank fishing. There is a new fishing lodge, tackle shop and cafe on site.

Harding, E. W. Colonel Harding fished with Skues on the Abbotts Barton water of the Itchen in the 1920s. Harding set up an observation tank at his home at Iwerne Courtney and was astonished by what he saw. A large part of the water surface was opaque; flies floating on the surface could not be seen as flies, only as the imprints and light sparkles, or blobs, caused by the pressure of their hackles on the surface. Only when the flies came into the trout's window could they be seen as flies, though the wings appeared to float away from the body and only gradually rejoined it. Curiouser and curiouser, said Harding, just like being in *Alice in Wonderland*. Encouraged by Skues he wrote a book, *The Flyfisher and the Trout's Point of View*, published in 1931, which was largely ignored by the chalkstream fisherman at the time.

See Goddard *and* Clarke.

Hardy, House of   For well over a century the House of Hardy has had the reputation of making the finest game fishing tackle in the world, and today the name is synonymous with quality and excellence.

The business began in 1872 when William Hardy established himself as a gunsmith in his home town of Alnwick, Northumberland; a year later he was joined by his brother John James, and the Hardy partnership came into being. Despite their success the Hardy brothers' passion for fishing soon dictated a change in direction, their favourite hobby became their profession, and the reputation of Hardy rods and reels was born.

In those early days rods were made from lancewood, hickory and greenheart, but by 1880 bamboo had been added to the range. Hardy's were the first to invent a system for building hexagonal rods from bamboo, and the Palakona rod won their first gold medal in 1881. In 1891 the first Hardy Perfect reel was patented, and, despite one or two minor changes, this design has stood the test of time; for the same basic model is still manufactured today. Throughout its long history the company has been responsible for some of the most radical advances in tackle design. It was the first to market bridge rings, spiral lockfast joints, stud lock joints, split end joints and 'W' and screw grip fittings for salmon and trout rods. It developed ball-bearing reels and was the first to feature the check mechanism housed within the reel arbor.

Alnwick itself became famous as the birthplace of this angling institution, and the annual Hardy catalogue became the bible for all those who sought either knowledge of the best of fishing equipment or the equipment itself.

To ensure that some of the fishing tackle memorabilia in the company's possession was preserved for posterity the House of Hardy decided to build a museum at its Alnwick headquarters and this was opened by HRH Princess Margaret in 1987. The Alnwick factory manufactures over 90 per cent of all parts used in the Hardy range of fishing tackle – from split-bamboo, glass and carbon-fibre rods to a most extensive range of fly reels.

Opposite St James Palace in London's Pall Mall, the House of Hardy's retail shop has been a mecca for the world's game fishing enthusiasts for over a hundred years. In 1998 Hardy's acquired Farlow's of Pall Mall.

James Leighton Hardy's *The House the Hardy Brothers Built* traces the history of the firm and the personalities responsible for its success and provides a great deal of technical information which will be of interest to collectors of fishing tackle. The Appendices include details of the catalogue numbers of rods produced from 1883 to 1983 and all the reel production figures. John Drewett's *Hardy Brothers: The Masters, the Men and Their Reels* is the definitive work on the development of Hardy reels from 1873 to 1939, the Hardy brothers and the reelmakers.

House of Hardy Ltd, Alnwick, Northumberland NE66 2PF.

Hare's Fleck Sometimes known as Hare's Flax. A very old and probably a West Country, fly; not dissimilar to some other traditional flies:

> *Body:* hare's fur, often ribbed with fine flat gold tinsel or thin wire
> *Hackle:* rusty blue cock, or sometimes a red gamecock
> *Whisks:* three or four fibres of the same colour
> *Hook:* 14-12

Harris, J. R. A lecturer in the zoology department of Trinity College, Dublin, Dr Harris wrote *An Angler's Entomology*. The book marked an important stage in the understanding and classification of trout food insects, some of which were seen in colour photographs in a book for the first time. Harris's work has been compared with the great step forward in knowledge made by Ronalds 116 years earlier, as well as providing encouragement and pointing the way to the work of Goddard in the 1960s. Harris's book is of lasting value, not least for the clarity of the writing and the enthusiasm of a dedicated fisherman.

Hartley, J. R. A fictional character who featured in a long-running and extremely successful advertising campaign for Yellow Pages. 'Hartley' went on to 'write' an equally successful book, *Fly Fishing*, published in 1991, followed by a sequel, *J. R. Hartley Casts Again*, the following year.

Hawthorn Fly (*Bibio marci*) A terrestrial, hatching in late April and early May, often blown onto the water in large numbers during the week or so long as the hatch lasts. When trout are taking a fall of hawthorn they will often look at little else. The hawthorn fly, when flying, is recognised by its long trailing legs. This is a traditional dressing:

> *Body:* black ostrich herl
> *Wings:* pale starling
> *Hackle:* black cock with two long strands of stripped black ostrich herl to suggest the legs
> *Hook:* 12

If the fly is inclined to sink below the surface an ordinary black palmer floats perfectly and can be twitched now and then to suggest the struggling fly.

Helmsdale A delightful salmon river in the far north of Scotland, in Sutherland, which has always had the reputation of being private. Owners keep the river generally to themselves, and it is rather a closed shop. However, locals do manage to get rods, and so do friends of friends who know the right people.

Henderson, John From just before the death of Queen Victoria until well after World War II, John Henderson fished almost every kind of lake, loch, and reservoir you can imagine in all parts of the United Kingdom. He died in the late 1970s aged 95 plus, a great fly fisherman and one of the longest-serving members of the Flyfishers' Club. His father contributed the chapter on dry fly fishing to Halford's *Dry Fly Man's Handbook* (1913).

One of Henderson's techniques of bank fishing on large lakes and reservoirs was to cast out a dry fly with the wind coming over his left shoulder and walking along the margin of the lake, keeping time with the fly as it floated with the wind.

One fisherman tells a charming story of John Henderson whom he met in the 1950s fishing at Weir Wood in Surrey, a stocked trout fishery:

> I saw this old man, rather sad-looking, sitting by the wall of the dam, rod in hand, doing nothing, and somehow I felt sorry for him and asked how he was. He was quite cheerful and said he was waiting for the hatch and he thought there might be one soon. I realised he was going to fish dry and felt even more sorry for him, because I'd never seen the dry fly fished on a reservoir before and I didn't think it was much good. I told him a wet fly would do better and he smiled and said it might, but made no move to change. An hour or so later there was a rise and I saw him coming back along the bank with a fish, a good one. That taught me a lesson.

Henzell, H. P. Another book about Scottish lochs but from a man who was devoted to the fly; Henzell's *The Art and Craft of Loch Fishing* (1937) is well named and contains illustrations of traditional wet and dry flies.

Hills, John Waller (1867-1938) One of the most charming fishing books of our time was J. W. Hill's *A Summer on the Test* (1924), and one of the most informative was his *History of Fly Fishing* (1921), though perhaps rather biased to the chalk streams. He wrote other books, including an autobiography, *A Sportsman's Life*, but none reached the level of these two, although *River Keeper: The Life of William James Lunn* (1934) came close. Hills was a long-time member of the Houghton Club, where William Lunn was keeper.

Hills was a solicitor, Member of Parliament (first for Durham and finally Ripon) and Financial Secretary to the Treasury. When nearly fifty years old, Hills joined the Durham Light Infantry where after two years he rose to command a battalion in France. He was, said *The Times*, 'a man of great character and courage'.

Hobbs, A.E. *See* Thames.

Hodder *See* Ribble.

Holiday, F. W. Authentic glimpses of fishing in Wales are rare but some of the best are in F.W. Holiday's *River Fishing for Sea Trout*. Wales has many miles of association water open for visitors and, though spinning and worming seem to dominate these lovely bright rivers, if there is more use of the fly it is largely due to enthusiasts like Holiday. Some of his advice on night fishing with a slack line may raise the eyebrows of those who have learnt their fishing elsewhere, but it seems to work well in Wales.

Hook Sizes The variation in hook sizes is considerable. The hooks used in America bear no resemblance to the Redditch scale sizes in use over here (an American size 24 hook is something like our size 18 or 20). Our new scale, or Pennell, scale of hook sizes, in use up to the 1930s, has now been replaced by the revived Redditch scale. This is the approximate comparison:

Redditch	6/0	5/0	4/0	3/0	2/0	1/0	1	2	3	4	5
Pennell	20	19	18	17	16	15	14	13	12	11	10
Redditch	6	7	8	9	10	11	12	13	14	15	16
Pennell	9	8	7	6	5	4	3	2	1	0	00
Redditch	17	18									
Pennell	000	0000									

Eyed hooks were in use in the earliest times, and the British Museum has some examples. The Forge Mill Needle Museum at Redditch has a good collection of Redditch fishing tackle, including hooks, some of which date from the 1800s. The modern eyed hook was developed by H. S. Hall in conjunction with G. S. Marryat in the late 1800s.

Hope, Loch A Sutherland loch some eight miles long, not too wide and with good shallows. A quick run into the sea brings in fresh and vigorous sea-trout of six and seven pounds or more which take out line like a torpedo. Dapping on the drift is the main method, using a black parachute fly or a palmer, though preferably the local fly, a Willy Ross. Anglers must be careful to use strong leaders. The Altnaharra Hotel has good beats on Hope for visitors and also on Loch Naver, which from time to time will produce heavy salmon of twenty to thirty pounds. Gillies and boats are provided by the hotel and beats are fished in rotation, with occasional outings for salmon on the Mudale and Mallart, productive tributaries of the river Naver.

Houghton Club   For over 175 years members of the Houghton Club have fished some of the loveliest fly water in England on the Test above and below Stockbridge. A former Honorary Secretary, P. K. George, wrote:

The Houghton Club was established in June, 1822, with twelve founder members, representative of the church, the arts and other professions. Then, as now, the club's headquarters were the Grosvenor Hotel in Stockbridge, though to ensure their evening fishing in those early days of slow travel members used to dine in a tent pitched on the river bank two miles below the town.

Initially, members relied on the grannom and mayfly for their sport. The floating fly had not been invented; dapping and fishing downstream with two flies were the order of the day. It was not until 1888 that the first fish is recorded as having been taken on the dry fly. Little fishing took place after early June. For the first 25 years or so grayling, introduced to the Test in 1818, competed with trout in popularity. The average weight of trout and grayling caught well into the twentieth century ranged from 1¾ to 2lb. For a number of years in the latter part of the nineteenth century club waters were stocked with bought-in fish; but in 1890 William Lunn, who came to Houghton in 1887, started a hatchery.

His arrival, coinciding with the advent of the dry fly, constituted a milestone in club history. A self-taught naturalist, he invented, amongst other flies, the Lunn's Particular and the Houghton Ruby. He was succeeded by his son, Alf, in turn to be followed by Mick Lunn, who retired in 1996. Ray Hill, himself the son, grandson and great-grandson of riverkeepers, was appointed in 1991.

The club consists of 24 members, and its waters are bounded to the north and south of Stockbridge by Leckford and Bossington estates. There are no written rules, but anyone wishing to become a member must have fished at least once as a member's guest before his name may be entered in the candidate's book.

Fish, bred from club stock, both brown and rainbow, average a little over 3lb. Around 1,700 are taken annually.

Houghton Ruby   A trout fly that imitates the spinner of the iron blue, created by W.J. Lunn, river keeper of the Houghton Club from 1887 to 1932.

Body: red hackle stalk showing crimson silk underbody
Tail: three rather long white hackle fibres, spread
Wings: two light blue hackle points at right angles to the hook shank
Hackle: bright red cock, clipped under, so that the fly lies low in the water
Hook: 16 or 18

Companion creation to the Houghton Ruby is Lunn's Particular, which imitates the spinner of several of the olives.

Hughes-Parry, J.   A well-known fisherman on the Welsh Dee for many years, Hughes-Parry is the author of *A Salmon Fisherman's Notebook*, which A.G. Street described as 'the best book on salmon fishing I have ever read'. Hughes-Parry's book is admirably written and, though he had a partiality to bait, his advice on fly fishing is sound. His favourite flies were the Torrish and the Jock Scott, diminishing in size as the water temperature increased. Hughes-Parry, like all great salmon fishermen, had a humble approach:

The span of human life is too short to enable one to gain even the rudimentary knowledge necessary for the successful catching of salmon.

Hybrids   Crossbreeding of trout and char, of rainbow and steelhead, rainbow and brook trout, have been common among fishery managers since the 1880s but although some interestingly marked fish have been produced, with attractive names – sunbeam, tiger, cheetah, and so on – they do not seem to survive the experimental stage. Some hybridisation of fish takes place naturally at times.

International Fly Fishing Association (IFFA)   Evolved out of the old National Angling Clubs Association, when at their AGM in 1927 it was agreed to hold an annual competition between clubs representing England and Scotland. The first international was held on Loch Leven on 29 May 1928, which England won by a narrow margin. Ireland and Wales joined in 1932, but a formal constitution was not forthcoming until 1951.

Hon. Sec. Ian Campbell, 16 Marindin Park, Glenfarg, Perth & Kinross PH12 9NQ.

See also Competitive Fly Fishing

Invicta   An invaluable and versatile wet fly for lake trout and sea-trout, designed originally by James Ogden of Cheltenham around 1845. The dressing has been modified since:

> *Body:* yellow fur, ribbed gold twist
> *Body hackle:* red cock palmered down the body and held in place by gold ribbing
> *Shoulder hackle:* red cock with a beard hackle of blue jay in front
> *Wing:* hen pheasant tail feather slips
> *Tail:* golden pheasant crest
> *Hook:* 14 to 8

A pleasant variation is the Silver Invicta, which dispenses with body fur and palmered hackle in favour of an all-silver body made in several ways – mostly plain silver tinsel, sometimes with a silver wire rib.

Ireland   The game fisheries of Ireland bring visitors from many parts of the world, but it is more than the fishing which keeps them coming back. There is a certain magic about Ireland which is difficult to describe. It is the atmosphere, the kindness of the people, the beauty of the land, the humour and charm of the boatmen who take you out on the huge inland

seas and the great loughs of the west, after the salmon. Nor is the salmon the only attraction. Everywhere from small streams to great rivers are the wild trout – brown, *ferox* and many others – that give you some splendid fly fishing, mayfly hatches that last for nearly a month and fishing the drift with wet fly and dap. Salmon sometimes arrive in the very early spring, the grilse in June, and it is a good boatman who knows where they can be found and whether they will be taking the fly or a silver spoon.

The boatmen of the western rivers and lakes are professionals; it is their life. Not only do they know the places where fish are certain to be, but they look after your rods, are concerned for your enjoyment and welfare, and will make tea with a volcano kettle, guard the sandwiches, and feed the gulls that follow wherever you are. And always there is a lovely stretch of water still to come that can be fished comfortably for the rest of the day.

Moreover, there are good fishing hotels, with their own fishing and their own tackle shops, where you can spend some time discussing the varied merits of a Bibio or a Bumble. Ireland has its own fly patterns but if the visitor has a good selection of the Scots, such as a Hairy Mary and a Dunkeld, then he will do well enough.

Visitors to the Republic of Ireland should note that a state licence is needed for salmon and sea-trout, but not for brown or rainbow trout. There is much free brown trout angling, but privately owned fishing requires a permit from the owner. The Foyle Area, which has its own peculiar regulations, is in both the Republic and Northern Ireland, and fishing there is administered by the Foyle Fisheries Commission, 8 Victoria Road, Londonderry BT47 2AB; a rod licence is required there to fish for both brown trout and salmon, and this applies to anglers under the age of 18. In two areas of the Republic, the Northern Fisheries Board and the Upper Shannon, it is mandatory to purchase a Share Certificate before fishing; persons under 18 years or over 61 are exempt. A good many fishing festivals and fly fishing competitions take place during the season on the larger loughs and these should be avoided.

Your main problem will be deciding where to go, and for that you will need a copy of *The Angler's Guide to Ireland* and *The Great Fishing Houses of Ireland*, both available, free of charge, from The Irish Tourist Board, Baggot Street Bridge, Dublin 2. For more local information you should contact the appropriate regional fisheries board: Central and Eastern Fisheries Board, Mobhi Boreen, Glasnevin, Dublin 9; Southern Fisheries Board, Anglesea Street, Clonmel, Co. Tipperary; North Western Regional Fisheries Board, Ardnaree House, Abbey Street, Ballina, Co. Mayo; Western Regional Fisheries Board, Weir Lodge, Earl's Island, Galway; Shannon Regional Fisheries Board, Thomond Weir, Limerick; South Western Regional Fisheries Board, 1 Nevilles Terrace, Masseytown, Macroon, Co. Cork; Northern Regional Fisheries Board, Station Road, Ballyshannon, Co. Donegal.

Recommended reading: *Irish Game Fishing*, Paul Sheehan; and three books by the knowledgeable Peter O'Reilly, *Trout and Salmon Flies of Ireland*, *Trout and Salmon Loughs of Ireland: A Flyfishers' Guide* (third edn); and *Trout and Salmon Rivers of Ireland: A Flyfishers' Guide* (fourth edn); *A Man May Fish*, T. C. Kingsmill Moore; *An Angler's Entomology*, J. R. Harris; *Irish Trout and Salmon Flies*, E. J. Malone; *A Review of Irish Salmon and Salmon Fisheries*, Ken Vickers; *The Angler's Guide to Irish Fisheries*, Joseph Adams; and *Fly Fishing in Ireland*, Thomas J. Hanna.

See also Arrow, Ballynahinch, Beltra, Burrishoole, Careysville, Conn, Corrib, Costelloe and Fermoyle, Currane, Delphi, Eriff, Moy, Newport, and Shannon.

Iron Blue (*Baetis pumilus, B. niger*) One of the smallest and darkest of the *Baetis* family of flies, the iron blue is found on most rivers of the British Isles. It is a small, dark, inky-blue fly which, once identified, can generally be recognised again without difficulty.

Various wet fly patterns suggest or are based upon the natural iron blue, the Infallible in Devon and the Dark Watchet in Yorkshire among them. A number of good patterns suggest the floating dun, of which this is one:

Body: peacock quill, dyed inky-blue, or mole fur dubbed thinly, showing two or three turns of crimson tying silk at the tail
Whisks: white or pale blue cock
Hackle: dark blue or dark green cock
Wings: starling, dyed inky-blue
Hook: 16

The spent fly is best suggested by W. J. Lunn's Houghton Ruby, and Skues has a good dressing of the iron blue nymph.

A characteristic of the iron blue which endears it to

fishermen is its apparent indifference to cold and rain; it will sometimes hatch on the most unlikely of days in March and April. The best hatch will be in mid-summer, and, though it may tail off a little, there can be sudden flushes again in the autumn. Plunket Greene in *Where the Bright Waters Meet* paid the best tribute ever to the iron blue (the winged fly, not the hackle):

> It is not merely a Test fly, for I have caught a two-pound trout with it in a little Scottish burn, casting it dry on chance upstream into likely places. There used to be a superstition that the iron blue was a bad weather fly only useful in a thunderstorm but my experience is that it is the best of them all on glass-smooth water in bright sunshine. In fact it is often the only fly they will take in such conditions and it is certainly the only thing they will look at when they are smutting . . . .
>
> There may well be some physical reason for it. They may be very fat or tasty – why else should they [the trout] be so partial to mere hors d'oeuvres like the smuts? – or else they may look very luscious against the light; whatever it is the trout could not have a greater affection for it than I have.
>
> It is, no doubt, imagination, but the iron blue always seems to me to be happier and keener and have better manners than all the rest. He is an aristocrat, a prince of the wing, far above the world of underwater hacklers, as he sails down serene on the streams, oblivious to wind or rain or sun, above board in his every thought, and ready to work for you again and again till he disintegrates and falls to pieces from very exhaustion.

Itchen Quite a short river (only 32 miles long) flowing through Hampshire to the sea at Southampton Water, the Itchen is fed by a thousand or more springs that come from the chalk downs. The source is generally recognised to be at the head of one of the tributaries, the Tichborne Brook. There are two other main tributaries, the Candover Brook and the Arle, and the three of them join together within a few hundred yards to form the true Itchen, just downstream of the town of Alresford. Ron Holloway writes:

> If the Test is recognised as the king of the chalk streams then the Itchen must, indisputably, be the queen. Between Ovington and Winchester lie some of the famous beats where men like Lord Grey of Fallodon, Skues and, in later years, Dermot Wilson pursued their love of dry fly fishing. These beats, with such

evocative names as Ovington, Itchen Abbas, Lovington, Itchen Stoke, Chilland, Martyr Worthy, Easton, Abbotts Worthy and Abbotts Barton, are regarded as the cream of wild brown trout stream fishing in our country, or perhaps the world.

The uniqueness of the Itchen, with its constant flows of pristine spring water at constant temperatures, are of interest these days to far more people than dry fly chalk stream enthusiasts. Because of its very nature, this river is ideal for fish farming, and the pressures which the river has to sustain with several large fish farms only adds to the other pressures which the waters now have to bear. Only through wise ownership and management of these beats has the nature of the river been maintained at its present standard, although the balance is very precarious, necessitating constant vigilance on the part of the keepers and managers and owners.

How wise Ron Holloway was to warn of the dangers facing the chalkstreams. The Itchen was where G. E. M. Skues fished on the Abbotts Barton beats from 1883 to 1938, and where he pioneered the development of nymph fishing and yet in the 1960s this famous fishery was allowed to fall into disrepair. Sluices which fed carriers became blocked; huge deposits of silt and mud fouled the streams, and dense beds of Norfolk reed marched uncontrolled through the water meadows. This unique, beautiful and famous fishery was all but finished. Then came the rescue.

Roy Darlington writes:

During the winter of 1973–4, Roy and Ron Darlington obtained the lease on the fishery and set about its recovery. With the help of a number of like-minded friends and scant funds, they gradually re-instated sluices, dredged some of the carriers, re-established the appropriate width of channels where possible, and put into place regular river management practices. In 1979 a memorial stone seat was placed on a length which had been a favourite haunt of old Skues and where, in 1949, his ashes were scattered by Mullins the keeper. The fishery is now in good heart and provides exciting and exacting trout fishing for a restricted number of season rods. Despite the expansion of modern Winchester, the meadows are an oasis of wildlife and quiet calm. The area is currently designated as an SSSI and soon to be further protected by the European classification of Special Area of Conservation (SAC).

Along with the ghosts of some of the greatest names in the development of modern trout fly fishing, today's Abbotts Barton anglers savour much the same ambience and fishing experience.

Access to the Itchen is limited to the few waters which allow day tickets, but mainly it is held by riparian owners and their tenants and various fishing clubs. The Rod Box, London Road, King's Worthy, Winchester SO23 7QN is sometimes able to provide rods on the Itchen, but applications should preferably be made well in advance.

See also Chalkstream fishing.

Ivens, T. C.   No one had more influence on the development of reservoir fishing than T. C. Ivens with the publication in 1952 of his *Still Water Fly Fishing* which went through at least four editions and was reprinted several times.

Ivens and his friends fished the Midland reservoirs and developed new simplified types of fly and new techniques of fishing them. He divided fly patterns into two categories: attractors and the deceivers. The attractors were lure-type flies, like the Alexandra and his Jersey Herds; the deceivers were nymph or larva-type patterns, not tied to imitate any one creature, but to suggest a number. One of the most important of the latter which has retained and even increased its popularity, is the Black and Peacock Spider.

Ivens was one of the first reservoir fishers to emphasise the importance of long casting, which he demonstrated in a series of photographs. His deceiver flies, which he preferred to fish wherever possible, were fished very slowly, so that their shape and movement coincided with those of a trout's usual food. The attractors were generally used in heavy water or when trout were sticklebacking, and were fished fast. Though there were exceptions, as there always are, in general he regarded dry fly fishing as a waste of time. His aim was to put reservoir fishing on as scientific and simple a basis as possible, and his book and his whole philosophy had an instant appeal to large numbers of men who were being attracted to reservoir fishing for the first time since World War II, as well as to those who had previously been fishing traditional wet flies without knowing quite why.

J

Jacques, David (1906 - 1983)   A leading entomologist, angling editor for publisher A & C Black, and contributor to many journals on fly life and fly fishing, David Jacques was awarded a fellowship of the Royal Entomological Society for his brilliant ecological research.   His essay on the life of the grannom is contained in *Fisherman's Fly*.   In 1974 Black published his *Development of Modern Stillwater Fishing*.   He also revised the third edition of Courtney Williams' *Dictionary of Trout Flies* and wrote a life of Viscount Grey.   At the time of his death Jacques was preparing a commentary on *The Boke of St Albans*.   Among his many friends was John Goddard, who encouraged him to write his first book, *Trout Fly Recognition*, to which Jacques devoted lavish care.

He was a good fisherman on the Test, Avon and at Two Lakes as well as being a good entomologist, and would often break off in the middle of fishing, take out a lens and study some tiny insect, not minding in the least that he might be missing the only fish of the day.   In an appreciation, John Hillaby wrote:

> Although my good friend David Jacques could not be described as an academic, he was in his own particular way at college all his life.   He was forever learning, exploring, getting down to the fundamentals of whatever stimulated his agile mind.   He grasped the essentials of Hebrew, Yiddish, Latin and a fair amount of Greek and applied them to his impeccable English, a fact attested by all his books on fishing . . . .   Should all this sound over-austere, many of us will remember a loving and learned man.

Jardine, Charles   Almost certainly one of the best-known names in fly fishing today, Charles Jardine lives in mid-Wales, but was born in Canterbury, Kent, where he caught his first trout at the age of six.   Fly fishing and his other principal interest, wildlife painting, were encouraged by his father, Alex

Jardine a noted artist in his own right.

Charles has written articles for many fishing, country, in-flight and travel magazines, and is now in his fifth year writing and illustrating for *Trout Fisherman* and *Trout & Salmon* magazines. He is also feature writer for the Kent Messenger group of newspapers, a contributor to the *American Angler* and illustrator for the German magazine *Fliegenfischer*. He has written several books on fly fishing including *Dark Pools, Small Water Trout Fishing, The Sothebys' Classic Guide to Fly Fishing for Trout* (now in its third edition, translated into five languages, and believed to be one of the most successful books of its kind) and *The Pocket Guide to Fly Fishing for Trout*. He provided the watercolour illustrations for the late Trevor Housby's *The Illustrated Angler*.

Charles holds the Federation of Fly Fishers' masters certificate in fly casting, is APGAI qualified and also has the Salmon & Trout Association's STANIC qualification in casting and fly tying; he demonstrates these specialities at all the major angling shows in the UK, Europe and the USA. He has also featured on a number of television and radio programmes, and is the only Englishman to have received the prestigious American Federation of Flyfishers' 'President's Pin', an award for conservation and services to the world of fly fishing.

In 1993, Charles was a member of the winning English team in the Commonwealth Championships held in British Columbia and again when the same team retained the championship in 1995, gaining an individual bronze medal in the process. He is currently manager of the English Ladies' Fly Fishing Team, and European secretary of the Federation of Flyfishers, and is on the council of the Handicapped Angler's Trust. Charles is the UK and European game fishing consultant for Sage Rods of America and fly line and accessory consultant for Ryobi Masterline.

Jed Water A tributary of the Teviot, the little Jed has affinities with most of the Border trout streams whose names, not without too much imagination, sound like a chime of bells – Whiteadder and Blackadder, Till and Teviot, Ettrick, Gala and Leader Water.

Chalk stream fishermen who think that spate rivers are easy had better try a river like the Jed. It can be as clear as the Test, or sometimes clearer, and the trout do not wait if they see you

– they are gone, and the river is emptied for the next thirty yards. The truth is that to fish any of these Border rivers, especially in high summer and low water, demands the highest qualities of presentation and rivercraft; one false move, one splashy cast, and all will be lost.

Upstream fishing is obviously the best – one accepts that now the lessons that Stewart sought to teach have gone home – but there are times and places where across and down seem inevitable. There are no rigid rules to stay the hand, so one can fish according to the way of the stream. Small flies of the spider type, size 16 and 18, do well in the surface film, a dry olive or an iron blue if there is a hatch, or else an 18 or 20 black gnat. It is also rewarding and satisfying to fish a Greenwell in its home waters.

Permits to fish the Jed can be obtained through enquiries at Jedburgh, the Jedforest Angling Club (Teviot, Jed and Oxnam waters) or the ironmongers. The fishing associations welcome visitors and provide day tickets.

Jersey Herd An attractor pattern, a minnow fly for reservoir trout, designed by T. C. Ivens, named because the copper-coloured foil used for the body came from the top of a bottle of Jersey Herd milk:

> *Body:* an underbody of wool formed in minnow shape, covered by copper-coloured tinsel or foil tied in at the tail and wound to the head
> *Back:* about 12 strands of bronze peacock herl, with the ends projecting beyond the bend of the hook as a tail, and the ends by the eye wound round to make a head
> *Head hackle:* two turns of bright orange hen
> *Hook:* 8 or 6

Jock Scott The most elaborate of traditional salmon flies. A good modern dressing is by Veniard, but some of the feathers may now be unobtainable:

> *Tag:* silver tinsel and yellow floss
> *Tail:* topping and Indian crow
> *Butt:* black ostrich herl
> *Body:* in two equal parts: first, yellow floss silk ribbed silver tinsel, butted with toucan and black ostrich herl; second, black floss silk ribbed silver tinsel with black hackle over
> *Throat:* guinea-fowl

Wings: two strips of dark mottled turkey tail, golden pheasant tail, bustard, grey mallard, peacock wing, blue and yellow swan, red macaw, brown mallard and topping
Sides: jungle cock
Cheeks: blue chatterer
Horns: blue macaw
Head: black
Hook: almost any size from 5/0 down to 1 or 2

Kelson, George M. (1886–1902) *See* Salmon Fishing: A Short History

Kennet The river Kennet is one of southern England's loveliest chalk streams, rising in the Marlborough Downs, and flowing in a great curve through Avebury and Marlborough and on to Hungerford. Although Peter Rennie wrote only about a small part of the river he captured the spirit of the whole:

> My knowledge of the Kennet is restricted to the stretch from Ramsbury upstream to Axford – rather less than two miles in which the water flows gently and the trout grow strong on a seemingly endless supply of freshwater shrimp, larvae and other delicacies. The water level scarcely ever varies save in the worst drought and even in so short a stretch the country through which it flows changes from iris-filled water meadows at one end which are kept neat by a flock of Jacobs sheep, to fly-tangling woods at the other where I once counted no fewer than thirty-four swans.
>
> When we first took rods at Ramsbury there was no chance of the thrill of a mayfly hatch. Two years ago we counted half a dozen or so and last year (1983) many more. So, despite the fame of other stretches of the Kennet we are only now able to look forward to enjoying the same heart-lifting, hand-shaking trauma of a serious mayfly hatch in future years.

Season, and some day, tickets on the Kennet can also be had from Barton Court, Kintbury, near Newbury which has approximately three miles of bank fishing; from the Craven Estate, Hampstead Marshal; and from the Denford Fisheries, Lower Denford.

Kennet: The Hungerford Water The main A4 road, the old Great West Road, crosses the Kennet at the ancient town of Hungerford (a name meaning a ford leading to poor or

unproductive land). The Hungerford town water has a unique history. John of Gaunt (1340–1399), who married Blanche of Hungerford, one of the daughters of the Duke of Lancaster, is said to have granted the inhabitants of Hungerford the right to fish the Kennet in perpetuity, so the town water – controlled by the Constable of Hungerford and the Trustees of the Town and Manor of Hungerford Charity – has a continuous history of many centuries. Each year at the Hocktide Lunch in Hungerford fishermen still drink to 'The Immortal Memory of John of Gaunt'.

Ownership of the river was challenged over the years but the Hungerford residents appealed to Queen Elizabeth in 1574 and she confirmed to the inhabitants 'such liberties and profits and benefits as heretofore, time out of mind and remembrance of man they have used and enjoyed.' So, if you are lucky to fish the town water, you are very conscious of its history. One of the lovely pools is known as the Wine Cellar and another is the Bathing Place.

Day rods are sometimes available. Enquiries should be made at the tackle shop, Roxton's in the High Street.

Ketting's Duck Fly   An unusual fly, introduced to this country by Dutch fishing journalist Kees Ketting in 1979, which had a remarkable success at Kimbridge on the Test. The odd thing about the fly is the hackle, which gives the impression of a grey mist:

> *Body:* brown tying silk or nylon, tied thinly from the bend of the hook to the head
> *Hackle:* a transparent-looking grey feather taken from the preen gland of the mallard duck, about four turns. The feathers have long fibres, and, when tied in, these fibres are pulled forward over the eye of the hook and clipped at the ends so that they do not appear too long, as they suggest the wings
> *Hook:* 14, 16 or 18

It could be that the fly suggests a black gnat or a chironmoid but it is taken freely during the evening rise to spinner. Whatever it may suggest, there are times when it is highly effective. The only trouble is collecting anus feathers.

Kingsley, Charles   The Rev. Charles Kingsley, author of *The Water Babies*, also wrote 'Chalk Stream Studies' an essay contained in *Prose Idylls* (1844). It is frequently quoted at the time for his praise of the alder fly:

'Oh, thou beloved member of the brute creation . . . would that I could give thee a soul if indeed thou hast not one already.'

Kingsmill Moore, T. C. One of the best books about trout and sea-trout in Ireland is Kingsmill Moore's *A Man May Fish*. First published in 1960 and reprinted several times, it is described by one specialist bookseller as 'A book to enchant every angler. An Irish classic of which the first edition is becoming difficult to obtain.' Kingsmill Moore's own tyings of the Kingsmill and Bumble sea-trout flies are in the Flyfishers' Club museum in London.

It was once said of him that quite apart from being a judge his real profession was fishing. His wife, Alexandra, a lifelong companion, persuaded him to write *A Man May Fish*, and he was pleased as well as surprised by its considerable success, both here and in America. The main character in the book, Jamesie, is a classic portrait of an Irish boatman.

Kite, Oliver One of the great names of nymph fishing who claimed he created the phrase known as the 'induced take', Major Oliver Kite wrote the standard work, *Nymph Fishing in Practice*, first published in 1963 and subsequently reprinted on at least two occasions. Oliver Kite was an army officer stationed at Bulford on Salisbury Plain who fished the service's water from 1955 onwards. He lived from 1958 to 1968 in a cottage at Netheravon. Frank Sawyer, the keeper, taught him to fish the nymph, and Kite went on to develop his own style, which he named the 'induced take' method. (For Kite's description of the technique of the induced take *see* Nymph Fishing).

Quite apart from nymph fishing, Kite was also a good dry fly fisherman, and one of the flies he designed, Kite's Imperial, was still in the best-selling lists in the late 1980s and is very much used today. For the last five years of his life he had his own successful programme, *Kite's Country*, on Southern Television. He died, while fishing, in the summer of 1968. The weekly articles he had written for the *Shooting Times* were edited by Philip Brown and published posthumously in 1969 under the title of *A Fisherman's Diary*. Those who fished with Ollie Kite, as he was always called, and those who saw him on television, were always drawn to his home-spun personality, soft voice and friendly charm.

Klinkhammer Special   'I doubt if any fly pattern devised in the last twenty years is as effective,' says John Roberts in the *Illustrated Dictionary of Trout Flies*. Peter O'Reilly is equally enthusiastic, calling it 'a wonder fly'. Designed by Hans van Klinken for grayling fishing, this dry fly has been found to be equally successful for trout. Most of its body is entirely submerged, with just its hackle keeping it afloat. It was originally tied as an emerging sedge imitation, but it works well in most situations. Its high profile and white polypropylene wing makes it highly visible in the water. There are now many variations, but the following is standard:

> *Body:* light tan polypropylene or feather fibre ribbed with fine silver wire
> *Thorax:* bronze peacock herl
> *Wing:* white polypropylene tied upright
> *Hackle:* ginger cock hackle tied parachute fashion round the base of the wing
> *Hook:* long shank, size 12-22, bent – Partridge make a special hook for this pattern – to give a curve half way along the body

Knots   Knots are older than man's recorded history, and the variety is almost infinite; to add to the confusion a knot may be known by many different names. For the flyfishers' needs only a few basic knots are required as it is increasingly common for leaders and lines to be supplied with looped ends to make life easier. For most purposes the Blood Knot and the Half Blood Knot (or Cinch) will suffice, and these knots are illustrated on page 133.

All knots reduce the breaking strain – a well-tied knot by perhaps 5 per cent, the all-too common-wind knot in a leader by as much as 50 per cent. A test of leader materials conducted by Dick Stephen and John Maitland, published in *Trout & Salmon*, May 1997, found that a badly formed or ill-tightened knot would fail at well below the expected shock load.

There is a considerable literature on knots, but the two most useful books are Alan B. Vane's *The Hardy Book of Fisherman's Knots* and the more recent *Hamlyn Book of Knots* by Geoffrey Budworth who co-founded the International Guild of Knot Tyers in 1982. The latter has twenty pages devoted to angling knots, but not all suited to the requirements of the flyfisher.

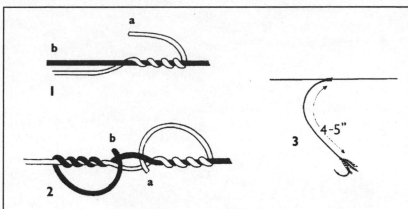

The Blood Knot for joining two lengths of nylon. *1.* The two ends are laid side by side, overlapping. End (a) is twisted four to six times round end (b); it is then brought back and goes through the junction of the two lines. *2.* Line (b) is twisted round line (a) and is brought back in the same way but goes through the junction in the opposite direction to (a). The knot is then snugged down and pulled tight and the ends trimmed. *3.* To make a dropper, one end is left uncut for four to five inches

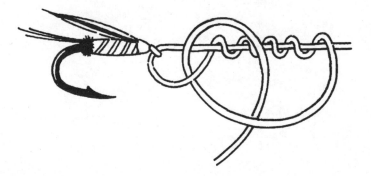

The Half Blood or Cinch Knot is useful for tying on a fly. The end tucked through one loop and then through the other gives a very strong grip

Landing There are two ways of landing a fish you are going to release. The first is to net it, and, keeping the fish in the water, take out the hook with artery forceps, lower the net and help the fish to recover in the water, making sure it does not turn over. However, much the best way to release a dry fly is to use a barbless hook and wind the line down until the top ring of the rod is in contact with the fly; press the rod forward against the fly in the fish's mouth, which will then be unhooked without damage.

Never beach a fish. It causes unnecessary pain. So does tailing with a tailer. Net the fish you are going to keep, lift the net out of the water, keeping the fish in the net, take it away from the water and kill the fish quickly with a blow on the head. Gaffs are mainly outlawed, and so are knotted nets in England and Wales as from April 1998.

Lambourn The Lambourn is a chalk stream that rises on the Berkshire Downs and flows into the Kennet. It can sometimes be seen from vehicles on the M4 which crosses the river just above the water fished by Howard Marshall, and commemorated in his book *Reflections on a River*, first published in 1967. In it he wrote:

> Always I shall come back to the little River Lambourn. The fact that I am fortunate enough to live on its banks is beside the point. If I lived a hundred miles away I should still return to this limpid stream and its golden trout.

Much of the Lambourn is now private fishing. Howard Marshall's water at Easton has been taken over by a syndicate. Apart from industrious local enquiries it is doubtful whether there is now any way of fishing the Lambourn unless you own a stretch. This is a pity for it is one of the most charming little rivers in southern England.

Lane, Joscelyn   Colonel Lane's book *Lake and Loch Fishing* (1966) set high standards in the study of the development of still water fishing techniques. He was among the first to produce good fly dressings of lake olive nymphs, damselfly nymphs, shrimps, water boatmen and stickleback lures. His trimmed-hackle sedge preceded those of Richard Walker and others. A thoughtful and useful book.

Lapsley, Peter   A former army officer, at one time owner of a fishery at Rockbourne, near Fordingbridge, is the author of two exceptionally good books: *Trout From Stillwaters* and *River Trout Fishing*. Lapsley goes into great detail about the fish themselves, and examines their life style, their environment, food, flies, tackle and techniques.

Last Hope   A fly designed by John Goddard to suggest a pale watery. It is also useful as a spinner, also in a *Caenis* hatch and when trout are smutting:

> *Body:* natural stone or buff condor herl, but in the absence of condor a light-coloured or off-white silk or wool might do
> *Whisks:* four to six fibres of honey dun cock
> *Hackle:* very short cream cock
> *Tying silk:* pale yellow
> *Hook:* 18–20

Lawrie, W. H.   A great authority on the history of anglers' flies, his book *A Reference Book of English Trout Flies* is the standard work and gives dressings of some 700 flies from the fifteenth century onwards, created by more than 70 anglers and fly dressers. An earlier work, *Scottish Trout Flies*, is also invaluable for reference purposes. Lawrie's *Border River Angling* is a useful book dealing with classic wet fly methods.

Leaders   There is a bewildering choice of branded leader material: from the widely used nylon to the copolymers and the more recent fluorocarbon. The advantages of fluorocarbon are many: it sinks faster because of its higher specific gravity, it has a refractive index close to that of water, making it virtually invisible when submerged; it does not absorb water; it has a much higher breaking strain for a given diameter; and it is more abrasion-resistant than nylon. It is, however, more expensive, and knotting can be a problem (though tests have shown the Half Blood Knot, which pulls down on itself, to be the answer). The invisibility factor is obviously a great advantage when fishing crystal clear waters, and for marine fly fishing fluorocarbon is said to be unsurpassed.

The less expensive monofilament nylon remains the most commonly used material but is likely to give way to the newer fluorocarbon before very long. Some enthusiasts still prefer to construct their leaders from progressively thinner-diameter strands of monofilament nylon, but single-stranded tapered leaders are preferred by most anglers. The other choice is the braided tapered leader, which is claimed to be more supple, thereby reducing drag, absorbs shocks better, transfers energy more efficiently and allows for faster changing.

Tapered monofilament and braided leaders are generally available in lengths ranging from 7½ to 15 feet and in size from 0X to 7X. The X specification is a throw-back to the time when leaders were made from natural gut material. The X number refers to specific diameters of the tippet as shown in the following table:

	Diameter	Approx breaking strain (lb)
0X	0.011"	6.5
1X	0.010"	5.0
2X	0.009"	4.5
3X	0.008"	3.8
4X	0.007"	3.1
5X	0.006"	2.4
6X	0.005"	1.4
7X	0.004"	1.1
8X	0.003"	0.75

For many years these specifications were universal, irrespective of the material. But today, whilst the X-rating and diameter are still used, the breaking strain will vary from manufacturer to manufacturer and with the type of material used. For example, a typical monofilament knotless tapered leader rated 5X with a diameter of 0.006" has a breaking strain of 3lb, which is higher than that quoted in the table. A copolymer and resin material (available only in reel form as yet) has a stated breaking strain of 6lb in 4X; compare that with a fluorocarbon, from the same manufacturer, where a 4X is rated 4.75lb (but then fluorocarbon has many other advantages over copolymer, and is twice as expensive). It is all very confusing and specifications are changing all the time.

Dick Stephen and John Maitland conducted a series of practical tests on the leading 18 brands of monofilament leader materials, the results of which were published in *Trout & Salmon*, May 1997: the costs per metre ranged from 3.2p (standard nylon) to 32.81p (fluorocarbon); the stated diameters from 0.15 to 0.22mm with stated breaking strains of 4.5 to 6lb. Their findings make interesting reading.

Among many other conclusions they make the point that badly formed knots failed well below the shock load – the four-turn water knot was used as standard. Knot efficiency tests ranged from a low of 70% (and this was not the cheapest line) to an equal number scoring 80% and 90%. A copolymer costing nearly twice the price of the cheapest nylon, but less than the fluorocarbon, performed well across the test range. Information of this calibre allows the angler to make informed choices.

See also Knots.

Leane, Lough   The largest lake in Killarney, Co. Kerry, noted for its salmon and trout fishing and also for the beauty of its surroundings. The best salmon months are from January to June; trout fishing can be good in the spring with hatches of duck fly. There are plenty of boats and boatmen for hire and fishing is free. Accommodation: Ross Castle, Killarney, Co. Kerry, and Tara, Fossa, Killarney, Co. Kerry.

Lee, Art   An American fisherman whose book *Fishing Dry Flies for Trout on Rivers and Streams* has had some influence in Britain. He concentrates on presentation of the fly, rather than precise imitation of the natural insect, and as a result of his experience recommends fishing the dry fly across or slightly downstream rather than in the traditional upstream fashion. His book was published after some thirty years experience of fishing the Catskill rivers and other American streams, as well as the Test.

Lines   The first fly lines were made of horsehair, then a mixture of horsehair and silk, and by the 1860s of silk dressed with linseed oil. These silk lines had to be religiously dried after each outing to prevent rot and required oiling or greasing to make them float. The advent of synthetic materials in the late 1940s introduced nylon, which overcame the problem of rot, although these lines stretched and were difficult to float.

The next improvement came about in the early 1950s with the development of plastic coatings and the ability to control the density of lines; this meant that lines could now be made either to float or to sink (in theory at least – in practise many early coated lines were prone to breaking, did not float very well and suffered from 'memory'). These problems were largely overcome by the mid-1980s with the use of non-stretch synthetic cores, with the added bonus of increased abrasion-resistant coatings. Continuous research and development, both here and in the USA, ensures the regular appearance of improved lines and adds to the bewildering choice on offer to the sophisticated fly fisher.

Silk lines were described by diameter, and the new synthetic substitutes were at first treated the same way, but for a variety of reasons this was found to be confusing and inadequate. In 1961 the American Fishing Tackle Manufacturers (AFTM) devised a new numeric code which graded lines by weight, irrespective of the material used or their calibre. The scale runs from 1 to 15 with a No. 1 line weighing 60 grains, as measured by the first 30 feet of line, and a No. 15 weighing 550 grains, with a tolerance of ± 10 per cent. (Sage introduced an 'ought' (0) line in 1998, but the technical specifications were not available at the time the *Encyclopaedia* went to press.)

These new size numbers, which have been adopted universally, are used with letters that describe the type of line: WF = weight forward; DT = double taper; L = level; F = floating; S = sinking; I = intermediate; ND = neutral density; TT = triangle taper; and ST = shooting taper. Sink tip is denoted by F/S after the line size. WF6F indicates a weight forward No. 6 floating line, and DT8S a double-taper No. 8 sinking line. Rod manufacturers mark all their products with the recommended line number to use for maximum performance.

Weight Forward (WF): This line has most of its casting weight in the belly, approximately 30 feet or so immediately behind the front taper, and is the most popular line in use today. WF lines are easier for distance casting than a double taper (DT). Shooting heads (ST) are a variation on the basic WF, but with the level running line replaced by a finer-diameter material, which can achieve greater casting distance.

Double Taper (DT): At one time these lines had the reputation of giving a more delicate presentation than WF, but that is no longer true because most of today's WF lines are made with a more gentle taper. There is however, no denying their superiority when it comes to fishing small streams with restricted access, for it is an easier line to roll cast. The other obvious attraction is that of economy – when one end becomes worn the line can be reversed.

Intermediate: Sinking lines are denser, and therefore thinner, than floating lines of the same AFTM rating. Intermediate, or neutral-density, lines are easier to cast in high winds and have the added advantage that they tend to land more lightly on the water. Useful in still water fishing, these lines slowly pull the fly and the leader down into the water and keep it down as you retrieve.

Floating: Ideal for dry flies, or nymphs, that are to be fished on, or in, the surface film of the water; they are also used for deep nymph fishing on rivers. The floating line also acts as a take indicator and is the preferred line for the novice.

Sinking: Available in slow-, medium- and fast-sink versions, with the latter being first choice for deep fishing in a reservoir or from a boat. The whole of the line sinks – unlike the sinking-tip line, where only the first 10- to 20-foot section sinks and the remainder of the line floats. The sink-rate is indicated on the line carton and can range from one foot per second to ten feet per second.

Triangle Taper: Invented by Lee Wulff in the mid-1980s, protected by US and UK patents and generally misunderstood by many anglers, who believe the whole of the line is triangular in cross section. The name describes just the profile of the casting head: the tip section is relatively fine, then the line diameter increases steadily for the next 40 feet; it then decreases and tapers rapidly down to a thin running line. This line is a compromise between the characteristic delicacy of a double taper and the improved casting ability of a weight-forward line. Versatile in so far as it handles well in a variety of casting situations – a light tip for close presentations, ideal for extended casting and without equal when it comes to roll casting. Available in floating, intermediate and fast-sinking, and for salmon, saltwater fly and sea-trout fishing.

Level: A line which has a constant diameter. Inexpensive and sometimes included in novice outfits, despite the fact it is difficult to cast. Its only value is to the angler who likes to

construct his own line system by attaching a shooting or a fast sinking-head.

Specialist lines are available for salmon, pike and salt water fly-fishing.

See also Rods, Leaders.

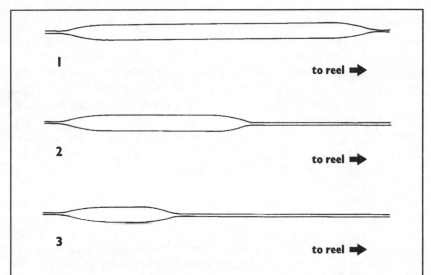

Line Tapers. 1. The double-tapered line is very useful because when one end wears out the line can be reversed on the reel and the other end used. 2. The forward or 'rocket' tapered line has only one working end (the front) so it cannot be reversed as the double tapered line can be. It has the advantage that longer casts can be made as more of the thinner part of the line can be 'shot' in casting. 3. For extremely long casting a line about 30 feet long, known as a shooting head, is attached either to a thin braided line or to nylon monofilament backing, allowing this to be shot more easily than a forward-taper line.

Line Care The use of a cleaning pad, generally supplied with the line by the best manufacturers, is recommended to be used from time to time. Scum, grease, algae and microscopic particles of grit are picked up by lines and can damage their surface; in the case of floating lines this will increase their weight to the point where they will begin to sink. Lines can be damaged by various chemicals, oils, petrol, detergents, insect repellents and certain kinds of line floatants, as well as by excessive heat (leaving a line in the back window of a car in direct sunlight for many hours, for example). Worn rod rings can slice a line to pieces in no time at all. Bad casting, treading

141

on the line with nailed boots and pulling it violently from branches and brambles are also a common cause of damage.

Some fishermen with experience of the old silk lines affirm that, if properly treated, they would last three times longer than their modern counterparts – but do admit, sometimes reluctantly, that the newer lines are less trouble to use.

Line Colour   Controversy and continued debate surround the choice of line colour. Experiments have been conducted over the years, but there is no conclusive evidence to support any of the several conflicting theories. Currently lines are sold in the following colours: ivory, ivory white, natural green, light green with a dark green tip, olive, dark olive, pale green, buckskin tan, light green, grey, olive-green, black-grey, deep grey, mist green, blue, optic orange, mist green, white, orange, fluorescent yellow, off-white, pale green, peach, ice blue, ice blue and green tip, dark moss green, yellow with green head, and more recently, crystal clear.

It is generally thought that sinking lines should be dark (as they are believed to be less noticeable to fish) and that floating lines should be of a light colour, or even completely transparent – but all cast a shadow both in the air and on the water. Some anglers opt for a garish-coloured floating line for the simple reason that it is more visible than other shades, particularly in low-light conditions of early morning and late evening.

Little Red Sedge   A pattern of a sedge fly, made popular by G. E. M. Skues, which can be fished whenever sedges are hatching:

Body: dark hare's ear
Body hackle: red cock, tied in at the shoulder and taken down sparsely to the bend
Rib: fine gold wire binding down the body hackle
Wing: rolled landrail or substitute landrail, tied sloping well back and close to the body
Front hackle: red cock tied in front of the wing
Hook: the usual size is 14, but it should be larger when the big sedges are about

Lochy and the Western Highlands   A vast area with dozens of salmon and sea-trout rivers and lochs, and some of the sea-trout lochs like Eilt, Shiel and Morar, are among the most

productive in Scotland. The mountains – including Ben Nevis, 4,408ft (1,344m), the highest in Britain – are most spectacular, and the rivers – fed by fresh-water lochs – fairly short and fast flowing, with rock gorges; some of the sea lochs into which they run are so steep-sided they give the impression of Norwegian fjords.

A good centre is Fort William, where the tackle shop can make a number of reservations for rods. A good stretch of the Lochy is available but is soon booked up. The Spean Bridge Hotel has water on the Spean, the main tributary of the Lochy. For Eilt and Morar the centre is the Loch Morar Hotel. It is worth remembering that the fishing in practically all these Western Highland rivers depends very much on water levels.

Lomond, Loch   A great loch for pleasure boating as well as fishing, Lomond has plenty of room, for it is the largest fresh-water loch in Scotland (24 miles long and several miles wide). Salmon are taken in many areas, but the most popular place is the south shore between Balloch and Balmaha. It is spinning early in the season, but it is fly-only on the Endrick Bank from May. Boats and permits can be obtained at Balmaha, Balloch and Luss, and hotels along the lochside can also make arrangements for the fishing. The loch is so big, and the lies so widespread, that a local boatman is essential if one is to feel confident of covering fish. There is good sea-trout (no sea-trout can be killed before 1 April) and brown trout fly fishing on the drift, with a team of two or three flies on the cast, and when the water is clear, which it generally is, quite small flies will bring up the fish. Because there are big fish around it is advisable to have a flexible rod and fish not too fine. Recommended flies: Burton Black, Mallard and Claret, Silver Invicta, Peter Ross and for salmon, Ian Wood, Brown Turkey, Green Highlander and Willie Gunn.

The newly formed Loch Lomond Angling Improvement Association are actively engaged in restoring the loch's reputation which had been in decline since the 1980s. Membership applications should be made to the LLAIA, PO Box 3559, Glasgow G71 7SJ.

Accommodation information is available from the Argyll, Loch Lomond and Trossachs Tourist Board, Dunoon PA23 7UZ.

Lunn   Three generations of the Lunn family have been river keepers on the Houghton Club water of the Test at Stockbridge. The first, W. J. Lunn, began work in 1887 at the age of 20 and retired 55 years later in 1932. Even at an early age he was a fine practical naturalist, and Halford and Marryat and others frequently consulted him and took his advice. He was a splendid fly designer and tyer, had an almost unrivalled knowledge of the ecology of rivers, and so many fishermen relied on his judgement that it was not surprising that J. Waller Hills wrote about him and his life and times in *River Keeper* (1934).

Alfred Lunn, his son, succeeded him in 1932 and was responsible for the layout of the hatchery and the stews at Stockbridge. One of Alfred Lunn's many achievements was the substitution of borehole water for stream water in the rearing of fry, which increased the survival rate from 50 to 80 per cent.

When Alfred's son, Mick Lunn, took over in 1963, he had already absorbed an enormous amount of river lore as part of his family background but was never content to rest on tradition. He made considerable advances in modern methods of fish farming, studying the use of chemicals and the improvement of fish diet. Before his retirement in 1996, Mick Lunn published *A Particular Lunn: One Hundred Glorious Years on the Test*, which he wrote with Clive Graham-Ranger.

Lunn's Particular   One of the famous flies designed by W. J. Lunn, tied first in 1917 as a suggestion of an olive spinner. It was said to attract shy feeders when the trout were being 'particular' about their choice of fly.

> *Body:* undyed hackle stalk from the Rhode Island red cock
> *Hackle:* medium Rhode Island cock
> *Whisks:* four fibres from the same bird, rather long
> *Wings:* two medium blue hackle points, tied on flat and at right angles to the body (the spent position)
> *Tying silk:* dark red
> *Hook:* 14

Many fly dressers like to clip a V in the hackle underneath so that the fly floats in the surface film. Some fishermen prefer to fish a Particular upstream wet, on the assumption trout prefer drowned flies.

Lunn's Spent Gnat *See* Mayfly.

Lune   The river Lune rises on Ravenstonedale in Cumbria, where it is a wild and open moorland stream.   Well past Sedbergh it turns down into the wild valleys and broadens out, flowing through farmland, joined by small streams, flowing past Kirkby Lonsdale and Hornby, to be glimpsed briefly by motorists on the M6 motorway as it goes into the estuary at Lancaster.

The Lune is a wonderful mixed fishery. Oliver Kite in *A Fisherman's Diary*, recounts a splendid few days there with Reg Righyni and Arthur Oglesby, during which he caught one roach, nine brown trout to 2lb 6oz, eight sea-trout, including three three-pounders, and two salmon together weighing 20lb. He caught his best two sea-trout – in Lancashire they are called morts – in blazing mid-afternoon sunshine, on a small and sparsely dressed nymph. The country is lovely and open with a variety of secluded valleys, and the up-stream wet fly fishing for trout in the classic style is among the best in the North Country. In recent years the salmon runs have declined, as they have done in so many other rivers.

Lures   Lure fishing was probably carried out by the ancient Egyptians and the Chinese several thousand years ago. Jacques records that Homer wrote of fishing rods, hooks and casting in the twelfth century BC. The Greeks and Romans used what they called a plume, rather similar to the feathers that the Cornish use for mackerel.

The Romans fished plumes, and it is likely that they brought the habit over to this country during the colonisation of Britain. Fishing for salmon with a 'dubble' is mentioned in the *Treatyse of Fysshynge Wyth an Angle* in 1496, though what a dubble on a hook looked like is uncertain. A hundred years later several writers were describing flies for salmon which had several 'wings'. The plumes, dubbles and wings give a tantalising glimpse of feathered lures that were dressed according to an oral tradition passed down from one fishing generation to another, changing little over the many centuries.

The more one tries to define a lure the less likely one is to succeed except, in the broadest terms – that it is almost any creation of fur and feathers that is not a copy of an insect. The modern lure has developed from the artistic creations of early Victorian fly dressers, leading up to Kelson. Salmon and sea-trout flies are visibly lures, though at least some patterns may give the impression of small fish. In reservoir fly fishing many large double and treble-hook lures are specially designed as a result of American influence – for example, the popper bug and the lead-headed jig, known here as a Nobbler. An interesting comment on reservoir lures was given by Richard Walker in an article in *Trout & Salmon*, republished in *Dick Walker's Trout Fishing*:

> There is a great deal of debate about the ethics of lure fishing. I should be sorry to see any restriction placed on it in large water-supply reservoirs and other sheets of water of comparable size, where there is no evidence that its use leads to too high a catch rate. When trout are eating fry, or when they are obviously not eating insects, the use of an appropriate lure may catch a fish or two and save an angler, who may have travelled a long way, from a blank day. In these conditions, using a lure is perfectly reasonable.
>
> I am, however, sorry for the anglers who have no ideas beyond casting out a lure as far as possible and stripping it in as fast as they can, regardless of what the trout are doing. They don't know how much pleasure they are missing. That they often catch a lot of fish is undeniable, but they never learn what fly fishing is all about.

Lyd A small tributary of the Tamar, rising on Dartmoor, creating picturesque falls in the National Trust area of Lydford Gorge, then passing in a sequence of pools and stickles through farming valleys to join the Tamar south of Lifton. Though small, the Lyd has an excellent run of sea-trout from late June or early July, and a small run of salmon. The Arundell Arms at Lifton has several miles of fishing for hotel guests.

Lyn A small Exmoor stream in *Lorna Doone* country. Fishermen should avoid the tourist area of Watersmeet. There is good fishing for small trout around Rockford, where permits may be had, and then two little rivers, East and West Lyn, join up and speed down a steep wooded and rocky gorge to the sea at Lynmouth. Salmon do run up the Lyn (the Environment Agency, Devon and their local agents issue permits), but it is mostly local inhabitants who know best when to fish.

M

McCaskie McCaskie's Green Cat Fly, mentioned by Skues (*see* Williams, A. Courtney) was designed by Dr Norman McCaskie, author of *Fishing – My Life's Hobby* which contains an eleven-page introduction by Skues. McCaskie's Corner on the Abbotts Barton water, named after him, was taken over for Winchester town development in the 1970s and is now closed to fishermen. Dr McCaskie's brother, Dr H. B. McCaskie, also a fisherman, was the author of *The Guileless Trout*.

McLaren, Charles Author of *Fishing for Salmon* and other books on fishing, Charles McLaren is a great exponent of long casting and the use of fine tackle to take fish in clear water. He won a number of English and Scottish fly casting championships and in the 1970s opened his own fly fishing school at Altnaharra, Sutherland.

Mallard and Claret A wet fly for trout in use almost everywhere, abroad as well as at home. It is used mostly for lake fishing, for fishing the drift and for sea-trout:

> *Body:* claret-coloured seal fur or wool, ribbed with fine gold wire or gold tinsel in the larger sizes, sometimes with a small gold tag
> *Tail:* golden pheasant tippet
> *Wings:* two strips of dark bronze mallard
> *Hackle:* red cock
> *Hook:* 14 for lake trout, up to 8 or 6 for sea trout

March Brown (*Rhithrogena haarupi*) A pleasant-looking ephemerid fly, about the size of the Large Dark Olive, with noticeable speckled wings. It has a localised distribution in Wales, Devon, Yorkshire and parts of Scotland. Fished dry on rivers like the Usk, a good artificial can be deadly. Jean Williams, of Sweet's Fishing Tackle, Usk, Gwent, changes the body colours of her dry March Brown because of the way the

natural fly varies in colour:

Body: hare's ear or red or yellow or green wool
Rib: fine oval gold tinsel
Tail: four or five reddish fibres from a cock pheasant's tail
Hackle: one brown partridge hackle in front of two medium red cock hackles, the partridge, which gives the speckled look being slightly longer than the red cock
Hook: 12 or 10

Jean Williams also has an interesting pattern of the nymph of the March Brown, imitating the male:

Body: weighted with fine lead wire
Tail: short cock pheasant tail fibres
Body: first half (abdomen), cock pheasant tail fibres; second half, (thorax), hare's ear and red wool fibres mixed together
Casing: fibre strips over the top of the thorax taken from the darkest cock pheasant tail fibres
Hackle: grouse
Hook: 12

The female March Brown nymph is similar but the red wool is absent from the thorax, which is plain hare's ear, and the tail fibres and throat hackle are not pheasant but partridge.

The wet fly March Brown is similar to the dry, but with less hackle and the addition of strips of feather taken from the tail of the hen pheasant, sloping backwards, with a brick-red wool body.

Maree, Loch   A deep loch in Ross and Cromarty which lays claim to being 'the fairest in Scotland', and which certainly produces some record sea trout. Geoffrey Snutch gives this description:

The loch is a magnificent setting in Wester Ross, bounded on the inaccessible northerly shore by wooded slopes tumbling sheer from the bare faces of Silioh mountain, where circling eagles are sometimes seen. The road follows the southerly shore through unspoilt woods and rocky moorland. About 11½ miles long and 2 miles wide at its broadest point, Maree is studded with wooded islands which add much to its beauty and also its fishing potential.

The fishing is for sea-trout and salmon, which ascend the short and often productive outfall river Ewe. The major part of the fishing is controlled and organised from the Loch Maree Hotel, situated half way along the southern shore. There is a fleet of motor boats and their attendant ghillies are employed to take the angler to dap the sea-trout drifts around the ten hotel beats, bearing names such as Coree, Grudie and Fool's Rock. Ash Island is reckoned the best and to produce the biggest trout. In the rotation, the far beats enjoyed a brief popularity due to several appearances of a naked female bather.

Marryat, George Selwyn Once described as 'the finest dry fly fisherman in England', G. S. Marryat served as a Guards officer and retired from the army in 1870 when he was only 30. Most of the time for the next 26 years was devoted to fishing. He was involved with H. S. Hall in improvements to the eyed hook, which had been introduced in an early form some 40 years before. Marryat met Halford by chance – a meeting described by Donald Overfield in *Famous Flies and Their Originators* – which began their partnership. Marryat, to begin with, knew far more than Halford about the dressings of floating flies. Halford certainly thought that the result of their researches should be published under their joint names. For some reason, Marryat refused. It is possible that this might have been because of Halford's rigid insistence on the use of the dry fly at all times. Marryat, so far as we know, did not share this view. A box of his flies, seen in a rummage sale at the Flyfishers' Club in London, contained many wet-fly patterns.

Marryat died in 1896 and is buried near Izaak Walton in Winchester Cathedral.

Marshall, Howard (1900–1973) Howard Marshall's only book on fishing, *Reflections on a River*, was widely admired for delicate and perceptive essays that took their inspiration from the river Lambourn. He was interested in fishing all his life and was the co-founder, with Bernard Venables, of *Trout & Salmon* magazine. In his last years Marshall lived at Easton Lodge, Easton, near Newbury, close to the Lambourn, whose charms he shared with his friends. His favourite flies were the Greenwell, the Gold-Ribbed Hare's Ear, the Blue Upright and the Little Red Sedge.

Marshall became famous for his radio commentaries for the BBC on great national and sporting occasions. He was educated at Haileybury and Oriel College, Oxford, became a sports writer for the *Daily Telegraph*, and joined the BBC in 1927. One of his many famous commentaries was on the

Coronation of King George VI in 1937. He was Director of War Reporting for the BBC from 1940 to 1945. He died in 1973 and is buried in Welford churchyard, not far from the Lambourn.

Martin, the Rev. James   A great advocate of dry-fly fishing, James Martin was the author of *The Angler's Guide*, published in 1854, which among other things gave this advice:

> Never throw your fly on the water in a wet state, for if you do it will sink the moment it gets there, which is not well. To prevent this, whisk it once or twice through the air before you let it fall on the water . . . so that it shall appear in its descent exactly like a real fly.

Mask, Lough   An enormous limestone lough in Co. Mayo, ten miles long, four miles wide and covering some 20,000 acres, famous for its free trout fishing. Brown trout taken on the fly weigh up to 3lb or more, but the average is just over a pound. Apart from dapping, dry fly and wet fly on the drift, a great attraction is to troll 10 or 30 feet down for what are known as *ferox* trout which can weigh over 20lb. Experienced boatmen are essential, as there are hidden rocks close to the surface. Accommodation: Cong Gateway, Lackafinna, Cong, Co. Galway. Ballinrobe is the main angling centre, and there are a number of guest houses which cater for the angler.

Mayfly   In America all ephemerid flies are called mayflies, in Britain the term is applied to only three. The most important is the big mayfly, *Ephemera danica*; the other two, less frequently seen, are *E. vulgata* and *E. lineata*. Hatches vary from year to year and place to place. The chalk streams are liable to have profuse hatches during the last week in May and the first week in June, and in certain years hatches are so heavy that passing cars have their windscreens spattered with so many insects that drivers have to stop and wipe them off.

The mayfly occurs in other districts apart from the chalk streams – in the West Country, parts of northern England and Scotland – but the hatches are generally sparse and nothing like the abundance of fly in the Hampshire-Wiltshire area.

The common name for the mayfly dun is the Green Drake and for the spinner, the Spent Gnat. The most popular flies to suggest the Green Drake are Peter Deane's Shadow Mayfly and Lee Wulff's Grey Wulff. This is Deane's Shadow Mayfly pattern:

Body: none
Body hackle: palmered grizzle cock, long, from eye to bend
Whisks: none
Wings: two red cock hackles, points clipped square, standing up well from the body, tied in about half way between the centre of the hook and the eye
Hook: 10 long-shank

At times a badger or a grizzle hackle can be used for the wings, but the original is red game cock, the hackle points curving inwards towards each other. Peter Deane writes:

I was taught to tie the Shadow Mayfly by post by J. Arthur Palethorpe of Hungerford Priory in 1950. Believe me it was the only fly tying lesson I ever had and I trust the last as he was an extremely hard taskmaster. In the hand it looks nothing like a real mayfly and it took me some 16 years after I first tied it before I had sufficient confidence to use it myself, and what a surprise when I did so! It is most effective and creates an illusion or impression of a fly, possibly because it casts the right kind of shadow.

Among other dressings are Horace Brown's Fore and Aft, and Skues' Straddlebug:

Body: raffia
Whisks: brown mallard
Ribbing: fine gold wire
Hackle: ginger cock palmered from the eye of the hook to the bend, held down by the gold wire

The Grey Wulff, from America, was one of the first dry flies to be tied in such a way that the whole fly was lifted off the water, leaving only the imprint of the hackles and the tail on the surface:

Tail: long and thick fibres to help lift the hook from the water
Wings: fibres from a bucktail with white points, leaning forwards
Hackle: long grey or dark blue cock to lift body and head of the fly from making contact with the water
Hook: long-shank 12 or 10 for the mayfly, ordinary hook 12 or 14 for the duns

This is Lunn's Shaving Brush:

Body: thin white wool, ribbed with black or brown tying silk, the closest turns at the head
Whisks: two or three fibres of teal, grizzle or pheasant tail, according to taste

Wings: grey hackle points tied forward and divided for the spinner; for the dun, grey hackle and black mixed thickly to give a nice bushy appearance
Hook: 12 or 10 long-shank

Veniard's dressing of the Spent Gnat:

Body: white floss silk or dun-coloured raffia
Tail: three cock pheasant tail fibres
Hackle: badger cock
Wings: dark blue dun hackle points, tied spent
Hook: 12 or 10 long-shank

John Goddard's Spent Gnat:

Body: natural raffia
Tail: three fibres from a cock pheasant's tail
Rib: fine oval silver
Wings: a very stiff black or dark blue cock hackle wound in the usual way, the hackle then split into two equal halves and tied spent
Hook: 12 or 10 long-shank of fine wire

Mayfly Nymph There are various opinions about the use of a nymph during the mayfly season. On many chalk streams nymph fishing is not allowed, or only after the mayfly season is over. An outspoken rejection of fishing a mayfly nymph during a hatch is in Oliver Kite's *Nymph Fishing in Practice*:

> If I can't reach them with [a dry Mayfly] I give them best although I know there are days when trout taking the natural Mayfly can be damnably difficult. The point is they do take it, and for me, personally, deceiving them is part of the challenge. In such circumstances it would be spiritual prostitution for me to put on a nymph on a No. 5 hook [Redditch scale 10] and use this to butcher trout with. For that is what using a large Mayfly nymph amounts to, in my opinion.

Melvin, Lough Partly in the Republic and partly in Northern Ireland, Lough Melvin holds both salmon and trout. There are said to be four genetically distinct species of trout in the lough: brown, *ferox*, gillaroo and sonaghan trout. The angling activities, with boats and boatmen, are centred mainly at Kinlough, Garrison, and Rossinver. Fishing competitions are held there from time to time. For accommodation contact: Gillaroo Lodge, West End, Bundoran, Co. Donegal.

Midge (*Chironomidae*)   A large family of mostly non-biting midges or gnats belonging to the order of two-winged flies (*Diptera*).   There are some 400 types.   On still waters, midges are a major trout food, and on rivers they are of growing importance.   The midge larvae, known as bloodworms because of their colour, live on or near the bottom; they are sometimes copied by a thin thread of red wool or red rubber on a hook, fished deep.   The more usual method is to fish the pupae; these rise to the surface with a wriggling motion and then hang in the surface film before ecdysis.   The winged midges can sometimes be seen in a swarm, generally of a dark colour, rising and falling in their mating dance by the edge of still waters.   The larger ones can sometimes be identified on sight by the slight hooked shape of the body.

Midges were frequently taken by using spider patterns prior to the 1920s.   So far as we know, the first artificial specifically tied to imitate a midge, came from Blagdon in the 1920s, or earlier.   The best known, however, which was tied a few years later, was Dr Bell's Blagdon Buzzer (see that entry for the dressing).

In *Lake Flies and Their Imitations* C. F. Walker emphasised the great importance of midge pupae patterns, and he used gut or nylon for the abdomen and ostrich, condor or peacock herl for the thorax.   In *Fly Fishing Tactics on Stillwater*, Geoffrey Bucknall introduced the Footballer; the name, some say refers to the colours of Newcastle United:

Body: alternate turns of black and white horsehair carried round the bend
Thorax: mole fur
Head: peacock herl
Hook: 14–16

One of the most elaborate of all midge dressings is John Goddard's:

Body: according to the colour of the midge being imitated, black, brown, red or green marabou silk, ribbed silver lurex, then covered with PVC
Tag: white hen hackle fibres, projecting about one-eighth of an inch, tied in well round the bend of the hook
Thorax: green peacock or buff condor herl
Head filaments: loop or bunch of white hen hackle fibres, tied through the thorax to face upwards and forwards over the eye of the hook
Hook: 16, 14, 12

An interesting variation was Frank Sawyer's Bow Tie Buzzer, which had detached head filaments. For river fishing, most anglers use a small Black Gnat or flies such as Kees Ketting's Duck Fly or the Blae and Black.

A new development of the midge pattern for lake fishing came in the late 1970s. Steve Hare of Hucklebrook Trout Lake, near Fordingbridge designed a midge pattern made almost entirely of lead wire:

Body: turns of lead wire
Hackle: a fluff of white deer hair at the head

This was at first used to reach deep-lying river trout in fast water but its disadvantage for lake fishing was soon realised, and Bill Sibbons, a portrait painter with a studio near Fordingbridge, who had experience of fishing at Damerham and Rockbourne, developed this adaptation:

Abdomen: lead wire over a base of brown tying silk, the lead turns slightly apart to give the impression of the ringed body of the natural
Thorax: mole fur
Head: a small fluff of white deer hair, or similar
Hook: 14 –10

A variation, giving a brighter appearance, was to use copper wire for the abdomen.

Midland Flyfishers Formed in 1932 with Courtney Williams as chairman. Owns salmon fishing on the Welsh Dee and has trout fishing on Shropshire brooks. Neville Chamberlain was president, 1934–1940, and, among others, Lord Chobham, 1964–1977.

Mill Brook A tiny chalk stream rising at Blewbury in Wiltshire and flowing into the Thames at Wallingford. David Barr writes:

The Mill Brook is believed to be the stream in Kenneth Grahame's *The Wind in the Willows.* For many years a good head of trout lived amicably with shoals of roach. A trout of 5lb 2oz was caught on a sunken Dunkeld at East Hagbourne. Sadly, Mill Brook has become a winterbourne.

Missionary Ancestor and inspiration of many a reservoir lure, the Missionary originates from early this century and is

believed to have been first tied by Captain J. J. Dunn for the Blagdon sticklebackers. Later the pattern emigrated to New Zealand and, after being ignored in its own country for a while, became popular again among Midland reservoir fly fishers.

Body: white wool
Tail: white cock
Wings: a few fibres of dark turkey tail, with the side strips of dark teal extending well beyond the bend of the hook
Beard hackle: white cock
Throat hackle: as for the tail; white hackle fibres are sometimes used
Hook: originally 8 or 10 standard size, but now long-shank is more usual

Mottram, Dr J. C. (1880–1945) An experimental fly designer of the late Halford period, James Cecil Mottram broke away completely from conventional styles and pioneered the art of creating illusions and suggestions: silhouette flies and flies without bodies which he described in *Fly Fishing: Some New Arts and Mysteries, c.*1915.

Moy, River Has the reputation of being the most prolific salmon fishery in Ireland. It is difficult to obtain accurate figures of rod catches, and they are not available since 1990, but in that year the catch was in excess of 6,000 for the whole of the river. Since then, in common with all other rivers, catches will have declined. One of the most popular beats is the Ridge Pool in Ballina. It is a tidal pool, and boatmen are booked well in advance. In low water, flies such as Garry Dog, Yellow Goshawk, and Hairy Mary in size 12 doubles or 14 trebles on fine leaders are often used. The local anglers' association has good fishing. Permits from the Moy Fishery Office, Ridge Pool Road, Ballina; Gannons Guest House, Foxford; Mount Falcon Castle, Ballina; and Links Lodge, Castleconnor, Ballina, Co. Mayo.

Muddler Minnow At least one, and possibly several, fly patterns that have become popular on Midland reservoirs in recent years have been designed by American fly dressers. The Muddler was introduced from America in 1976 by Tom Saville, from a design by an American fisherman and instructor, Don Gapen of Minnesota. The Muddler, buoyant because of its deer hair body, was an immediate success as a reservoir lure, as an imitation of a small bullhead or minnow and as a surface lure for sea-trout fishing:

Body: flat gold tinsel
Tail: turkey or hen pheasant fibres, well bunched
Head: deer hair spun round the hook and clipped to form an oval or round shape, some of the fibres lying backwards along the hook and mingling with the wings
Wings: bunched or rolled turkey or hen pheasant fibres, projecting from immediately behind the head
Hook: 10 - 6 long-shank

Munro Killer   A salmon fly, originally marketed in the 1970s by Munro of Aberlour for the Spey, now popular on many rivers. It has affinities with the Stoats Tail and the Torridge Special. The Munro dressing:

Body: black wool or floss
Ribbing: two turns of round gold tinsel at the tail and three or four turns up the body
Whisks: none
Underwing: a few fibres of squirrel tail, the tips dyed yellow, not projecting much beyond the bend of the hook
Overwing: a few sparse fibres of black bear or black squirrel, long (almost twice the length of the body)
Beard hackle: wisps of bright blue and hot orange feather fibres, not mingled, tied on either side of the hook
Hook: generally small doubles, 6, 8, 10 and 12

N

Nadder A delightfully clear river, rising on the borders of chalk stream country near Shaftesbury, with good stocks of trout and grayling as well as coarse fish. The Tisbury, Burford, Teffont and Salisbury fishing clubs have good stretches for fly fishing. There is, on the whole, a sparse hatch of mayfly, but there are many midge, black gnat and sedge and, occasionally, profuse hatches of olives. The Nadder trout are known to be reasonably accommodating in their choice of artificial, a number of large trout are taken each year, and a five-pounder taken near Compton Chamberlayne in 1983 ((by John Barclay of Sussex on a Wee McGregor) is a splendid example of what this small stream can produce.

Ness A great area of the Highlands is drained by the river Ness and its feeder streams and lochs – Ness and Oich, Moriston and Garry. The town water at Inverness has permits from the local angling club. Further upriver the Dochfour Estate lets rods on the Ness, and the Glenmoriston Estate on the Moriston; rods on the Oich may be obtained from the fishing tackle shop at Fort Augustus. The Garry is largely private.

There is good trout fishing but the salmon vary considerably according to the height of water. The lochs, especially Loch Ness, are mostly fished by trolling from boats, and local knowledge is essential.

Netboy, Anthony The standard textbook on the salmon, containing valuable information and covering the seaboards on both sides of the North Atlantic, is Netboy's *The Atlantic Salmon: A Vanishing Species*, published in 1968, which he followed with *Salmon: The World's Most Harassed Fish* in 1980.

Newport, River A small stream in Co. Mayo which drains from Lough Beltra and travels less than seven miles to the sea

at Clew Bay. It is fly-only water with good pools most of the way: the Cement Bridge, Sheridans and many others. Floating lines are generally used with local fly patterns, such as the Beltra Badger – fairly small in clear water, a little larger if coloured. Permission to fish and good accommodation at Newport House, Newport, Co. Mayo.

Nith A Border river, though a long one, the Nith rises deep in Robert Burns country in south Ayrshire, flows through scenic Nithsdale, past Sanquhar and Thornhill to Dumfries and the Solway Firth. At most of these towns fishing can be had on association water through local hotels. The Drumlangrig Castle Fishings, on the Duke of Buccleuch's Queensberry Estate at Thornhill, leases beats. The Nith has a run of salmon towards the autumn, with sea-trout in summer, and so does its tributary, the Cairn. The river is on the whole slow-runnng but with occasional fast spates.

North Atlantic Salmon Conservation Organisation NASCO was established by a convention in October 1983 for the conservation and care of salmon in the North Atlantic ocean. A new inter-governmental organisation was set up under the convention, and fishing for salmon beyond areas of fishery jurisdiction was prohibited. As a result, the salmon fishery in the northern Norwegian sea, which at its peak amounted to 960 tonnes per annum, ceased to exist. During the winter of 1989/90 reports came in that some salmon long-lining vessels which had been registered in non-NASCO states were fishing for salmon north of the Faroes. Action was taken by diplomatic intervention, adoption of a protocol for signature, and international co-operation on surveillance; as a result there have been no sightings in these waters since February 1994.

Since NASCO's establishment regulatory measures have been agreed in most years for the West Greenland and Faroese fisheries. Agreements for the Faroese fishery have resulted in the establishment of catch limits, together with limits on the fishing season and the number of licences issued. Under these agreements the allowable catch has been reduced to 380 tonnes in 1997 in conjunction with an effort-limitation programme (catches in this fishery peaked at 1,100 tonnes in 1981). For the West Greenland fishery the quota has been reduced to 57 tonnes in 1997 from a peak catch of 2,500 tonnes in 1981.

Regulatory measures have also been agreed for the Newfoundland and Labrador commercial fishing, which exploits North American stocks.

In recent years NASCO has been able to turn its attention to the many threats to the health of the salmon, such as disease, parasites, climate change and other matters. Further details of NASCO's operations and activities can be obtained from NASCO, 11 Rutland Square, Edinburgh EH1 2AS.

Northumbrian Water manages eight fisheries (nine counting the wild brown fishery at Cow Green) and leases another ten waters to local angling clubs. At Derwent Reservoir, one of the most popular trout fisheries in the area, special family day tickets are available. Disabled anglers are catered for at several of the fisheries and are granted concessionary rates, as are senior citizens and persons under 17 years old. The reservoirs are as follows:

Fontburn (87 acres). Six miles south of Rothbury, off the B6342. Darlington. Wild brown, stocked rainbow and brook trout. The British record Brook Char (cultivated), weighing 8lb 3oz was taken here in April 1998 by Ernest Holland. Bank fishing.

Kielder Water (2,700 acres). Nine miles north west of Bellingham in the north Tyne Valley. Wild brown and stocked rainbow. Bank and boat fishing.

Derwent (1,000 acres). Off the A68, near Consett. Wild brown and stocked rainbow. Bank fishing.

Tunstall (66 acres). North of Wolsingham in Weardale. Wild brown and stocked rainbow. Bank and rowing boat fishing.

Grassholme (140 acres). West of Mickleton and south of the B6276 in Teesdale. Wild and stocked brown and stocked rainbow. Bank fishing.

Blackton (66 acres). Between Hury and Balderhead in Teesdale. Wild and stocked brown and stocked rainbow. Bank fishing. Fly only.

Hury (125 acres). Baldersdale, west of Romaldkirk in Teesdale. Wild and stocked brown and stocked rainbow. Bank fishing.

Scaling Dam (105 acres). Between Guisborough and Whitby in the North York Moors. Wild brown and rainbow. Bank fishing.

Cow Green (770 acres). Ten miles north-west of Middleton-in-Teesdale. Claims to have one of the best natural populations of brown trout in England. Bank fishing.

Northumbrian Water publish a most attractive, and informative, free game fishing guide to still waters in the north-east of England. Available from their Recreation and Conservation Department, Abbey Road, Pity Me, Durham DH1 5FJ.

Nymph Fishing 'A very exacting form of fishing, infinitely more exacting than the dry fly', said Oliver Kite in *Nymph Fishing in Practice*. Nymph fishing has various meanings. On reservoirs the term is widely used to describe fishing an artificial representation of a variety of underwater creatures, larvae, pupae and shrimp. On rivers it is generally limited to the nymphs of the olives and iron blues in hook sizes no larger than no. 14.

Nymph fishing was pioneered by G. E. M. Skues towards the end of the nineteenth century on the Abbotts Barton water of the Itchen just above Winchester. Skues was a dry-fly fisherman to begin with, a disciple of Halford. One day, however, he was fishing a dry fly to a trout which refused it several times. The fly was a poor floater and on the last cast it sank, whereupon the trout immediately took it. This experience led Skues to experiment with fishing the upstream wet fly and in due course to tie patterns of the nymphs which he found in the trouts' stomachs. All his nymphs were unweighted and were what we might call emerger patterns, which are generally fished in, or close to, the surface of the water. Most of them were on size 15 or 16 hooks, very delicately and sparsely tied. Some of the originals are in the Flyfishers' Club Museum in London. Skues came into conflict with Halford and the dry fly purists; and this continued for most of his life.

One day, Skues' friend Sir Grimwood Mears showed him some new patterns of nymphs tied by a water-keeper on the upper Avon, Frank Sawyer. These were the size and shape of the Skues nymphs but tied very simply with the reddish fibres from a cock pheasant tail twisted around fine copper wire. These were swimming nymphs (as distinct from the emergers of Skues), intended to be fished deep when the nymphs were active. Sawyer's patterns dispensed with the hackles that Skues used to suggest the nymph's legs, because when nymphs swim their legs are almost invisible, being held close to the body. Skues was impressed, urged that Sawyer should be encouraged, and helped in the preparation of Sawyer's book, *Nymphs and the Trout*.

A new stage was being reached in the development of the nymph. Skues, with his unweighted emerger patterns, had always insisted that nymph fishing was not to be considered as a separate form of fishing but one that was ancillary to the dry fly. Whether this was to placate the purists is difficult to say. With the arrival of the weighted nymph, though this could no longer be sustained. It was obvious that fishing a nymph pattern several feet below the surface of the water was very different to the dry fly.

In the atmosphere of the 1920s and 1930s, the idea of a weighted fly seemed to many to be a contradiction in terms. No 'fly' could be 'weighted'. Sawyer found the same opposition that Skues experienced when he introduced his emergers. In some cases opposition was even more bitter and contemptuous, for Sawyer was a water-keeper and did not have the skill to argue with his critics in the way that Skues could. It was some consolation that Sawyer ultimately had the satisfaction of knowing that his Pheasant Tail had a world-wide reputation and was being sold and used in more than 60 countries.

Fishing the nymph was popularised by Oliver Kite in the late 1950s and early 1960s. He describes it in his book, *Nymph Fishing in Practice*:

> When things were quiet when I was fishing at Choulston one day in the 1957 season he [Frank Sawyer] suggested to me that I might do better if I went higher up and tried my hand with a nymph. I had nymphs, shop nymphs, which I did not consider worth using. He gave me a couple of his small Pheasant Tail Nymphs and I went off to see what I could do.
>
> Above Choulston is the famous Court Reach at Netheravon, just at the back of the cottage where I now live. There, below Haxton Bridge, I found a good trout swinging to and fro in a streamy current where it emerged from between two clumps of starwort. The trout refused various dry flies. I put on one of the nymphs I had been given, casting it accurately a few feet ahead of the trout. As it passed the fish's head without being taken I raised the tip of my rod to withdraw it. As I did so, I saw the trout turn, so I stayed my hand. Momentarily, then, as the trout turned back, I struck. And that was how I caught my first trout on the artificial nymph.

That was also the inspiration of my nymph fishing technique.

The method of activating the nymph as it passes or comes near to the fish Kite called 'the induced take.' It was also the method used by Sawyer, and he felt hurt by the way Kite used the phrase 'induced take' as something that he, Kite, had created. Kite was a great publicist and Sawyer was not.

Recommended reading: *Nymph Fishing in Practice* by Oliver Kite; *Nymphs and the Trout* by Frank Sawyer; and *Masters of the Nymph*, which contains contributions by Brian Clarke and Frank Sawyer, among other famous names on both sides of the Atlantic.

Nymph Patterns   Modern unweighted emerger patterns which follow Skues' principles are numerous, but the Hare's Ear nymph or the Gold Ribbed Hare's Ear are among the better known:

Abdomen: hare or rabbit fur, ribbed with fine gold wire
Whisks: none, or a few short dun hackle fibres
Thorax: a slightly thicker dubbing of the grey fur or heron herl
Hackle: one turn, two at the most, of a short dun hackle
Hook: 14 - 16

For the nymphs of the pale watery, Sawyer's Grey Goose, tied unweighted, is as good as any:

Abdomen: pale grey fur or heron herl, ribbed with yellow silk
Whisks: a few fibres of grey feather, very short
Thorax: a thicker dubbing of the grey fur or heron herl
Hackle: one turn, two at the most, of pale grey or pale grey-blue feather
Hook: 15 or 16

Sawyer's Pheasant Tail Nymph is probably the most important nymph ever tied, and the original dressing by Frank Sawyer is known in some 60 countries (with, of course, many variations by many expert fishermen). Here is the original dressing, or close enough to the original:

Body: fine copper wire, wrapped round the hook from bend to eye
Thorax: build up with wire and then return wire to the bend
Tail: four centre fibres of a brown-red cock pheasant tail, tied in with the wire and projecting about an eighth of an inch
Rib and wing cases: the four pheasant tail fibres spun on the wire and lapped evenly to the hook eye; the fibres are then separated

from the wire, taken over the thorax, bound behind the thorax, doubled back to the eye, and tied down.
Hook: 14–16

Some fly tyers use brown silk instead of wire to tie off the wire at the head of the nymph, but this is not really necessary. Some use a clear varnish to set the wire.

Ogden, James An inventive fly dresser of the mid-1800s who had a fishing tackle business in Cheltenham and is best known for the design of that invaluable fly, the Invicta. He also claimed to have tied the first dry flies. Author of *Ogden on Fly Tying* (1879).

See Dry Fly Origins.

Olive Dun A name given to several fly patterns designed to suggest most of the common olives of the *Beatis* species. The duns of these are also represented by a number of other patterns, including the Blue Dun, Greenwell, Olive Quill, Olive Upright and Kite's Imperial. The pattern most likely to be an Olive Dun – and there are several – must have dark green about it somewhere:

> *Body:* medium olive-coloured fur
> *Hackle:* dyed olive-green cock
> *Whisks:* three fairly long fibres of the same colour
> *Wings:* starling primary
> *Hook:* 14 - 16

Olive Quill The same dressing as the Olive Dun but with a stripped peacock quill body, dyed olive-green. The Olive Quill is often used as a hackled pattern, without the starling wings.

Olive Upright The same as the Olive Quill but a West Country pattern. The stripped peacock quill is dyed a yellowish apple green and it seems to be always used as a hackle pattern.

One-Fly Man Quite a number of dry fly fishers use only one fly pattern throughout the season. Richard Threlfall fished only one pattern of dry fly wherever he went – Itchen, Lambourn, Teme, Vyrnwy, the Yorkshire becks, Blagdon and

the great lakes of Ireland and Scotland. This was the fly:

> *Body:* a reddish or black hackle palmered from eye to bend,
> making sure that the hackle at the head of the fly slopes forward
> and not to the bend
> *Hook:* 10 - 18

Howard Marshall who watched Threlfall fish on the
Lambourn said he cast very accurately and delicately. If a fish
refused him he would try once or twice more, but then moved
on to the next fish. Marshall said he knew many a chalk
stream man who fished a single pattern throughout the year,
'and Threlfall caught as many trout in all conditions as the
next man and decidedly more than most of us'.

Orange Quill   The dressing of the Orange Quill, favoured by
Skues when blue-winged olives were hatching, is:

> *Body:* pale condor quill, stripped so as to show no dark edge, dyed
> hot orange
> *Whisks and hackle:* bright red cock
> *Wings:* pale starling, rather full, as the natural insect has wings
> longer than the ordinary olive duns
> *Tying silk:* hot orange
> *Hook:* 13 or 14

Both J. W. Dunne and David Jacques were doubtful about the
Orange Quill representing the sub-imago of the blue-winged
olive; both thought it was more likely to suggest the imago, the
sherry spinner. Photographs in John Goddard and Brian
Clarke's book *The Trout and the Fly* confirm their opinion.

O'Reilly, Pat   Angling and wildlife author and broadcaster
Pat O'Reilly began fishing in 1947, when he learned to cast a
fly on Ireland's river Slaney. He has written a dozen books
(most recently *Matching the Hatch*) including several on fly-
tying and fly-fishing, and is a regular contributor to *Trout &
Salmon* and various newspapers.

   In 1981 Pat, an APGAI, STANIC and REFFIS fly-fishing
instructor, established the West Wales School of Flyfishing. He
chairs the Regional Fisheries Advisory Committee for Wales
and is a member of the Government's new Salmon and
Freshwater Fisheries Review Group.

O'Reilly, Peter   Lives at Boyne Hill, County Navan, Meath, within sight of the beautiful river Boyne. He is angling adviser with the Central Fisheries Board and one of Ireland's leading authorities on game fishing. His *Rivers of Ireland: A Flyfisher's Guide* (fourth edn), *Loughs of Ireland: A Flyfisher's Guide* (third edn) and *Trout and Salmon Flies of Ireland* are considered to be the definitive works in their field.

Peter is an APGAI and a STANIC fly tying and fly casting instructor. He is a prolific fly tyer and is in much demand as a speaker at angler gatherings and as a demonstrator at game fairs. Every year he conducts fly-fishing courses at the Delphi Lodge and Ballynahinch Castle Hotel Fisheries in Connemara. He is especially interested in encouraging more young people to take up fly fishing and ensuring that adequate measures are in place to provide sustainable angling for wild fish in a natural environment.

Orkney   Lying off the north coast of Scotland, the Orkney Islands offer both wild brown and sea-trout fishing. Boat fishing is the most popular, but wading can be equally successful on some lochs; whilst bank fishing in late evening and early morning in the middle of the season will often produce excellent results.

Orkney's five most popular waters are all within a ten-minute car journey of each other and can be fished by all without a permit or a licence. The only exception is Skaill, a minor Mainland loch which is reserved for members of the Orkney Trout Fishing Association (who, incidentally, maintain a watchful eye over all aspects of freshwater welfare – by becoming a member you will help to protect and support the country's finest wild brown trout fishery).

When it comes to fishing techniques, location, timing and choice of fly it is useful to seek local advice, and advisable to have a gillie with you in the boat (to avoid the ubiquitous skerries which can tear the bottom out of a boat and damage motors).

Stan Headley's *The New Trout Fishing Guide to Orkney*, which is essential reading, gives the following selection of flies for Orkney waters: *Wet Flies*: Irishman's Claret, Olive Dabbler, White Hackled Invicta, Octopus, Doobry, Hutch's Pennell, Gold Mini Muddler, Hedgehog and Muddled Hare's Ear; *Nymphs* : Blushing Buzzer, Mini Stick and Black Buzzer; *Dry Flies* : Black & Claret Emerger, Sedgehog and Fiery Brown Emerger.

For accommodation write to the Orkney Tourist Board, 6 Broad Street, Kirkwall, Orkney KW15 1NX.

Orvis   Founded by Charles F. Orvis in Manchester, Vermont, USA, in 1856, the company specialises in quality fly-fishing tackle and caters for all outdoor pursuits. It claims to be the oldest fishing-rod manufacturer in the world (it originally made and sold only fly rods and did not branch out into reels, flies and other tackle until later).

Orvis is one of the few major mail-order companies still in private hands, having had only three owners since its formation: the Orvis family from 1856 to 1939, D. C. 'Duckie' Corkham from 1939 to 1956 and finally, the Leigh H. Perkins family from 1956 to the present day.

In 1956, when Leigh Perkins bought the company, sales were in the region of $500,000; today Orvis distributes in excess of forty million catalogues and has net sales of $200,000,000 worldwide. Orvis's innovation record is impressive. It started in 1874, when Charles Orvis developed the first narrow-spool ventilated fly reel, which is still the prototype for the modern fly reel. In 1946 the company patented the world's first impregnated bamboo rod, making rods completely waterproof and warp-free; it opened the first American fly-fishing school in 1966 and introduced the world's first Zinger in 1967. In 1972 it developed the first modern exposed-rim skeleton-frame, super-light fly reel, the CFO and in 1974 introduced its first graphite rods. Orvis was the first manufacturer to provide a 25-year guarantee against breakage of its fly rods, regardless of the cause. As recently as 1996 Orvis launched its Trident series of rods using Maximum Vibration Reduction Technology, and in 1998 it put an end at last to the hitherto vague rating of rod-tip action with the introduction of the Flex Index system.

Otter   The river Otter rises in Somerset on the slopes of the Blackdown Hills, flows through Honiton and Ottery St Mary and into the sea by Budleigh Salterton. It is a small limestone stream, like its sister the Culm, and has a good head of wild brown trout. Even when it gets to Honiton the Otter is quite small, only a few feet across, so that it has to be fished with care: a small rod, the lightest of lines, a fine tippet and dry flies up to 18s or even 20s. Fishing is mostly upstream, wet fly or dry.

Several hotels have water, the best-known being the Deer Park at Honiton. Seaside visitors to Budleigh Salterton should enquire at fishing-tackle shops for permits for sea-trout fishing in and above the estuary.

Ouse (Sussex) A long tidal stretch of the river Ouse up to and above Lewes has a good run of sea-trout in mid-summer but above is mostly coarse fishing. Tackle shops at Lewis, Cuckfield and Newhaven are helpful about sea-trout permits.

Outer Hebrides *See* Western Isles

Overseas fishing Argentina, America, Iceland, Australia, Mexico, Costa Rica, Russia, Norway, Mongolia, Iceland, New Zealand, Canada, Africa, Bahamas, Panama . . . these are just some of the countries where you can go for wilderness fishing on disease-free rivers. (*See* Pollution: Danger From Overseas.) It is recommended that for the more exotic countries you book with one of several travel agents operating in this field, for they provide specialist guides and will advise on such matters as rod type, reels, lines, clothing, flies, etc., and most important of all, medical precautions relevant to the country you are visiting.

Check list: Ensure that your passport is valid for at least six months and that you have a visa if required. Insurance for both health and cancellation. A sturdy rod case and at least one spare rod. You will almost certainly need a heavier line together with spools loaded with wet and dry lines and lots of backing. Chest-high neoprene waders for cold climate fishing and wading jacket (one of the automatic inflatables; and obtain written permission in advance from the airline concerned because some companies treat CO_2 operating cartridges as hazardous cargo and may decline to allow them aboard), waterproof or specialist clothing appropriate for your destination. A money belt for your cash (American dollars preferred, for in many parts of the world cheques and plastic cards are unacceptable). Spare rolls of film if you are taking a camera, a multi-function knife (which must be stowed in your luggage), a small torch and spare batteries, insect repellent and a small first-aid kit. Farlow's of Pall Mall offer a complete specialist service for the overseas angler.

Frontiers International operate on an international basis, with fly fishing holidays throughout the world:

Christmas Island for bonefish and trevally.

New Zealand for brown trout, rainbow trout, kahawai ('the trout of the sea'), yellowtail, trevally, and kingfish.

USA: Montana, Idaho, Colorado and Oregon for brown trout, cut-throats and brook trout.

Mongolia for taimen, lenok and grayling.

Alaska for salmon, trout and char.

Russia: Rivers Ponoi, Kharlova, Eastern Litsa and Rynda on the Kola Peninsula for Atlantic salmon.

Argentina for freshwater dorado.

Midway Atoll for trevally.

Iceland for salmon.

Mexico for permit and bonefish.

Bahamas for bonefish and permit.

Canada: British Columbia for steelhead.

Argentina: Tierra del Fuego for sea-trout.

Belize for bonefish, snook, permit and tarpon.

and many more exciting destinations.

Frontiers International, 18 Albemarle Street, London W1X 3HA

Anglers have been travelling to Norway for over a hundred years, attracted by the large, early-running salmon. The Norwegian Flyfishers Club offer fishing and accommodation centred on Trondheim. Their prime fishing is on the river Gaula which rises in the mountains near the Swedish border and flows through magnificent and unspoilt country before entering the sea at Trondheim. The salmon season in Norway runs from 1 June to 31 August. The first part of June is the time for sunk-line fishing, whilst later in the month intermediate and floating lines with smaller flies are the norm. Norwegian Flyfishers Club, % Manfred Raguse, Robert-Blum-Str, 5B, D-22453, Hamburg, Germany.

On the Kola Peninsula in northern Russia the river Yoanga provides some fine salmon fishing. The river runs through long classic stretches of shingle and rock-strewn flywater, interspersed with deep holding pools. The season is from mid-June through to mid-September. In the early and late season sunk lines and big flies fished off a long, two-handed salmon rod are essential. As the water warms through July and August the salmon spread out, and a single-handed rod with skated flies can produce excellent results. In order to preserve the river's future, fishing is restricted to catch and release with single or double barbless hooks.

KolaCo, Little Saxbys Farm, Holywich Lane, Cowden, Kent TN8 7DX.

Go Fishing provide a wide selection of fishing holidays around the world:

Canada: New Brunswick for Atlantic salmon and trout; Nova Scotia, Labrador and Quebec for Atlantic salmon, brook trout and Arctic char; Ontario for trout, muskie, carp, walleye, large- and small-mouth bass and blue gill; Alberta for trout; British Columbia for Pacific salmon, steelhead, trout, halibut and sturgeon; Northwest Territories and the Yukon for lake trout, Arctic char and grayling.

USA: Montana, Idaho and Wyoming for trout; Alaska for Pacific salmon and trout.

Russia: Kola Peninsula for Atlantic salmon.

Bahamas for bonefish, permit, snapper, barracuda, blue marlin, white marlin, sailfish, broadbill swordfish and tuna.

The Falklands for sea-trout.

New Zealand (North and South Islands) for trout.

Argentina: Tierra del Fuego and Patagonia for sea-trout and trout.

Australia: for black marlin, sailfish, tuna, snapper and grouper.

Costa Rica for tarpon and sailfish.

Mexico for bonefish, tarpon and permit.

Africa: Egypt for Nile perch and tiger fish; Madagascar for sailfish, marlin, and trevally; Zimbabwe and Namibia for tigerfish; Kenya for sailfish, marlin, tuna, and barracuda; Mozambique for bonefish, tuna, kingfish, dorado, bonito, pompano and barracuda.

Go Fishing, Voyager House, 162 - 164 Fulham Palace Road, London W6 9ER.

Saltwater fly fishing for bonefish on the island of Eleuther in the Bahamas is the speciality of Bonefish Adventure, 75 Bargates, Christchurch, Dorset BH23 1QE.

Roxton Bailey Robinson are another world-wide operator:

Cuba for bonefish, tarpon and permit.

Argentina: Patagonia and Tierra del Fuego for sea-trout, brook trout, rainbow trout and land-locked salmon.

Bahamas for bonefish, tarpon and permit.

Russia: The Varzuga river on the Kola peninsula for Atlantic

salmon.
Mexico for bonefish, tarpon and permit.
Iceland for salmon.
Norway for salmon.
Alaska for salmon.

Roxton Bailey Robinson, 25 High Street, Hungerford, Berkshire RG17 0NF.

Fly fishing in the eastern Tyrol for wild trout, char and grayling is offered by Kings Angling Holidays, 27 Minster Way, Hornchurch, Essex RM11 3TH.

Oykel   A first-rate salmon fishing river in the Kyle of Sutherland – not a large one, but can be prolific, sometimes even in low-water conditions. The river is in a low strath with birch woods and deer, and a fishing hotel with good beats – the Oykell Bridge Hotel – just by the river. For spring fishing the Collie Dog and Garry Dog on aluminium tube flies are popular, the tubes giving way in summer to doubles and singles: Hairy Mary, Shrimp and Stoat's Tail, in sizes 6 and 8. Benmore and Assynt Estates have water and enquiries can be made through Renton Finlayson, estate agents, at Bonar Bridge.

P

Pale Watery   A fly fisherman's description of some five or six species of ephemeral flies which are of a pale watery colour. The natural flies generally belong to *Beatis* and *Centroptilum* species.   The most common artificials in use when pale wateries are about are the Tups, Blue Quill, Blue Upright, Little Marryat and the Goddard's Last Hope.   This is Skues' pattern:

> *Body:* cream coloured seal fur
> *Whisks:* cream dun cock
> *Hackle:* the same, fairly full for the hackled pattern
> *Wings:* young starling
> *Tying silk:* cream
> *Hook:* 15

Most of the dun patterns will do for the spent fly, providing they are made to lie low in the water.

Palmer Flies   These trout flies have a long history, going back five hundred years or more.   The style of dressing is a simple one: a hen or cock hackle wound the whole length of the hook, from eye to bend, producing a bushy appearance. The fly can be thinly or thickly palmered depending on how it is to be used.

The name is associated with the mediaeval Crusades: knights, travelling friars and pilgrims brought back palms from the Holy Land, and the word 'palmer' was used in various contexts, in one case being applied to the pilgrims and in another to travelling woolly caterpillars or 'palmer worms'. Red or black palmers are the most usual.   A good dressing for lake and sea-trout is the Soldier Palmer:

> *Body:* scarlet wool, the colour of a guardsman's tunic
> *Rib:* gold wire or tinsel
> *Hackle:* bright red cock from head to tail, kept in place by the ribbing
> *Hook:* 14–8

Palmer Nymph   An adaptation of the palmer principle of fly dressing to a wet fly, mainly for lake fishing.

Underbody: two strips of lead foil on the hook
Tail: very short golden pheasant topping
Overbody: yellow seal fur, finely dubbed
Rib: thin gold wire
Body hackle: an olive-green hackle, very short in the fibre, wound from the neck about three turns towards the tail where it is secured by the gold wire which is then wound through the hackle to the head and tied off
Head hackle: about three turns of dark red cock hackle, short in the fibre
Hook: generally 14

Parachute Adams   The parachute style of dressing trout flies was developed in 1930, when an American visitor, William Brush or Bush from Detroit, called in at Alex Martin's shop in Exchange Square, Glasgow, and asked if anyone could tie what he called 'a side-hackle fly'. The request was given to the lady fly dressers in the back room, and one of them, Helen Todd, tied the first parachute fly this side of the Atlantic.

Dressings of Parachute Flies are readily available. There is no need to have different patterns. One pattern will represent all duns, emergers and spinners:

Body: muskrat or similar dubbing
Wing spike: an upright bunch of white calf tail, tied well back from the eye of the hook
Hackle: strip off the fluff from a grizzle cock feather and tie it down both behind the wing spike and in front. Take several turns of the hackle round the spike and in front, so that the fibres spread all round the hook.

Mr E. J. T. Matthews of Winchester says that in fading light a wing spike of white antron improves visibility. Herb Wellington of Montana says a black spike is better in bright sunlight.

Parr   Before the young salmon puts on its silvery coat, young trout and salmon of about three to six inches long are difficult to tell apart, the markings are similar. The salmon parr, however, does not have a coloured adipose fin (the small stunted fin between the dorsal fin and the tail). A young trout's adipose fin is either red or has a red-orange tinge. It is

illegal to kill a salmon parr, and they must be put back into the water unharmed.

Parton, Steve   His informative book on boat fishing techniques on reservoirs such as Grafham and Rutland Water, *Boatfishing for Trout*, gives detailed information on the many ways that the fly can be fished from a boat; some will be new to most reservoir fishermen.   Parton has a nice sense of humour:

> The boat is really the refuge of free spirits among stillwater fishermen. It provides the chance for the enterprising to seek out their quarry without being unduly squeezed for elbow room.

Partridge and Orange   A versatile and charming-looking trout fly of the spider type which has its home in the Borders and Yorkshire, a strong following in Wales and the West Country, and on the chalk streams. 'Try bulging fish with a rough olive, or your favourite nymph or, what is best of all, an orange partridge', J. W. Hills, *A Summer on the Test*.

The partridge hackles should be fairly sparse. The body, when wet, takes on an attractive reddish-orange colour, very similar to the colour of both nymph and spinner bodies:

> *Body:* orange floss silk
> *Hackle:* partridge
> *Hook:* 14 –18, usually 16

There is another fly, the Yellow Partridge, with a yellow floss body, and this is said to be more use than the orange when fished upstream on spate rivers when pale wateries are about.

Pertwee, Roland   Actor and dramatist Roland Pertwee wrote one of the finest short stories about fly fishing ever written: 'The River God', published in Faber's *Best Fishing Stories*, edited by John Moore.

Peter Ross   A spectacular and deservedly popular wet fly for trout and sea-trout, a variation of the Teal and Red. Designed by Peter Ross (1873–1923), who kept the village shop at Killin in Perthshire:

> *Body:* the abdomen of flat silver tinsel, the thorax red seal fur, both ribbed with fine silver wire
> *Whisks:* golden pheasant tippet

Hackle: black
Wing: matching slips from the breast feathers of a teal
Hook: 14 - 8

Pheasant Tail   A Devon trout fly which dates back something like a hundred years, if not more, which probably accounts for several variations in the dressing. This, so far as one can tell, is fairly close to the Devon patterns of 90 years ago:

Body: dark herl from the tail feather of a cock pheasant
Rib: four or five turns of fine gold wire
Whisks: two or three fibres from the cock pheasant tail
Hackle: red cock
Hook: 12 - 16

The main variations are: a blue hackle, and red cock fibres for the whisks.

Phillips, Ernest   The author of *Trout in Lakes and Reservoirs* (1914), Ernest Phillips listed some 152 reservoirs in the British Isles which were then open for trout fishing, of which 134 allowed worming or bait fishing for the reason that '. . . the vital principle of angling is to catch fish by any method. It does not matter that you offer a Zulu, a real mayfly, a worm, a minnow, or a caddis grub . . . .'
   The various types of reservoir fishing that were allowed varied considerably. At Ravensthorpe, for example, boat fishing was fly only, yet minnow fishing was allowed from the bank. The Elan Valley reservoirs allowed the worm, as well as other methods, yet at Thirlmere every method was allowed except the worm.
   Mixed angling methods persisted in many reservoirs for another forty or fifty years and some continue now in smaller reservoirs, particularly in Wales.

Pike   Fred Buller writes: The sport of fly fishing for pike was first described by Robert Venables in the second edition of *The Experienced Angler* (1665). During the next 300 years, references to the sport have regularly appeared in angling literature. Even such an eminence on fly-tying as Blacker, described and tied pike flies.
   In an anthology called *The Flyfishers*, written by members of the Flyfishers' Club to mark their centenary (1984), and with a foreword by HRH The Prince of Wales, there is a chapter on

the history of fly fishing for pike. Chapters on the same subject appear in Fred Buller's *Pike* and *Pike and the Pike Angler.*

Just as the sport of fly fishing for marine species has greatly increased in popularity, so has fly fishing for pike – especially in the USA after Ted Trueblood, one of the most famous angling writers in America, spread the gospel during the 1960s.

Piscatorial Society   One of the oldest fly fishing clubs, the Piscatorial was founded in 1836. The society rents water on such rivers as the Wylye and the Avon, where it has a club house. It is largely a dry fly fisherman's club. The rule book is interesting for what one member has described as a 'modified Halford' rule:

> The style of fishing required by the fishing regulations on these [waters] is dry fly and upstream nymph. The weighted nymph is not permitted, only the unweighted Skues'-type pattern.

Plunket Greene, Harry (1865–1936)   Towards the end of the nineteenth century, and in the early part of the twentieth, Plunket Greene was a singer of world fame. For practically all his life he was a devoted fly fisherman, and all the character which *The Times* ascribed to him at the time of his death – generous, warm-hearted and full of humour – survives in his classic book, *Where the Bright Waters Meet*, first published in 1924 and in print ever since. The book title was taken from a poem by Tom Moore: 'There is not in this wide world a valley so sweet, As that vale in whose bosom the bright waters meet.'

Pollution   Years ago, salmon and sea-trout were able to recover from disasters, from over-fishing, from disease and the emptying of rivers by pollution; but since the late 1970s there has been a certain doubt in our minds, a certain feeling of anxiety over threats that seem to be increasing in scale.

Water pollution is principally caused by organic wastes (waste products of humans and animals and rotting plant matter), but it can also be caused by inorganic matter, such as chemicals or silt. Most major pollution incidents are caused by industry and agriculture, but private individuals can also be responsible.

Industrial pollution takes many forms, and, although the discharge of waste products is strictly controlled, accidental

spillages occur from time to time. Farming accounted for some 18 per cent of all serious incidents in 1977 and pollution caused by farm run-off is increasing. If slurry (an organic waste which is 100 times stronger than domestic sewage) enters a watercourse the result is more often than not catastrophic. Bacteria feeding on the organic waste multiply rapidly and consume all the oxygen in the water, with disastrous consequences to fish and other forms of aquatic life. Liquor produced in the making of silage is an even more serious pollutant for not only is it highly corrosive both to concrete and metal, but it is 3,000 times stronger than human sewage, so even small leakages into the water system will result in loss of fish and plant life.

Yet another source of farm contamination is the highly toxic formulations used for sheep dipping; synthetic pyrethroid (SP) is approximately 100 times more toxic than the organophosphorus (OP) which it has in part replaced.

Water enrichment by nutrients, a process known as eutrophication, caused by the leakage of farm fertilisers or sewage waste, leads to a lack of dissolved oxygen and creates severe problems for all forms of aquatic life. With an excess of nutrients the imbalance of the aquatic environment causes algae to increase, producing algal blooms, and as these die and decay, the bacteria feeding on them multiply and use up the oxygen in the water. The so-called blue-green algae can also produce poisonous toxic substances, which have been responsible for the death of wild and farm animals and domestic pets and have caused skin rashes, stomach disorders and pain in muscles and joints in humans.

But not all algal growth is man-made. Newspapers on Thursday 5 March 1998 carried reports and photographs of what was thought to be a major pollution incident on the river Dun – a tributary of the Kennet, near Hungerford – which wiped out thousands of coarse fish and 150 tonnes of trout at the Berkshire Trout Farm. Subsequent investigation by the Environment Agency revealed that the cause was a combination of naturally occurring chemicals associated with algal growth. Scientists discovered large quantities of polysaccharides (starch-like substances) in the water, which clogged the fishes' gills, leading to suffocation. Only one similar incident has ever been recorded, and that was in New Zealand in 1994.

Over-abstraction of water can also accentuate the effects of any pollution: current joint efforts by the ACA and the S&TA

may eventually lead to a new national policy in the management of our water resources.

The Legal Position

Pollution of rivers or lakes is subject to legal action under both Common Law and Criminal (Statutory) Law. It is, says the Anglers' Conservation Association (ACA), important to distinguish between them. Under the centuries-old common law every riparian owner or tenant is entitled to have water flowing past his land in its natural state of purity; if there is any infringement of this right, the owner or tenant (with the assistance of the ACA, if required) can apply to the courts for an injunction to restrain the polluter. If the offender disobeys the injunction and continues the pollution, he is guilty of contempt of court and can be imprisoned. Where riparian owners or tenants have suffered material or financial loss, or loss of enjoyment of their fishing or amenities, damages can be awarded. This law applies to rivers, streams, lakes, ponds, canals, tidal rivers and to estuaries in some cases.

Nearly all river pollution has been illegal under criminal law since the Rivers Pollution Prevention Act of 1876, and the Environment Agency has powers to prosecute an offender. If the offence is proved, the polluter can be fined, but the fine is not paid to the riparian owner or tenant.

It must be understood that in the case of pollution you cannot bring an action in the courts unless you own the water, or have a legal lease of the water you fish, or an exclusive right to the fishing.

Reproductive Changes

Changes in the reproductive cycle of wildlife, and humans, have been documented for many years. There is increasing evidence that exposure to certain chemicals released into the environment is responsible. Sources of this form of pollution, which disrupts the hormone system, include chemical manufacturing, textile processing, pesticide applications and domestic sewage. One of the most striking examples of this type of pollution was the identification around the coast of a condition known as 'imposex' in dog whelks, which involved females acquiring male characteristics that prevented them from laying eggs. Some types of male fish in the rivers Lea and Aire, downstream of discharges from a sewage treatment works, have also shown signs of feminisation.

Water Monitoring

The Environment Agency is charged with the monitoring of surface and underground water, which is under constant threat of pollution. Agency staff not only carry out thousands of routine tests but are also on 24-hour standby to react as quickly as possible to reports of pollution, tracing the source and taking action to prevent further pollution. The continuing vigilance of anglers is absolutely necessary in the continuing fight against water pollution and the protection of the environment. All pollution incidents should be reported to the Environment Agency using their 24-hour hotline number: 0800 80 70 60.

Dangers from Overseas

Fish in our rivers and lakes are largely free from the most serious fish diseases that occur in other countries. Tight restrictions on the imports of live fish, eggs and fry into this country play a major role in keeping our fisheries disease-free. All imports of live salmonids, other than from Ireland, are banned to prevent the introduction of *Gyrodactylus salaris*, which can cause heavy losses to wild Atlantic salmon stocks. *G. salaris* has been found in salmon in Norway, Sweden, Finland, Russia and other countries bordering the Baltic. The parasite, which cannot be controlled or cured, has also recently been detected in Denmark, France, Germany, Spain and Portugal.

Exotic Diseases

There are a number of other serious exotic diseases and parasites which, if introduced to this country, would cause high mortalities in both farmed and wild freshwater fish and salmon. These include Infectious Salmon Anaemia (ISA) – the first outbreak of which was recorded in Norway in 1984, and by 1991 some 80 Norwegian fish farms were infected. This killer disease has been found on at least two fish farms in Scotland (May 1998). Infectious Haematopoietic Necrosis (IHN) and Viral Haemorrhagic Septicaemia (VHS) are two other fatal diseases which so far have not been reported here.

The Ministry of Agriculture, Fisheries and Food urges all anglers returning to Great Britain from fishing abroad to clean all fishing equipment thoroughly (including nets, sacks, tackle, footwear and clothing) and then dry it for at least 48 hours. Chemical disinfection of pre-cleaned protective clothing and footwear can be achieved by spraying or wiping with a solution containing a concentration of iodine at 250 mg/litre, leaving for five minutes and then rinsing with uncontaminated water, such as tap water. Fishing equipment should be immersed for a minimum of 15 minutes in the same solution before rinsing. Other chemicals, such as caustic soda (sodium hydroxide), 'Vircon' or 'Wescodyne', may also be used to treat equipment. Similar precautions are also recommended when moving from river to river in this country to guard against the spread of crayfish fungus.

For further advice on fish health, import rules, cleaning and disinfecting fishing tackle and clothing, or to report suspected illegal imports or abnormal mortalities in fish stocks, contact:

England and Wales
Centre for Environment Fisheries and Aquaculture Science (CEFAS),
Weymouth Laboratory, Fish Health Inspectorate, Barrack Road, The Nothe, Weymouth, Dorset DT4 8UB. Tel. 01305 206673/4.

Scotland
Scottish Office Agriculture, Environment and Fisheries Department, Marine Laboratory, Fish Health Inspectorate, PO Box 101, Victoria Road, Aberdeen AB9 8DB. Tel. 01224 211446.

Another threat is posed by the thousands of tons of artificially bred salmon being bred in Atlantic coastal areas – in sheltered bays, in sea cages off the coasts of Norway, Scotland and Ireland. This sudden concentration of captive fish has produced a plague of sea lice, *Lepeoptheirus salmonis*, which feed on the skin of fish. In a short time – a matter of a few months – they multiplied in millions upon millions, fastening themselves not only to the caged salmon but also the free-swimming wild salmon and sea-trout coming and going in the estuaries and shallow seas. There is unfortunately no cure that is known, visualised, or can be applied to the wild fish: the sea-trout and the salmon coming from the rivers to the sea and returning from the sea to the rivers. Since 1989 it has been established that neither heavy lice infestation nor a collapse of the wild salmon population has occurred in any trout fishery on Ireland's western seaboard that has no salmon farm in its estuary – and the same applies to farms and fisheries elsewhere.

See also UDN

Polystickle   A minnow lure designed by Richard Walker in 1966 for reservoir fishing, which has blossomed out into various colours and methods of tying. There must be at least a dozen variations, but this seems to be one of the simplest:

Body: white floss ribbed with silver tinsel and over-wrapped with clear polythene strip
Back and tail: various dark fibres or imitation raffia, dark coloured, tied along the back and down the hook bend where it is opened out to imitate a fish's tail. Dark coloured backs seem most popular, but some fishermen use vivid yellow or orange
Hackle: a fluff of red wool at the throat, or coloured fibres
Head: built up with tying silk, varnished black or red, often with a fish's eye painted on it

Poult Bloa   A North Country trout fly. Poult is a young gamebird or chicken; bloa is (probably) blue. The fly suggests a drowned dun or spinner and is fished upstream.

Body: yellow silk, dubbed with red squirrel fur
Hackle: slate-blue feather from the underwing of the young grouse
Hook: 16

Price, Sydney Derek   Better known as 'Taff' Price, he was born in Barmouth, North Wales, where he started fishing as a small boy, but has lived in Sidcup, Kent for most of his adult life. Taff's interests, in order of importance, are fly fishing and fly tying; entomology and photography are natural adjuncts, and he is much in demand throughout the UK and overseas as a lecturer and demonstrator.

An accomplished artist, he illustrates his own books and the work of other authors. His latest books, *Angler's Sedge, Tying and Fishing the Sedge* and *Tying and Fishing the Nymph* are considered to be the definitive works on these subjects. The last contains descriptions and illustrations of nymphs from all over the world and reflect his extensive travels.

For over thirty years Taff has been a regular contributor to every British fly fishing magazine, and his work has been published in Italian, South African and Spanish journals. Vice President of the Fly Dressers' Guild and an honorary member of numerous angling clubs throughout the country; he is a consultant to a major fly materials supplier and also to an international fly manufacturer.

Pritt, T. E.   A great advocate of the North Country style of fishing. Pritt, who was on the staff of the *Yorkshire Post,* wrote many essays and four books: *The Angler's Basket* (1896) which was full of quaint Yorkshire sayings and stories; *North Country Flies* (second edn 1886); *Yorkshire Trout Flies* (1885); and *The Book of the Grayling* (1888).

Pulman, G. P. R.   Has the reputation, given to him by J. Waller Hills, of being 'the father of the dry fly'. George Pulman had a newsagent and fishing tackle business at Axminster, with branches at Dorchester and Totnes. He fished the river Axe from shortly after the end of the Napoleonic wars until he retired in the late 1840s. His best-selling book on fishing, which ran into several editions, is *The Vade Mecum of Fly Fishing for Trout* (1841). In it he recommended that when the floating fly became saturated the best way was to take a dry fly from the box and use it. The phrase 'dry fly' finally replaced the 'floating fly' in popularity.

Purism   Dictionary definition: 'over-fastidious insistence on purity'. Sometimes used as a term of abuse. Halford's definition which separated purists from ultra-purists, was given in his book *The Dry Fly Man's Handbook*:

> The dry fly is, as its name suggests, an artificial fly used dry, i.e. with no water suspension between the fibres of the hackle, wings and other feathers etc, used in its construction. When fishing dry the angler must in the first instance find a fish taking the winged insects on the surface, and it is essential that he should locate its position with the greatest precision . . . .   Those of us who will not in any circumstances cast except over rising fish are sometimes called ultra-purists and those who will occasionally try to tempt a fish in position, but not actually rising, are styled purists. The expressions are often used by angling authorities as a species of reproach or commiseration . . . [but] . . . I would urge that the first rule to be observed by every man who wishes to be deemed a dry fly fisher is to follow the example of these purists or ultra-purists.

R

Rabley, Charles A.   Rabley was a schoolmaster at Ashwater, West Devon, in the late 1800s and early 1900s. He fished the Tamar and Carey for over forty years and was the author of *Devonshire Trout Fishing*, published in 1913.   The book is of interest because Rabley always fished the floating fly and was unaware that trout would take a sunk fly as well. He describes an incident on the Carey when the trout were rising but would not look at his fly. He then cast up and across and allowed the flies to sink. He drew them towards him; this time the trout took:

> I now feel convinced that trout do feed freely below the surface on insects and can be caught with the artificial fly by touch as well as by sight.

Ransome, Arthur (1884–1967)   Journalist, foreign correspondent, essayist, children's story-teller. In the 1920s Arthur Ransome wrote a fishing column for the *Manchester Guardian* (as it was then) from which extracts have been quoted ever since, such as:

> Escaping to the Stone Age by the morning train from Manchester, the fisherman engages in an activity that allows him to shed the centuries as a dog shakes off water and to recapture not his own youth merely but the youth of the world.

The *Guardian* essays were first published as *Rod and Line* in 1929, reprinted as a paperback in 1980 and reissued in a limited edition by FCl, with a biographical introduction by Jeremy Swift. The title *Rod and Line* was used for a Granada Television production in 1982 in which Sir Michael Hordern, also a keen fisherman, played the part of Ransome. *The Times* (24 November 1982) said of the production:

> The camera watches him climb rocks, duck under trees, get the hook caught in his mittens, sees his hat blown off, and hears him

mutter 'sod it' beneath his breath as he bungles his backcast. This brings us near to the truth of things – an all-too-rare picture of what angling is all about.

It was particularly moving, said *The Times*, to see Hordern lost in thought beside the river and hear Ransome's farewell lines:

It is said that gardeners and fishermen make fine old men. That is not surprising. They have been caught up into Nature, grown old with a will and no hanging back, and are without misgivings about their own mortality.

Ravensthorpe Water   This Victorian 100-acre reservoir, at Teeton in Northamptonshire, is one of the smaller fisheries run by Anglian Water. In 1998 a catch-and-release policy was introduced (replacing a two-fish limit) requiring the use of barbless or de-barbed hooks, with the recommendation to use release tools which are available on site; no doubles, trebles or tandems; and boobies are prohibited. Another innovation is the opportunity to experiment with float tube fishing with the equipment available for hire. For more conventional boat anglers, electric outboards can be hired. A specially adapted boat is available for the disabled.

Local advice is to try floating lines from the bank; boats and tubes should not neglect the area in front of the lodge, with drifts to the Island giving excellent results. Lures will catch fish, but the angler who fishes imitative patterns is likely to take the better fish. Damsel nymphs, epoxy buzzers and, later in the season, corixa work well.

Fishery records: brown trout 8lb 6oz (1998) and rainbow 12lb 5oz (1991).

Record Fish   The official British rod-caught record fish (1997–8) include the following:

Brown Trout *Salmo trutta* (natural): 25lb 5oz 12dm 1996. Andrew Finlay, Loch Awe, Scotland
Brown Trout *Salmo trutta* (cultivated): 28lb 1oz 1995. David Taylor, Dever Springs, Hants
Rainbow Trout *Oncorhynchus mykiss* (cultivated): 36lb 14oz 8dm 1995. Clive White, Dever Springs, Hants
Rainbow Trout *Oncorhynchus mykiss* (resident): 24lb 1oz 4dm 1998. John Hammond, Hanningfield, Essex
Wild Sea-Trout *Salmo trutta*: 28lb 5oz 4dm 1992. J. Farrent, Calshot Spit, River Test, Hants

Grayling *Thymallus thymallus* (natural): 4lb 3oz 1989. S. R. Lanigan, River Frome, Dorset

Atlantic Salmon *Salmo salar*: 64lb 1922. Miss G. W. Ballantyne, River Tay, Scotland

Arctic Char *Salvelinus alpinus*: 9lb 8oz 1995. A. Fairbairn, Loch Arkaig, Inverness, Scotland

American Brook Trout/Char *Salvelinus fontinalis* (cultivated): 8lb 3oz 1998. Ernest Holland, Fontburn Reservoir, Northumberland

Pike *Esox lucius*: 46lb 13oz 1992. R. Lewis, Llandegfedd, Wales

These official records are not necessarily the biggest fish known to have been caught, but those which have been identified and recognised by the British Record (rod-caught) Fish Committee, which has its offices at 51A Queen Street, Newton Abbot, Devon TQ12 2QJ. Tel and Fax 01626 331330.

PROCEDURES

1 a) The claimant should contact the Committee Secretary or his agent.
b) Advice will then be given concerning preservation, identification and claims procedure.

2 Claims must be confirmed promptly in writing to the Secretary stating
i the species of fish, the weight, and if a game fish whether a natural or cultivated fish or in the case of the Rainbow Trout whether a cultivated, resident or wild fish
ii the date and place of capture, the tackle used, and in the case of sea fish whether Shore or Boat-caught
iii the names and addresses of preferably two witnesses both as to the capture by the claimant and the weight, who will be required to sign the forms supporting the claim (if no witnesses to the capture are available, the claimant must verify his claim by affidavit)
iv photographs of the fish must be made available which should be of good quality and preferably in colour. They should include shots of the angler, holding the fish in a normal manner, or in the case of a very large fish, standing alongside it, and also the fish lying on the ground on or next to, an identifiable object.

3 No claim will be accepted unless the Committee is satisfied as to the species, method of capture and weight. The Committee reserves the right to reject any claim if not satisfied on any matter which the Committee may think in the particular circumstances to

be material. The Committee requires a high degree of proof in order to safeguard the integrity of the list. As a high degree of proof is required, rejection of a claim imparts no reflection on the bona fides of the claimant. All costs incurred in submitting a claim must be met by the claimant.

Method of Capture

4 a) Fish caught at sea will be eligible for consideration as records if the boat used has set out from a port in England, Wales, Scotland, Northern Ireland, the Isle of Man or the Channel Islands and returns to a port in the United Kingdom without having called at any port outside the United Kingdom. Fish caught in the territorial waters of other countries will not be eligible.

b) Claims can only be accepted in respect of fish which are caught by fair angling with rod and line. Fair angling is defined by the fish taking the baited hook or lure into its mouth, and also in accord with the rules of the respective angling discipline.

c) Shore fishing shall mean fishing from any land mass or fixed man-made structure. In case of doubt the Committee will classify a claim on the information provided.

d) Fish must be caught on rod and line with any legal hook or lure and hooked and played by one person only. Assistance to land the fish (ie gaffing, netting) is permitted provided the helper does not touch any part of the tackle other than the leader.

Weight

5 a) The fish must be weighed on land using scales or steelyards which can be tested on behalf of the Committee. Where possible commercial or trade scales which are checked regularly by the Weights and Measures Department should be used. The sensitivity of the scales should be appropriate to the size of the fish, ie small fish should be weighed on finely graduated scales and the weight claimed for the fish should be to a division of weight (ounce, dram, gramme) not less than the smallest division shown on the scales.

b) A Weights and Measures Certificate must be produced certifying the accuracy of the scales used and indicating testing at the claimed weight.

c) In the cases of species weighing less than one pound, the claimed weight must be submitted in grammes.

d) The weight must be verified by two independent witnesses who, for example, should not be relations of the claimant.

Identification of the Species

6 a) The Committee is required from time to time to consider claims

for fish of species which cannot be determined to its satisfaction without inspection. For this reason and others, claimants are strongly advised not to liberate or otherwise dispose of a fish for which it is intended to enter a claim until an inspection of the body, dead or alive, has been made by a representative of the Committee and permission given for disposal.

b) While claimants should recognise that failure to produce the fish for inspection may prove prejudicial to the acceptance of a claim, the Committee does not bind itself to reject a claim solely because inspection has not been made.

c) All carriage costs incurred in the production of the fish for inspection by the Committee must be borne by the claimant.

7 Claims can be made for species not included in the Committee's Record Fish List.

8 The Committee will issue, at regular intervals, lists of British Record (rod-caught) Fish.

9 No fish caught out of season shall be accepted as a new record. Where a closed season or a ban on fishing is in force, for whatever reason, a fish from these specific areas cannot be considered as a claim for a British Record.

10 A fish for which a record is claimed must be normal and not obviously suffering from any disease by which the weight could be enhanced.

Game fish record claims should be made to the Salmon & Trout Association, Fishmonger's Hall, London Bridge, London EC4R 9EL. Tel 0171 283 5838.

Irish, Scottish and Welsh Records
Claims for fish caught in Northern Ireland are dealt with by the British Record (rod-caught) Fish-Committee.

Claims for fish caught in Eire should be made to the Secretary Mr K. Lennane, Irish Inspection Fish Committee, Balnagoan, Mobhi Boreen, Glasnevin, Dublin 9. Tel 01 8379206.

The British Record (rod-caught) Fish Committee has in membership both the Scottish Federation of Sea Anglers and the Welsh Record (rod-caught) Fish Committee; Scottish and Welsh records which are also British records are submitted by the respective organisation to which the initial claim is made. Barbour, the world-famous country clothing manufacturers, are sponsors of the official British Record Fish Lists, and for every record claim accepted by the British Record (rod-caught)

Fish Committee, the successful angler will automatically be entitled to receive a Barbour waxed cotton jacket of their choice.

There are many unofficial records. The biggest salmon ever seen on the bank was said to weigh 103 lb, and was taken off the River Devon in Scotland, but details are missing – even of the year it was taken (either 1902 or 1903).

Other big salmon include:

94lb. Eger. Norway. 1867
94lb. Tana. Norway. 1878 or 1879
84lb. Netted in the Tay. Scotland. 1869
69½lb. Aaro. Norway. 1921 (caught on rod and line by J. Aarven)
67lb. Nith. Scotland. 1812 (caught by a poacher, Jock Wallace)
60lb. Eden. England. 1888 (length 54 in, girth 27 in, caught on a fly by Mr Lowther Bridger)
59½lb. Wye. Wales. 1923 (caught on rod and line by Miss Doreen Davy)

The unofficial record British brown trout was 39½lb, caught on Loch Awe by Mr W. Muir in 1866. It was foul-hooked on a trout fly and took 2½ hours to land. Other big trout have been recorded, the next biggest being a 29lb slob trout from Loch Stennes in 1889 on a hand line, which might possibly be listed as a semi-sea-trout.

Sea-trout unofficial records are:

38lb. Tees. England. Said to have been caught by James Teasdale in the early 1800s
28lb. – Sweden. 1930 (caught by Mr W. H. Barrett)
26½lb. – Sweden. 1929 (ditto)
22½lb. Loch Maree. Scotland. A cast of this fish is in the Loch Maree Hotel
21lb. Frome. England. 1918 (caught at Bindon by Mr R. C. Hardy Corfe)

A grayling of 4½lb was caught by Dr T. Sanctuary on the Wylye at Bemerton in 1885 and one of 4¾lb was netted from the Avon at Longford, and returned, in the same year by Dr Sanctuary and Mr G. S. Marryat.

Red Quill An admirable dry fly and as much a favourite of many fishermen as the Pheasant Tail or the Greenwell:

Body: stripped peacock quill from the eye feather, tied to give a well-marked banded appearance, dyed red optional
Whisks: a few fibres from a bright red cock hackle
Hackle: bright red cock
Wings: pale or medium starling primary
Hook: 14–16

F. M. Halford was reported as saying that the Red Quill was 'the sheet anchor of the dry-fly fisherman on a strange river'.

Red Spinner Not so popular a trout fly as it used to be, having been overtaken by the Pheasant Tail and the Tups, nevertheless a good pattern when spent olives are on the water:

Body: red wool or red floss silk
Rib: fine gold wire
Hackle: red cock
Wings: blue hackle points, tied spent
Hook: 14–16

Red Tag A well-known grayling fly, sometimes confused with another North Country fly, the Treacle Parkin. The Red Tag has spread to Wales and the West Country.

Body: bright green peacock herl
Tag: bright red wool, cut short
Hackle: red cock
Hook: 14–16

Reed Smut A small humpy-bodied black fly, very small (less than an eighth of an inch long) frequently known with other small black flies, as 'smut' or 'curse'. It is a river fly – so far as is known, rarely or never hatching on still waters – and sometimes appears in vast numbers on rivers. It is on record that fly fishermen have been infuriated by reed smuts ever since the first imitation was tied – by Scotcher around 1800. Practically every fly-dresser of repute has tied his own version since. This is a fairly simple one:

Body: dark brown tying silk, slightly bunched and humpy
Wings: blue dun or badger hackle points, tied spent
Hook: 18–22

The difficulty of taking trout with this fly, as J C. Mottram pointed out, is that when trout are taking the natural there are so many of them on the water that the artificial has to be cast very accurately to drift precisely over the trout's nose.

Reels   Essentially the reel's function is to store line and backing and to provide tension, or drag, when a fish is being played.

The small river or still water angler more often than not retrieves and feeds line manually and therefore has no need for the more sophisticated, and expensive, reels. Providing the reel has a simple ratchet mechanism, as most do, and an exposed outer rim, then pressure applied by the fingers or palm will give all the control necessary. Irrespective of type, the reel should be capable of holding the line with an amount of backing appropriate to the type of fishing. However, if you take delight in the appearance, engineering excellence and silky smooth operation of your equipment, and cost is not an important factor, then there is a wide choice of reels costing up to several hundred pounds.

The first disk-drag reels appeared in the 1930s, working on similar principles to a car's disk brakes. The early models were very large and cumbersome, with fixed spool and non-change wind. There have, however, been many improvements in the ensuing years, both in size and mode of operation. Do not be tempted by cheaper disc-drag action reels, though, for, unless the operating mechanism is properly sealed there is a real possibility of it jamming up as a result of sand or grit getting in. Apart from being more expensive than the ratchet reel, this type of reel is heavier, and some models require a special tool to change the wind, to take apart for cleaning, or simply to change spools. It is favoured by some saltwater fishermen.

The large arbor reels, available in disk-drag or ratchet versions, are increasingly popular with anglers who appreciate the benefits of their very low start-up inertia which helps to eliminate breaks when a fish suddenly takes off – all too common with the trend towards lighter leaders, for the energy required to get a spool moving can sometimes exceed the breaking strength of the leader. The larger diameter spool also helps to prevent line memory.

Whatever the type of reel, a spare spool is an inexpensive luxury and well worth having for the convenience of switching lines with the minimum of inconvenience.

The multiplying reel is gear-driven, and its spool turns more than once (up to two and a half times) for every revolution of the crank handle. It is useful for the long caster, as it picks up line faster, but it has never really been popular with the trout fisherman because of its extra weight and increased bulk. The same is true of the so-called automatic fly reels. On these stripping out line tightens a circular spring which is then released by means of a trigger or lever; the action is sudden and somewhat difficult to control. Both these type of reel have the added disadvantage of limited line storage and lack the interchangeable spool function present in the basic fly reel.

For salmon and saltwater fishing the reel has to be more robust and able to take a heavier and longer line and longer backing. It should also be made of materials capable of withstanding the corrosive effects of brackish or salt waters.

See also Backing, Lines.

REFFIS The Register of Experienced Fly Fishing Instructors and Schools was formed in January 1993 with the following stated aims:

1. To accept onto the register only those professional fly fishing instructors and schools and guides who meet the various conditions of membership.
2. To set the conditions of membership at a high enough level to ensure that members of the public can seek professional instruction and guiding from REFFIS members with absolute confidence. Also to ensure that REFFIS members depict themselves honestly and accurately to the public.
3. Above all REFFIS is to be considered a trade organisation aiming to increase business for its members by setting and promoting high standards and by encouraging referrals between members.
4. To foster our close link with the Salmon and Trout Association and to discuss with them matters relating to fly fishing instruction if requested to do so. REFFIS members are expected to promote the S&TA by informing their clients of the vital role the S&TA plays safeguarding game fisheries and angling.
5. To publish an annual directory of its members by means of a newsletter magazine for distribution to the public.

Instructor members must be qualified by STANIC if living in mainland Britain, or be qualified by REFFIS from anywhere else in the world. Instructors accepted as members of the register become REFFIS Approved Instructors. There are two other categories of membership: REFFIS Approved Guides and REFFIS Approved Schools.

The officers (1998) are: Chairman, Charles Bingham. Hon. Secretary and Treasurer, Richard Slocock, Wessex Fly Fishing, Tolpuddle, Dorchester, Dorset DT2 7HF. Joint Vice Chairmen, Pat O'Reilly and Roddy Rae. Publicity Officer, Tony King. REFFIS is sponsored by Farlow's of Pall Mall.

See also STANIC, APGAI.

Reservoir Fishing A specialist branch of fly fishing in its own right requiring tactics, and tackle, different from those employed on chalkstreams or even small still waters. One of the fundamental differences is that much reservoir fishing is conducted from a drifting boat rather than from the bank. This calls for longer rods – 9½ to 11ft – with heavier, weight-forward lines, both floating and sinking, and sink-tip shooting heads. Floating lines are needed for surface, or sub-surface, trout feeding on daphnia, and sinking lines for really deep fishing at the start and back end of the season. The reel must be larger than the conventional trout reel in terms of width and spindle size, in order to accommodate the heavier line and the greater reserve of backing needed (the latter should be of 30lb breaking strain, rather than the more usual 20lb). *See* Reels.

Bob Church, an outstanding-fly fisher responsible for so many of the innovative reservoir techniques in common use today, was once asked the secret of his success, to which he replied, 'Boat handling'. A drifting boat will naturally head straight downwind, but Church resurrected the ancient technique of using a leeboard (a portable rudder is now used) to tack across the wind which allows for longer casting and recovery of the fly at a controlled speed. Trout tend to move upwind but with the controlled drift the fly is drawn right across the path of the surface, or sub-surface, feeding fish. Improved boat control, deep-water fishing and a number of successful lures are just some of Bob Church's contributions to the art of reservoir fishing.

Bob Church's favourite fly patterns, and how and when to fish them:

Lures and Attractors
Baby Doll (best on a sinking or sink-tip line until summer, when a floater is even better), Whisky Fly (an excellent catcher of rainbows), Muddler Minnow (early autumn, fished on the surface produces fantastic results), Jack Frost (floating, sink-tip or sinking lines and particularly effective when trout are on the fry), Black Chenille (fish on fast-sinking lines), Appetiser (also good for fry-feeding trout), Church Fry (a gaudy version of the perch fry for sinking lines), the tail-less Sweeney Todd (an early-season fly), Badger Matuka (effective when fished deep), Missionary (a late season small fry imitation for fishing in the margins), Ace of Spades (works best when fished slow), Poly-Butcher (has a curious capacity to catch when other lures don't), Mickey Finn (try in hot weather when nothing much is happening – strip it fast across the surface), Mrs Palmer (a lure for coloured water and fishes well in the summer months), Polystickle (fish it high and jerkily on a floating line), Leprechaun (another high-summer pattern, particularly useful when green algae is present) and White Marabou Muddler (a lure to be used when trout are taking large size fry).

Traditional Small Wet Flies
Claret and Mallard (one of the best-known traditional loch wet flies), Olive Quill (wet-fly adaptation of Halford's famous dry fly), Black and Peacock Spider (a great deceiver, fished high in the water as a bob-fly or on a sinking shooting head as a bottom grubber), Ginger Quill (an early-summer fly, best fished slowly through the ripple) and Butcher (try this on a slow sink shooting-head with a steady retrieve). All these small wets are tied on medium-shanked hooks in sizes 14, 12 and 10. Also Claret Hatching Midge (fish just under the surface) and Pheasant Tail Nymph (fish deep and slow with a floating line and a long leader).

Sedge Nymph Patterns
Brown and Yellow Nymph (a versatile fly – can be fished slowly through the surface during a sedge hatch or, with a copper-wire underbody, as a point-fly along the bottom), Green and Brown Nymph (July and August during the sedge hatch), Stick Fly (fish slow and deep on a floating or sink-tip line and a long leader), and Invicta (imitates the hatching or adult sedge – use on a floating line with a slow retrieve on or just below the surface). All the sedge patterns are on no. 12, 10 and 8 hooks, but the Brown and Yellow and Stick Fly are tied on size 8 long-shanks.

Miscellaneous Dry Flies
Tup's Indispensable (try it when the trout are feeding on *Caenis* – the angler's curse), Grey Duster (another pattern for the angler's curse), White Wulff (an excellent high-floating fly for mayfly time), Daddy Longlegs (the most important fly as autumn approaches – fish it static or drifting with the wind), Drone Fly (a 'must' for hot days in late summer), Flying Black Ant (a good artificial at 'ant time' when the trout are rising) and Floating Snail (fish just below the surface when trout are taking snails).

See Ivens, T. C.

Reversed Flies   A method of tying the dry fly with the hackle reversed – that is attached to the hook at the bend, just above the point. The wings are attached in the same place, and the whisks or tails project under the hook eye. The whole fly is therefore reversed.   This method of tying was first recommended by Alexander Macintosh, river keeper of the Driffield Beck, in his book *The Driffield Angler* (1808) and has been revived occasionally since.

Ribble   The Ribble and its companion river, the Hodder, come from the land of broad acres, rising in the high moors of the Pennines – small streams which are grand places for fishermen. There may be a worm here and there, but the upstream wet fly should be paramount (the Partridge, Bloas and Watchets) and the wild brown trout take well and savagely.   The Royal Oak Hotel at Settle can provide tickets for association water. There is also good fishing at Malham Tarn, a famous nature reserve a few miles away. The Inn at Whitewell, Forest of Bowland, has five miles of salmon, trout and sea-trout fishing on the Hodder.

Ritz, Charles   Hotelier, fly fisherman, designer of rods, instructor in casting, Charles Ritz wrote a charming and readable autobiography, *A Fly Fisher's Life*, first published in 1959 and reprinted several times most recently in 1996. In this book Ritz gives a fascinating picture of fly fishing adventures in most of Europe, England and America, together with an examination of the casting techniques of many fishermen.

Roadford Lake   A brown trout and fly-only reservoir of some 730 acres, off the A30, near Lifton, north Devon, operated by South West Water. At its deepest point the lake is over 120 ft deep. Part of the reservoir is set aside for dinghy sailing, and the northern area is designated as a nature reserve. Open from April to mid-October. Optional catch and release with barbless hooks. Boat and bank fishing. Recommended tactics: stalking, early and late in the day, using light tackle. For classic nymph fishing try Green or Black Buzzers on a long leader; Pheasant Tail Nymph, Damsels and Gold Ribbed Hare's Ear on floating or intermediate lines.

Roberts, John   Author of the standard work *Illustrated Dictionary of Trout Flies* which contains dressings for over 1,000 flies, (some 480 illustrated in colour) and was described by *The Times* as, 'a classic of its kind'. John Roberts has been a key contributor to game fishing magazines for over twenty years. Among his other books are *The Grayling Angler, To Rise a Trout, Trout on a Nymph* and *A Guide to River Trout Flies*.

Rods   The sophistication of fly fishing came with advancing technology. Individual hand-craftsmanship gave way to mass production, and space age composite materials have replaced natural fibres. L. U. Borenius writes:

> The fly rod gradually became differentiated from rods required for other forms of fishing, since progressive flexibility (action) became an essential requirement of what was essentially a casting instrument. The flexing and unflexing inherent in casting a fly placed a much greater strain on the rod and the traditional materials of which fishing rods were originally made. Hazel, willow and ash were replaced by rods of denser and much stronger materials: greenheart and hickory, both imported from abroad.
>
> The all-important change in the design of the fishing rod, from an instrument of placement to a casting instrument, took place during the last century, and the fly rod became a comparatively heavy rod throwing a silk line. The normal method of joining the rod sections together was by binding with leather thongs which were wetted before binding. As the thongs dried, the leather contracted, and the sections were held firmly in position (a knob was normally carved into the ends of the sections to prevent the thongs from slipping).
>
> The greatly increased range achieved by casting made the use of much longer lines necessary, and a mechanism for carrying the

line, i.e. the reel, came into common use. Previously fish were 'played' on a tight line, with the flexion of the rod as the only buffer between fisherman and fish. If all else failed the fisherman would throw the rod into the water, in the hope that eventually, when the fish had exhausted itself by pulling the rod through the water, rod and fish could be recovered.

Joining of the sections of a rod with thongs ('splicing') was both cumbersome and not entirely reliable. In the case of coarse fishing rods of whole cane it was possible to join the pieces simply by inserting the sections inside each other. This technique was adapted to rods made of non-tubular materials by using metal 'ferrules' for joining the pieces.

By the turn of the century, the fundamental design which today constitutes modern fly tackle was completed: a flexible rod, a line heavy enough to throw and a reel large enough to store all the line which could be thrown, together with 'backing' (a reserve of line enabling a strong fish to swim a considerable distance from the angler without breaking the line). All subsequent developments in fly-rod design and construction were founded upon the discovery and application of new materials to the fundamental requirement of throwing the fly line.

At the end of the nineteenth century split-cane rods were introduced. They were in fact longitudinally split pieces of bamboo glued together. The hard outer bark of the bamboo was utilised, and in a well-manufactured rod the tapering effect was achieved by reducing the thickness of the inner, pulpy side of the bamboo. To give greater stiffness without increasing the weight, the technique of heating the sections (before glueing and binding) was introduced. It was virtually impossible to make a thick enough handle out of split bamboo, so the modern cork handle (rings of cork sandpapered to the required shape) was introduced. This was eventually applied to all rods, including those made of greenheart, the handles of which had originally been made of the same material as the rest of the rod.

The introduction of the split-cane rod had a dramatic effect on fly tackle and ultimately on casting techniques. Trout rods, instead of weighing 15 or 16oz, weighed less than 8oz and by 1920 were normally between 5½ and 6½oz in weight. By 1930 refinement in manufacturing methods (notably the introduction of hollow-built butts) and the introduction of light-weight aluminium rod fittings enabled powerful 8ft rods to weigh as little as 4oz. The lightness of these rods made it possible to impart much greater speed to the tip of the rod during the forward (or power) cast. The result was that maximum casting distance achievable with ordinary tackle increased very substantially (since this is governed almost entirely by the speed of the rod tip during the forward cast and the lighter the rod the faster its tip can move through the air).

By 1930 split cane was the major material for all fly rods; only in Scotland were the older two-handed greenheart salmon fly rods widely used for Spey casting (largely because of their better resistance to the 'torque' involved in executing the Spey cast, and also because of their comparative cheapness).

The extreme lightness of split cane, combined with its virtual immunity to sudden fracture, was the determining factor in securing its ascendancy. If a greenheart rod dried out completely (by being kept in a warm atmosphere), it would fracture without warning. By contrast, a split cane rod which is weakened will almost invariably fail gradually, giving warning that replacement of the affected section is necessary.

One marked feature of split cane was the individuality of each rod. The precise stiffness and resilience of a rod depended largely upon the characteristics of the individual pieces of cane from which they were made, no two split cane rods, however identical in taper, ever having exactly the same 'action'.

The source of all split cane of quality was a district in north-west China (Tonkin), and the climatic conditions affecting each individual crop of cane would have an effect on the quality of the ultimate product. This individuality gave each fly rod its own inimitable 'feel' comparable to the difference between finely made violins.

From 1930 to 1950 split cane ruled supreme. In the 1950s, however, the worsening diplomatic relationship between China and the US (and a consequent embargo on purchase of further stocks of Tonkin by American tackle manufacturers) made it necessary for the Americans to develop an alternative synthetic material – 'Fibre' Glass. This material consisted of man-made artificial glass fibre cloth wrapped round a metal mandril impregnated with plastic and baked in an oven. The method of manufacture lent itself to mass production, and, once the teething troubles were ironed out, the resulting product was almost unbreakable, highly flexible and extremely light in weight. It was also possible to reproduce rods with identical 'actions' in large batches. By 1960 glass rods were a substantial threat to split cane. The growth of fly-fishing in reservoirs greatly increased the market for mass-produced, cheap, light and powerful rods, since reservoir fishing required single-handed rods capable of casting long distances all day without tiring the users; significantly, almost all trout and salmon distance tournament casters adopted the new material because of its extreme lightness. Increases in wages made split-cane rod manufacture increasingly costly. Glass fibre manufacture, on the other hand, cost progressively less as sales increased, and the manufacturers benefited from the resultant economics of scale.

Tubular glass rods however, did have certain disadvantages. Although light and resilient, they were inclined to cause a tiring vibration in prolonged use. Also, being tubular, they would not readily bend beyond a certain point without the whole tube collapsing inwards. By the mid-1970s fibre glass and split-cane rods were equally popular.

During the last twenty years the introduction of a completely new material, carbon fibre, has had a dramatic effect on the development of fly rods. This new material was developed in the English aerospace industry to combine extreme lightness with extreme strength. It reproduces almost all the qualities of hollow-built split cane in terms of responsiveness and 'steely' action, but with enormously reduced weight. For long rods (over 9½ft) there can be no doubt that carbon fibre has completely replaced the traditional materials, as a visit to any tackle shop will show. There will, however, always remain a specialist market for cane rods of up to 8½ft, individually designed and built for special applications, especially for dry fly work on rivers. [A list of makers is given below]. Indeed, cane rods are still being hand-made in England and America as a craft-built alternative to the mass-produced graphite (carbon-fibre) rods.

The introduction of a proportion of boron into the carbon material has produced rods with an action similar to that of cane. The methods of manufacture for all carbon-fibre or boron rods is similar to that used for glass fibre rods (making of a steel mandril, tapered exactly to reproduce the desired configuration), and then wrapping of carbon-fibre cloth round as before, impregnation with epoxy resin and baking. This technique makes 'one-off' manufacture entirely uneconomic, because the cost of the mandril cannot be recovered until several dozen rods have been produced on it.

Cane rod makers

Agutters, Marionville, South Stour Avenue, Ashford, Kent TN23 7RS

E. Barber Rod Co., Ham Hill, London Road, Newbury, Berkshire RG14 2BU

Farlow's of Pall Mall, 5 Pall Mall, London SW1Y 5NP
House of Hardy, Alnwick, Northumberland NE66 3PF
Shaun Lindsley, Jessamy Mill Lane, Stour Provost, Dorset SP8 5RA
Orvis, Vermont House, Unit 30a North Way, Andover, Hampshire SP10 5RW
Peregrine, 56 Haydon Industrial Estate, Radstock, Bath BA3 3RD
Sigman Cane Rods, 968 Admiral Callaghan Lane, Suite 182, Vallejo, California 94591, USA
Turners of Reading, 21 Whitley Street, Berks RG2 0EG

The confusion concerning the description of rod tip action may have been finally resolved by the recent introduction by Orvis of a new system called the Flex Index, which begins at 2.5 and currently finishes at 12.5. A rod with a Flex of 2.5 will have a very slow, soft action, while a rod with a flex of 12.5 will have a very fast, tippy action. Rods are available with Full Flex (2.5 to 5.5), Mid Flex (6.0 to 9.0) and Tip Flex (9.5 to 12.5), with the largest selection being in the Mid Flex range and all new Orvis rods will henceforth carry a Flex Index rating. In future the system will enable an angler to buy a rod made of a newly introduced material in the certain knowledge that it will have the same action he has already become accustomed to. It is hoped that all manufacturers will eventually adopt the system and label their rods in the same way as they now do with line weights.

Another interesting development is the so-called zero-weight fly rod from Sage. This ultra-lightweight, three-piece rod weighs less than 2oz, and comes with a revolutionary centre-axis reel and its own special line giving a total weight of under 5oz.

Rogan, Michael A famous Irish fly-dresser with many English admirers, Michael Rogan was born in Ballyshannon in 1834. He specialised in tying mixed-wing salmon flies with special dyes which he kept secret (one of them was said to have come from a donkey's urine) and won a gold medal and diploma at the London Fisheries Exhibition of 1883. The business was carried on by his son and grandson, also Michael Rogan, for many years. The business was taken over in 1996 by Mr and Mrs David Feeley, who carry on the Rogan tradition.

Rough Olive   A trout fly which suggests the large dark olive, popular in Ireland and in many rivers in England and Wales:

> *Body:* originally heron herl dyed a dark green-brown, but wool is often used as a substitute
> *Wings:* starling primary
> *Hackle:* brown-green cock
> *Whisks:* the same
> *Hook:* 14 –12

Ronalds, Alfred   Author of *The Fly-Fisher's Entomology*, first published in 1836, which has been described as 'one of the most important milestones in the history of angling literature'. The book contains nineteen hand-coloured copper plates depicting 47 artificial and 47 natural flies, and a first edition copy in clean condition sells at £1,500 (1998). The fifth edition of 1856, the last to be published in Ronalds' lifetime, is the one selected by FCL for publication.

Royal Family   Many members of the Royal family have been ardent fly fishers, including Queen Elizabeth the Queen Mother, Prince Charles and Prince William. Prince Philip was initiated by his brother-in-law, Prince Berthold of Baden, himself a dry-fly fishing addict. George IV was also a keen fisherman. One of the best stories about a royal fisherman concerned George V, and was told by Sir George Aston in *Mostly About Trout*:

> At the time of the Anglo-French *entente cordiale* it was customary for journalists to write flattering articles about the heads of state of the other country. These were vetted by the respective diplomatic representatives before publication. Here is the literal translation of an article by a French journalist about King George V written as a compliment to that monarch during World War I:
> He is an angler of the first force, the King of Britain. Behold him there as he sits motionless under his umbrella, patiently regarding his many-coloured floats. How obstinately he contends with the elements!   It is a summer day in Britain, that is to say a day of sleet and fog and tempest. But, what would you? It is as they love it, those who follow the sport.
> Presently the King's float begins to descend. My God! But how he strikes! That hook is implanted in the very bowels of the salmon. The King rises. He spurns aside his footstool. He strides

strongly and swiftly towards the rear. In good time the salmon comes to approach himself to the bank. Aha! The King has cast aside his rod. He hurls himself flat on the ground on his victim. They splash and struggle in the icy water. Name of a dog! But it is a 'braw laddie'!

The ghillie, a kind of outdoor domestic, administers the coup de grace with his pistol. The King cries with a very shrill voice: 'Hip, Hip. Hoorah!' On these red-letter days His Majesty King George dines on a haggis and a whisky grog. Like a true Scotsman he wears only a kilt.

Another story, about the Queen Mother, is related in *The Angler's Quotation Book*:

The salmon fishing skills of HM the Queen Mother are well-chronicled and there can be few more determined anglers, as indicated by the following incident. Having waited all day for conditions to improve, Her Majesty at last set out for the river in early evening.

An anxious staff waiting to serve dinner, by which time it was already getting dark, assembled with torches to begin an urgent search of the river bank. The staff should have known better for just then Her Majesty appeared with a twenty-pounder in her grasp. With a bravado, only appreciated by the really dedicated angler, came the explanation for her absence. '*This* is what detained me!'

Rusty Spinner   A useful chalk stream dressing of the Sherry Spinner devised by G. E. M. Skues:

Body: chestnut-coloured seal fur
Rib: fine gold wire
Hackle: rusty dun cock
Whisks: three fibres of the same-coloured spade feather
Tying silk: orange
Hook: 14–16

Rutland Water   Europe's largest and best-known trout fishery, this 3,100-acre Anglian Water reservoir is set in some of England's finest countryside. It is home to major national and international competitions, including, in 1998, the new House of Hardy Fly-fishing International Championship, the Youth International Championship, the International Championship for the Disabled and the English Youth Championship. The complete novice is not ignored, though, for expert tuition is available and helpful advice is always forthcoming from the well-equipped tackle shop.

It can be a challenging water for both the bank and the boat angler, and local knowledge is advisable for the best results. There is fishing from April to December, but the highspots are likely to be in May and June, when the abundant insect life begins to show, and again in September and October, when the large browns and rainbows start to feed on the fry.

Fishery records: brown trout 14lb 12oz (1993); rainbow 13lb 8oz (1993).

204

Safety Fly fishing can be dangerous, particularly when wading fast rivers (*see* Wading). But there are other hazards too.

An American ambassador was blinded in one eye while salmon fishing. The short rod he was using was not able to give sufficient velocity to a large single-hook fly he had just put on to replace a smaller one; the fly lagged, because of its weight, and swerved in flight. To prevent damage to the eyes wear sunglasses with side protection (polarised sunglasses have the added bonus of making fish spotting easier, particularly in bright conditions). If a fly is snagged and you have to pull hard to break, turn your face well away. When casting in high winds make sure the fly is travelling on the downwind side of the body. If on the other side wind pressure can blow the fly into the neck or face. If line speed is lost during a cast, do not try to recover it in mid-air. Let the line drop and start again.

Carbon fibre rods are excellent conductors of electricity. There are at least two cases of fly fishermen being electrocuted by casting too near power lines. Thunderstorms may also be a hazard especially when out in a boat.

Night fishing can be hazardous. Carry a torch and reconnoitre the banks and pools beforehand in daylight. Preferably go night fishing with a companion. If fishing alone, let someone know where you are.

Salmon
The Salmon: Life History The salmon is an anadromous fish – a word derived from the Greek which means that it runs up rivers to spawn. The name of the Greek goddess, Aphrodite, comes from a similar word that meant emerging from the sea.

From the time that the young salmon hatch from their gravel cots, or redds, in the spawning grounds of the rivers where their parents mated some 14 weeks earlier, the tiny fingerlings

(alevins) are in constant danger. When they shed their yolk sacs they are known as parr, and look more or less like small wild brown trout. A parr can be distinguished from a trout by the adipose fin (on the back nearest the tail): if this is coloured red or orange the fish is a trout, if colourless the fish is a parr.

After one to three years in the river the parr puts on a silvery colour, becoming a smolt, as it prepares to cross the salt barrier of the estuary and that takes time – a year, perhaps even two. Only one in ten of the fish which hatched are likely to survive to reach the sea, and of these only about four or five in a hundred will return.

After spending anything from a year to several years in their deep-sea feeding grounds the salmon and the grilse – the young salmon – feel the urge to make the long journey of several thousand sea miles to return to the rivers of their birth.

How do they find their way home? It is a problem that puzzles scientists, and the full answer is not yet clear, although a number of mechanisms are known to guide salmon at sea. These include guidance by the stars as well as the use of receptors (a receptor is an organ adapted to receive certain stimuli) which are attuned to the weak electrical impulses of the earth's magnetic field; ocean currents may also play an important role. Near the coast salmon are guided by a chemical memory which apparently allows them to identify and home on to their native river.

Salmon Fishing: A Short History Fly fishing for salmon is first recorded in English in the *Treatyse of Fysschynge Wyth an Angle*(1496), without any details. In 1651 Thomas Barker gave an inadequate description of a salmon fly which had 'six wings or four at least'. The Roman historian, Aelian was among others who mentioned 'a plume on a hook' which was used not only for trout and salmon but for fishing for mackerel, as we still do today off the Cornish coast. There are records of Roman soldiers using the plume when stationed at Hadrian's Wall and at the Roman barracks near the Severn. The recorded history can be said properly to begin with Andrew Young's *Angler's Guide*, published in Edinburgh in 1857, by which time the salmon fly was already a fairly sophisticated creation – and it was certainly used earlier than that on Scottish and Irish rivers and lakes.

Ever since the first railway services had been opened, the North Eastern and the Caledonian railways had been pushing to the north, to Edinburgh, Perth, Forfar and finally Inverness. The speed of those early trains was not very great – about 30 to 40 miles an hour – but they opened up a new world of enormous estates rich in fish and game, and the owners were not slow to take advantage of adventurous young men who were coming north in increasing numbers with their rods and guns. The flies they used at first were rather drab, but then the Irish developed brightly coloured flies like the Golden Parson, which came to Scotland via the tackle shops around St Pauls.

Salmon fishing was suddenly fashionable and the new brightly coloured flies became not only fashionable but a kind of mystique developed about these flies which were said to be irresistible to salmon. Towards the end of the nineteenth century the high priest of this new sporting cult was a great egotist, George M. Kelson. In Kelson's book *The Salmon Fly*, privately printed in 1895, were coloured drawings of something like sixty salmon flies, which were all listed as to when and where they were to be fished on what Kelson called 'well-established principles', though one was never quite sure what these were. Kelson admitted that he 'might seem now and then to be over-didactic' – and how right he was, poor man. None of his theories and only two of his flies survive. (Despite that, a first edition of Kelson's book, in good condition, sells for in excess of £650).

On different rivers in America there were many who fished the dry fly for salmon based on a book by E. R. Hewitt (*Secrets of the Salmon*, 1922). There were reports of dry flies being used on the Tyne in 1896 and on the Test, by Major R. G. Fraser, in 1906 and quite a few dry flies have been fished on Scottish rivers like the Dee, the Naver and the Don in recent years; but this was very much a minority cult, and it declined with the advent of new tackle after the 1940s, fast-sinking lines, tube flies and dressed trebles, and of course the demise of gut and the coming of nylon and many other wonders of new technology.

Salmon Fishing: The Present and the Prospect Reports coming in to the *Encyclopaedia* are that salmon catches in the British Isles are far worse in 1998 than even pessimists expected. We asked Sandy Leventon, editor of *Trout & Salmon*, how he views the prospects:

> Scottish salmon rivers are now in desperate straits, with catches of spring fish at an unprecedented low level. In 1997 the North-east

of England drift nets caught 22,000 salmon, an estimated 80 per cent of which were destined for classic Scottish east-coast rivers such as the Spey, Tweed, Dee and Tay. While this drift-net fishery is gradually being phased out, and the number of licences has been reduced from 141 in 1992 to 89 in 1997, the catch is completely unregulated, so that while there may be fewer boats fishing there is no reduction in fishing effort. Meanwhile the Scottish coastal nets continue further to deplete wild fish stocks.

At one time it was thought that the introduction of salmon farms to Scotland would be the salvation of the wild fish, lowering their market value and making it uneconomical to net them. Sadly, this has not proved to be the case. Moreover, the salmon farms have become a menace, polluting the sea-bed underneath the cages, threatening the integrity of wild stocks of whole river systems through farm escapees, and encouraging unnatural numbers of sea-lice that attach themselves to the wild fish. If that were not enough, in 1998 outbreaks of the notifiable disease Infectious Salmon Anaemia (ISA) were reported on Scottish west-coast salmon farms; while it is not known what effect this may have on wild fish, it proves that serious fish diseases can, and no doubt will, continue to find their way into Scottish stocks.

Add to the foregoing an explosion in the seal population and the continued commercial exploitation of sandeels and other salmon fodder, and you would be forgiven for thinking that the salmon's future is indeed in jeopardy.

Salmon Fishing: The Empty River   We asked David Barr, editor of *The Haig Guide to Salmon Fishing in Scotland*, what happened when he went fishing on one of the famous Scottish salmon rivers for the spring run of 1998, and this was his reply:

During the last two years, 1997 and 1998, I caught nothing. Almost worse was my feeling that the river – as beautiful as ever with a fine flow of water and lovely surroundings – was empty of fish. They were not there, there was no spring run, and as I fished on, hopelessly, I had the growing feeling that I was flogging a dead river.

What made it worse was the gillie trying to be helpful. 'Never give up sor', he would say, but there was a desperation in his voice which could not be hid. His job and his livelihood were on the line and he knew it and so did I. I never felt so sad and depressed in all my life. It was even worse in the evenings, for there was a good deal more whisky drunk than I ever remember, and the language was unprintable. 'Nobody doing a bloody thing: not even shooting the seals or banning the nets.'

More than a hundred salmon and sea-trout rivers of the British Isles are suffering a disastrous shortage of fish. The Scottish figures follow.

Salmon and Sea-Trout Catches: the Scottish Figures The Biennial Review (1995–1997) of the Freshwater Fisheries Laboratory, Pitlochry, published by the Scottish Office, says that the total number of wild salmon and grilse of all ages caught throughout Scotland by rod and line, net and coble and fixed engine in 1996 was 123,867. This was substantially less than in 1995 and the lowest recorded since records began in 1952.

The number of wild salmon and grilse caught and retained by rod and line in 1996 was 59,169 – substantially lower than in 1995 – as was the total number caught, 69,578, including 10,409 subsequently released.

The number of sea-trout caught, for all Scotland by all methods, over the period 1952–1967 rose steadily to a peak at 308,854. Catches then declined rapidly in the first two years and then gradually until a new low of 115,883 in 1987. In the North West region the all-catch total declined from 15,129 in 1957 to 1,187, the lowest on record, and the West Region shows a similar decline.

Salmon Farming: Mass Escapes Salmon farming began in Scotland around 1970, and by 1996 production had reached 83,000 tonnes, almost twenty times the number of wild salmon reported as caught and retained in Scotland in 1996.

The report of the Freshwater Fisheries Biennial Review 1995–1997 also contains a study of farmed salmon escapes from cages in the sheltered bays of the western coasts and islands, and is critical of the mass escapes which occur from time to time.

Salmon escape in small numbers from aquaculture sites as a result of errors in routine management. Mass releases occur sporadically as a result of catastrophic equipment failure. Losses occur at every stage of development. In each case some of the fish may survive and resume a normal or near normal life cycle.

Salmon Research Agency of Ireland   The report of the Agency for 1997 says the shortage of salmon is a matter of major concern. Urgent action is needed to arrest the pervasive decline of the wild salmon and the critical state of sea-trout stocks. It is possible that the increased loss of salmon at sea, in particular of the multi-sea winter-stock, may be due to a change of climate.

The Agency suggests that one of the remedies might be an agreed five-year moratorium on commercial catches. The report sets out in great detail the work that is being done (for example the development of sterile salmon for farms, so that fish that escape cannot breed with wild salmon and so cannot change the genetic basis of the wild salmon stock), and extensive statistics record the severe decline of both salmon and sea-trout. For example, the sea-trout run recorded in the Agency's traps totalled over 2,000 in 1970-74 but by 1997 had dropped to a mere 137.

The Agency, which has done important work in the 44 years of its existence, is now to be merged with the Marine Institute.

'Save Our Sea Trout' Campaign   The Irish have been most active in lobbying the public and government in Dublin for action to help deal with the salmon and sea-trout crisis. The most effective effort has been Ireland's 'Save Our Sea Trout' campaign. Save Our Sea Trout, PO Box 69, Galway, Ireland. Its Chairman, Professor Graham Shaw, told the *Encyclopaedia* that in the mid-to late 1980s the western Irish seaboard went into a steep decline, culminating in 1989 in a complete collapse of sea-trout angling. He went on:

> This included such renowned fisheries as Delphi, Costelloe, Ballynahinch, Gowla, Invermore, Beltra, Screebe and Kylemore. Fisheries in the South West and in Donegal also collapsed, and it became clear that the common factor in all the affected fisheries was the presence of a salmon farm in the estuary.
>
> Scientific investigation also quickly established another common factor. In all the affected fisheries, sea trout smolts and kelts were returning prematurely to fresh water in May with extremely high infestation with juvenile sea lice and with head and fin damage. Monitoring the adjacent salmon farms revealed high levels of lice infestation on farmed fish. Since 1989 it has been established that neither heavy lice infestation nor a population collapse has occurred in any Irish sea trout fishery without a salmon farm in the estuary.

Despite regular fish farm lice monitoring, the picture for most of the affected Western fisheries remains bleak. It is clear that sustained good lice control or fallowing of farms in the entire bay during spring leads to a partial recovery of the sea trout. Nevertheless it is also clear that one year of poor lice control can reverse this recovery. Anglers contemplating a trip to any of the affected fisheries to fish for sea trout are advised to seek local advice prior to arranging their visit. In some fisheries the salmon return has also collapsed but some have successfully introduced salmon ranching to compensate for the sea trout loss.

On a more positive note, reports from some of the rivers in Mayo and parts of the western coasts of Ireland are that the grilse run this year (1998) is slightly better than last.

Salmon: Transgenic Breeding   During 1995–97 a company based in America began licensing a new system of artificially breeding salmon. A report of the North Atlantic Salmon Conservation Organisation says that during 1995 the company began licensing what it called its transgenic technology with the claim that transgenic fish would grow more than four to six times faster than normal fish. One fish farm in Scotland began to rear these fish experimentally in 1995, but the latest news we have is that this may have been discontinued.

Transgenic salmon are salmon into which genes have been introduced from another organism, which may or may not be of the same species. NASCO says that, while transgenic organisms may offer potential environmental benefits, their use also raises important questions related to ecological consequences, product safety and consumer acceptance. The need to ensure the containment of transgenic salmon, so as to avoid interactions with the wild stocks, has been stressed by scientists, including those involved in the production of transgenic salmon.

Salmon and Freshwater Fisheries Review Group   A new body was set up by the then Agriculture Minister Jack Cunningham in April 1998. Its terms of reference are 'to review existing polices and legislation in England and Wales concerning the management and conservation of salmon, trout, eels and freshwater fish and make recommendations'. Chaired by Lynda Warren, Professor of Environmental Law at the University of Wales, its members are Dr Nick Giles, Dr Keith Hendry, Derek Heselton, David Hodgins, Mrs Jean

Howman, Mrs Jane James, Dr Mike Ladle, Frank Lythgoe, David Moore, Mervyn Mountjoy, Pat O' Reilly, Stanley Payne, Dr Anne Powell, Professor Kerry Turner and John Williams.

Salmon & Trout Association Formed in 1903 by the Worshipful Company of Fishmongers in the City of London, the S&TA is the only national body devoted solely to representing the interests of game anglers. S&TA has been an independent organisation since 1973 and has offices in London and Edinburgh. A membership of 15,000 individuals and 300 clubs support around 100,000 game anglers throughout England, Scotland, Wales and Northern Ireland. Its 52 branches across the United Kingdom provide a social focus for members and allow local issues to be closely monitored. S&TA is primarily a political lobbying organisation on all matters relevant to safeguarding game angling. It also has an expanding role in environmental issues and education and training, and a close link with the S&TA Charitable Trust, which supports conservation research work on game species and habitat enhancement.

Lord Moran, elected chairman in April 1997, reports that angling associations are joining together in a new committee (the Moran Committee) to make proposals for the government's review of fishery policy and legislation. Lord Moran also welcomed proposals for a reform of the S&TA to 'make it more democratic and more effective'.

For further information contact the Salmon & Trout Association, Fishmongers' Hall, London Bridge, London EC4R 9EL. Scottish office: 10 Great Stuart Street, Edinburgh EH3 7TN.

See also STANIC.

Saltwater Fly Fishing Paul Morgan writes: During the nineteenth century sea angling, and freshwater angling for pike and perch, were frequently pursued with fly tackle, either cast or trolled. The invention of multiplier and fixed-spool reels subsequently enabled adherents of both disciplines to cast further and more efficiently, and the fly was almost forgotten by sea and coarse fishermen.

It was not until the 1960s that this trend began to be reversed. In Britain this was largely due to the opening up of the large water-supply reservoirs to angling, the consequent accessibility of inexpensive trout fishing and the huge growth in the number of fly fishermen.

At this time in America anglers like George X. Sands, Joe Brooks and Lefty Kreh were pioneering the use of fly tackle in the pursuit of tarpon, bonefish, striped bass and other saltwater species. The proliferation of predatory, fly-taking, species of fish in America enabled flyfishers to widen their horizons enormously and the new sport grew apace. Gradually new methods and materials were developed for saltwater fly-tying and fly-fishing, and books and magazines on the subjects began to appear to satisfy the growing demand.

In northern Europe an existing flyfishing tradition had been given a boost by the Danish trout stocking policy which has led to a large population of sea-trout in the Baltic Sea and created a major new saltwater fly fishery. Anglers from Germany and the Low Countries, with little fly fishing background but with a pioneering spirit, have joined with the Scandinavians in this new sport. Indeed, Belgium and Holland, with hardly any recognised game-fisheries, have gained a reputation for skilled and innovative fly tying and fly fishing.

Through the medium of international magazines and television most anglers now know of the possibilities of exciting and exotic fishing in the far corners of the globe. Relatively cheap travel allows many British and Europeans to fish in the Caribbean and even further afield. (*See* Overseas Fishing.)

All this has given a boost to the sport of fly fishing in our own temperate waters. The principal quarry species here are bass, mackerel, pollack and coalfish, garfish and in the North Sea, sea-trout. Every still water trout fisherman already has the equipment necessary to fly fish in salt water. Early in the morning or late in the evening (the best times anyway), with a minimum of tackle, the holidaying angler can sneak away and be in with a good chance of excellent sport.

Recommended reading: *Angling in Salt Water*, John Bickerdyke; *Flyfishing in Saltwater*, Lefty Kreh; *Inshore Fly Fishing*, Lou Tabory; *Saltwater Flyfishing: Britain and Northern Europe*, Paul Morgan (contains a complete bibliography on the subject).

Samuel, William William Samuel's book, *The Arte of Angling* (1577), is said to be the model on which Izaak Walton based his *Compleat Angler*. The main characters are Piscator and

Viator, one the tutor, the other the pupil (as in Walton) but the book lacks the charm of Walton's. Only one copy is known to exist, and that is now held by Princeton University in the United States who issued a reprint in 1956.

The Flyfisher's Classic Library has announced a facsimile reprint of the Princeton edition with the addition of Professor Thomas P. Harrison's article from *Notes & Queries* which describes his researches into the mystery of the authorship (the original title page was missing). Professor Harrison established the identity of the author as William Samuel, a vicar in Huntingdon.

Sandison, Bruce The author of *Trout & Salmon Rivers and Lochs of Scotland* which gives details of every game fishing water in Scotland (over 6,000 lochs and 600 rivers) permission addresses, telephone numbers, OS map locations, costs, boats and gillies, recommended flies and tactics. A comprehensive guide.

Sawyer, Frank (1907–1980) The modern method of nymph fishing is largely due to the work of Frank Sawyer. His Pheasant Tail Nymph is now fished world-wide in more than sixty countries. Sawyer was born at Bulford, Wiltshire, and the river Avon, close to his home, occupied all his working life and most of his spare time for more than sixty years. He became keeper on the Officers' (later the Services') Fly Fishing Association water in 1928, which was then dry fly only.

By sheer persistence, skill and an almost unique knowledge of trout and insect life acquired by long observation of the river, Sawyer began to spread the doctrine of fishing a weighted nymph to subaqueously feeding trout. Originally he used the weighted nymph to remove unwanted grayling from the water and achieved remarkable results. His phenomenal underwater vision helped him to see a trout take a tiny nymph many feet below the surface.

Encouraged by Sir Grimwood Mears and G. E. M. Skues, Sawyer wrote articles on his methods and in 1958 his book *Nymphs and the Trout* brought him world acclaim. He had also published, in 1952, the charming *Keeper of the Stream*. Anglers in many countries honoured him: he received the Fario Club medal in France, presented by Charles Ritz, and at the Game Fair at Bowood in 1979 the Prince of Wales presented him with the long-service award of the Country Landowners'

Association. He was made an MBE in the Prime Minister's Honours List in 1978.

Frank Sawyer, *Man of the Riverside*, by Sidney Vines, contains much of Sawyer's unpublished writings and his observations of trout and insect behaviour.

Scotland   Noted for its fine wild salmon fishing, Scotland also offers quality sea-trout, brown and rainbow trout fishing, much of it among breathtaking scenery.   In addition to the migratory rivers there is a wide range of game fishing on the numerous lochs, still water fisheries and reservoirs.

A rod licence is not required in Scotland but there is very little free game fishing, so obtain a permit and always seek local advice before fishing.   Many rivers allow the use of bait and spinning for game fish, but by far the most popular method is the fly.

Salmon and sea-trout fishing on Sundays is illegal throughout Scotland.   In very general terms the game season in Scotland for migratory fish extends from early February until late October; there are however, many exceptions so you should seek precise dates locally.

Some of the angling locations are very isolated (an attraction in itself for most of us) so if fishing without a gillie do carry an OS map, a compass and a whistle for emergencies. When boat fishing always wear a buoyancy aid and *never* stand up in the boat. Another wise precaution is to tell your host where you propose fishing and your estimated time of return. At the end of a day's fishing thoroughly wash all your tackle, and in particular the reel, for the brackish water of some lochs will play havoc with the ferrous parts of your equipment including your flies. A midge repellent is advisable, particularly on calm days and especially in the evenings.

The game fisher's needs are well-served by regional tourist boards, all of whom produce free and informative angling guides, and at a local level there are many helpful tourist information centres.

Recommended reading: *Fish Scotland*, a free publication available from the Scottish Tourist Board, 23 Ravelston Terrace, Edinburgh EH4 3EU. *Trout and Salmon Flies of Scotland* by Stan Headley; *Trout and Salmon Rivers and Lochs of Scotland* by Bruce Sandison; *The Great Salmon Rivers of Scotland* by John Ashley Cooper; *Salmon* Fishing by Hugh Falkus; *A Salmon Fisher's Odyssey* by John Ashley Cooper; *The Art of the Atlantic Salmon*

Fly by J. D. Bates, and *The Haig Guide to Salmon Fishing in Scotland* by David Barr.

'Scott, Jock'   Probably the best book on salmon fishing for beginners ever written is Jock Scott's *The Art of Salmon Fishing* (1933), but unfortunately, all his advice about lines and rods is so outdated now that large parts of it are of little interest, but when it comes to tactics, and how a fly should be presented, 'Jock Scott' is unbeatable.

Scottish Anglers National Association (SANA) *See* Competitive Fly Fishing.

Scouts' Campaign   The Environment Agency has joined with the Scout Association in a campaign to award badges to Scouts who gain proficiency in fresh water and sea fishing and a knowledge of the environment. Scouts will have to learn about tackle, how to cast, and go fishing at least six times in three months. Contact: Environment Agency, Manley House, Kestrel Way, Exeter EX2 7LQ.

Scrope, William   *Days & Nights of Salmon Fishing in the Tweed* by William Scrope,was first published in 1843 and contains many good fishing stories. The book is quaintly written, a little discursive but full of interest. 'It is notable for its charm, humour, anecdote and description, as well as for sound information,' according to James Robb in *Notable Angling Literature*. Copies of the first edition are much sought after and sell for as much as £850. Reissued by FCL in 1991 and reprinted again in 1995.

Sea-trout   In an article in *Salmon and Sea Trout Fishing*, edited by David Wrangles, Gilbert Stanley, former Inspector of Salmon and Freshwater Fisheries, wrote:

> In Scottish law, sea trout are salmon; in English law they are distinct. Scientifically they belong to the single species of trout found in Europe.
> Ecologically they show a broad pattern of behaviour spanning the clear-cut distinction between the sea-going salmon and the riverine brown trout.

Not a great deal is known of the life of a sea-trout. The young spend two or three years in the river of their birth before going down to the estuary. Some remain there and come back within a few months. If they retain a habit of estuary feeding they are often called slob trout.

Their sea-going is almost as uncertain as their return for spawning. Hartley records that some sea-trout from south Devon have been found in the Tweed; on the other hand, sea-trout in the Fowey in Cornwall have been found to stray very little from the river of their birth.

It is not known whether sea-trout breed true or whether some offspring can remain in the rivers and give up their migratory habits forced on them by their environment. There is some evidence that male sea-trout can at times remain in a river and become sexually mature and indistinguishable from brown trout in appearance.

Identification Although scientifically they are brown trout (*Salmo trutta*) these silvery fish that ascend our rivers are so like salmon in appearance, and so unlike brown trout that many anglers think of them as a different fish. Even experienced anglers make mistakes; in one embarrassing case, only laboratory tests proved that a fish hailed as a Thames salmon was a large estuarine trout. The problem is complicated by variations in the appearance of salmon and by occasional cases of hybrids. The simplest tests are shown on page 218.

Feeding Sea-trout do feed in fresh water, especially in their first few days in a river or loch, but the habit of feeding diminishes fairly quickly, probably less quickly in a freshwater loch, but this is not proven.

River Fishing According to Roy Buckingham, in an article in *West Country Fly Fishing*, 'Night fishing is the best way of taking sea-trout and the deadliest method is with the fly'. Night is generally the best time to take sea-trout in rivers, but many sea-trout are caught during the day on big rivers like the Tweed and on big Scottish lochs. Kingsmill Moore recalls that in Ireland the rivers in Connemara are generally fished during the day while the Slaney is fished at night. In sea pools in the west of Scotland sea-trout will rise readily to a fly during the day. In general, however, night fishing, especially on the smaller rivers, is most productive.

Flies and fishing methods vary. In some rivers long thin lures are effective, in others less so. On the Torridge, in north Devon, some of the most effective flies are the small ones,

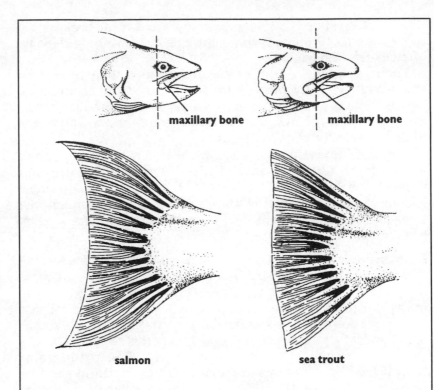

maxillary bone   maxillary bone

salmon   sea trout

Sea-Trout Identification Salmon have a forked tail with two tiny 'horns' at the extremities, and the rear of the eye is level or almost level with an imaginary line drawn from the top of the head down to the maxillary bone. Sea-trout have their eye well forward of this line, and they have square tails and no 'horns'. Other tests can be made.

G. H. Nall in *The Life of the Sea Trout* (Seeley Service, 1930) suggests counting the number of scales in an oblique line drawn downwards and forwards from the hind edge of the adipose fin to the lateral line. Salmon have 10 to 13 scales, usually 11. Sea-trout have more scales, 13 to 16, usually 14, rarely 12.

about size 12; yet only a few miles away on the Tamar no one fishes anything smaller than a 10, and mostly big bushy flies on 8, 6 and 4 low-water salmon hooks. On the Spey and Tweed many sea-trout are taken by salmon fishermen on large salmon flies, singles, doubles and tubes. On the Conway and Dovey, big tandem lures, demons and terrors will take sea-trout at night but alarm them in daytime.

The best kind of fly and the best ways of fishing are subject

to argument. In *Sea Trout Fishing* Hugh Falkus sought a compromise, a formula for success, involving frequent change between the various methods – floating lines, sunk lines, small lures, long ones, surface flies fished with a drag, fly-maggot and bait fishing. The important thing was to have confidence: 'There is a great truth in the saying that the best fly to use is the one you believe in'. Upstream wet fly, dry fly and nymph fishing can take sea-trout during the day but the sea-trout is easily scared. Small flies on fine long leaders are needed. Many modern reservoir lures – the Muddler Minnow, Ace of Spades, Whisky Fly, Black Lure to mention a few – are effective sea-trout flies as well, and traditional Scottish sea-trout flies, such as Peter Ross, are widely used in sizes from 10 to 8.

Practically all sea-trout fishing on rivers is wet fly downstream with a single fly, a strong leader and a flexible single-handed rod. Daytime reconnaissance of the water to be fished at night is essential. The angler must take into account not only where the sea-trout shoal is, or likely to be, but must know in advance where to stand, how far and where to put his cast, how far he needs to wade, the rock or gravel formations under water, the type of wading, and the dangers from potholes or other obstructions.

Fly fishing at night is difficult. Most good casters are inclined to speed up the rhythm of casting; there has to be a deliberate effort to keep the slow rhythm which comes naturally during the day. A slack line on the water cannot be seen and is often the cause of a lost fish – a trout will pluck at the slack fly and because of the lack of tension, will not be hooked. And night fly fishing can be alarming to those who have been brought up in cities. Strange sounds, rustles in the undergrowth, heavy breathing, can be frightening, even terrifying, to those who do not recognise country sounds. Many sea-trout fishermen at night go out in pairs, arrange where they are going to be, carry whistles or communicate by flashing a torch. In real wilderness country it is best to let someone know where you are likely to be if you go fishing alone.

For the Irish 'Save Our Sea Trout' Campaign, *see* page 210 .

Sedge Flies   There are some 200 varieties of sedge flies (*Trichoptera*) including very big ones and very small ones; most of the few which are of interest to fishermen look like moths and some are semi-nocturnal.

Hatching from an egg in the bottom of the river, the larvae protect themselves by making cases from an extruded fluid which they cover with microscopic particles of detritus, mud and sand. The cases are anchored on stones, the ends closed. The larvae pupates, bites its way through the end of the case and rises to the surface of the water, or crawls along the bottom and climbs to a resting place to hatch into the mature fly.

Trout take the fly on hatching and again when the females lay their eggs in the water. Sedges can be distinguished from a stone fly (*Plecoptera*) by looking at the wings. The sedge wings are slightly hairy and at rest are carried in the shape of a roof over the insect's body. The stone fly has hard shiny wings, without hairs, carried flat over the body.

Artificial patterns of the sedge are often localised. On the northern rivers of England a large sedge which hatches in the evening is known as the Bustard; this has several dressings but can be suggested by a large Red Palmer. Lunn's Caperer is a good pattern for some of the sedges often found on the chalk streams. The grannom (q.v.) is a medium-sized sedge which often hatches in large numbers, so do the grouse-wing on lakes and the little red sedge on rivers.

Sedge Pupae   These are often called caddis flies, from their case-building habits. In the seventeenth and eighteenth centuries the grubs were known as cods or cod-bait. Artificial sedge pupa patterns are mostly still water flies, generally fished just below the surface of the water. The best known is the Amber Nymph. Others that will take fish during a sedge hatch include the Invicta, Alder, Chompers and Palmer Nymph.

Senior, William   A former editor and fishing columnist for *The Field* who wrote under the name of Red Spinner. Senior gave invaluable encouragement to Halford and Marryat in their researches into fly life on the Kennet and the Test and wrote the introduction to Halford's autobiography.

Shadow Flies   These are purely palmer flies: no body, no whisks, simply a hackle palmered from the eye to the bend of the hook. Peter Deane's Shadow Mayfly (*see under* Mayfly) is a good example. One of the pioneers was Richard Threlfall, who explained in his book *On a Gentle Art* that the imprints of the

hackle on the water, as seen from below, gave the impression of a live insect. The colour of the hackles does not seem to matter: Threlfall's were red or reddish and black, and Peter Deane's Mayfly is grey. Threlfall's, fished dry, was the only pattern he used.

Recommended reading: *The Fly Fisher and the Trout's Point of View* by E. W. Harding.

See also One-Fly Man.

Shannon Fisheries Region   This comprises all the rivers that flow into the sea between Hag's Head in Co. Clare and Kerry Head. An Electricity Supply Board permit is needed to fish for salmon on the Shannon or any of its tributaries. The Board manages fisheries on the lower river at Limerick – Castleconnell and Mulchair. The Shannon is very much a mixed fishery, with a wide range of coarse fish and pike, as well as salmon and trout.

Probably the fly fisherman would do best to fish Castleconnell, which is recovering from the effects of a hydro-electric dam up river. There are eight beats on the fishery: five let by tender every season, and the remaining three let on day tickets. Bookings to the Manager, Electricity Supply Board, Hydro Group, Ardnacrusha, nr Limerick.

Accommodation can be had at the Angling Centre, Castle Oaks Hotel, Castleconnell, Limerick.

Sheringham, H. T. (1876 -1930)   Son of a vicar of Tewkesbury, where he fished as a boy, H. T. Sheringham was angling editor of *The Field* for many years in the early 1900s. He wrote a number of country books, and one, *Syllabub Farm*, was a considerable success; so too was *Trout Fishing – Its Cause, Treatment and Cure*, first published in 1925 – a most hilarious and charming book which was reissued in 1996 by FCL. Sheringham, a witty and thoughtful essayist, was one of the first to praise Blagdon fishing, and he wrote with perception on both the spate rivers and chalk streams.

Sherry Spinner   Originally an artificial to suggest the female spinner of the blue-winged olive (*Ephemerella ignita*), the angler's name seems to cover a large number of olives. Trout will also take other patterns – Pheasant Tail, Orange Quill, Rusty Spinner – when spent blue-winged olives are about.

Goddard gives Wooley's dressing of the Sherry Spinner:

Body: pale gold quill or gold-coloured floss
Whisks and hackle: pale ginger cock
Wings: glassy blue cock hackle fibres, or two pale blue cock hackle tips, in both cases tied spent, at right-angles to the hook
Hook: 14

Skues' dressing was:

Body: amber seal fur, slightly mixed with orange and green and a little hare fur
Rib: fine gold wire
Whisks and hackle: pale honey dun cock
Wings: none
Hook: 13 or 14

Shipley, William   A fisherman on the Dove who kept a fishing diary from 1780 onwards. This was edited and published, as *The True Treatise on the Art of Fly Fishing*, by his son, also William, together with Edward Fitzgibbon, in 1838. Shipley's description of fishing the floating fly on the Dove is frequently quoted:

> Let your flies float gently down the water, working them gradually towards you, making a fresh cast every two or three yards you fish. We distinctly recommend frequent casting, for . . . the quick repetition of casting whisks the water out of the flies and line and consequently keeps them drier and lighter than if they were left to float a longer time in the water.

Shrimp (*Gammarus pulex*)   An important trout food, shrimps are found in rivers and lakes among stones and weed, in most cases close to the bottom. Early patterns (Horsfall-Turner and Skues) were unweighted, but most of those tied in the past few decades have been heavily weighted for fast sinking, sometimes on hooks with curved shanks. The artificial shrimp is useful on lakes and reservoirs and on many spate rivers. On most of the chalk streams weighted shrimps are banned as being imitation bait. There are various dressings:

Underbody: lead wire or lead strip
Body: pale orange or yellow-brown seal fur mixed with olive seal fur
Rib: fine gold wire
Hackle: grey or olive, palmered over the body from head to bend

Back: a speckled dark feather laid over the back of the fly from head to bend, sometimes varnished
Hook: 14 –10

Silver Doctor A salmon fly dating from the mid-1850s. The modern simplified version is:

Body: flat silver tinsel
Rib: oval silver
Tail: golden pheasant tippet
Hackle: bright blue hen, dressed beard
Wings: strips of goose or swan, dyed green, yellow and red, flanked by grey mallard or teal

Silver Wilkinson A salmon fly designed by the Rev. P. S. Wilkinson in 1859 for fishing the Tweed:

Tag: silver tinsel
Tail: golden pheasant crest
Butt: scarlet wool
Body: silver tinsel wound silver wire
Throat hackle: guinea fowl fibres dyed blue
Wings: a mix of red and yellow swan with teal and jungle cock
Wing topping: golden pheasant crest
Cheeks: jungle cock

This is an approximation of the original design.

Sinkant A substance to make leaders sink quickly, often made by mixing fullers' earth and glycerine to the consistency of putty. There are several proprietary brands on the market under a variety of names.

Skues, G. E. M. (1858–1949) A London solicitor, George Edward MacKenzie Skues, had a profound influence on his own and subsequent generations of fly fishermen. He was the first to challenge the 'dry fly only' code of the chalk streams, the first to urge chalk stream fishermen to return to upstream wet-fly technique when trout were feeding underwater, and the first to tie imitations of the ascending nymphs on which the trout were feeding.

From the early 1900s for some thirty or forty years Skues was always in the centre of controversy with the purists. It was their antagonism and resentment of the man who was rightly called 'the father of nymph fishing' which ultimately

caused his resignation from the Itchen fishery at Abbotts Barton, just above Winchester, where he had fished for 56 years.

It took many years for Skues to formulate the theory of nymph fishing. He was at first a devotee of Halford, but doubts began when one of Skues' dry flies sank and was taken by a trout which had previously refused to take it on the surface. From this followed a series of articles in *The Field*, the *Fishing Gazette* and the *Flyfishers' Club Journal* in which he advocated the return of the upstream wet fly to the chalk streams when trout were feeding off the ascending nymphs.

By the end of 1909, H. T. Sheringham, angling editor of *The Field*, urged Skues to publish his articles in book form, with some extra material, and from this came *Minor Tactics of the Chalk Stream* (1910). This was followed by *The Way of a Trout With a Fly* (1921), *Nymph Fishing for Chalk Stream Trout* (1939) and, posthumously, *Itchen Memories* (1951). His angling letters, edited by C. F. Walker, were published in 1956, and a biography and many unpublished letters were skilfully put together by Donald Overfield in *G. E. M. Skues: The Way of a Man with a Trout*.

Skues defined nymph fishing in *Nymph Fishing for Chalk Stream Trout* with considerable precision. It followed an acrimonious debate in The Flyfishers' Club a year earlier, which is given in full in Overfield's book. This is Skues' description:

> Nymph fishing means to me the practice of presenting to a subaqueously feeding trout, in position, an artificial nymph representing as closely as possible the natural nymph he may be expected to be feeding on at the moment.
>
> The artificial nymph, if properly selected, more nearly represents the bulk of the trout's food than does any winged or hackle fly. I claim that the use of the artificial for subaqueously feeding fish is a definite advance in the chalk stream angler's technique of fishing for trout which are letting the hatched fly go by.

Skues' influence stretched far wider than the chalk streams. At Blagdon Lake, Dr Bell scooped out the trout he caught with a marrow-spoon, as Skues recommended, and from this developed still water nymph fishing. In time, in spite of much opposition, many chalk stream dry fly purists gave way. In 1938 a Piscatorial Society report had condemned nymph fishing because it took 'so many undersized trout'. Twenty years or so later the Society recanted; it allowed the use of unweighted Skues' nymphs, fished upstream, without drag, just under the surface, as being 'included in the term dry fly' on the Avon, Lambourne and Wylye – sophistry it may have been, but it was a useful compromise.

With his back to the wall, facing the purists of the 1920s and 1930s, unaware of his approaching triumphs, Skues was hurt and lonely. He never married. He died in 1949 at the age of 91. Thirty years later, as a result of an appeal by Roy Darlington, who was renting the Abbotts Barton fishery and was an admirer of Skues, a memorial stone seat was erected near the place where his ashes were scattered. The lower half of the Abbotts Barton fishery was taken over by Winchester Council in 1975 for town planning purposes.

Dry fly purists came to have a somewhat guilty feeling about their intolerance and of their treatment of Skues. They tried to make amends:

> When . . . Skues wrote *Minor Tactics of the Chalk Stream* he effected a revolution. The dry fly was at the height of an intolerant dictatorship, and the other method was discarded and ridiculed to such an extent that enthusiasts of the school of Halford regarded Mr Skues as a dangerous heresiarch. Much water has flowed under the bridge since then, and in that water many trout were caught on a sunk fly which would not have fallen to the dry. More and more each year does nymph fishing become a part of the modern angler's equipment and he who does not possess the art is gravely handicapped; and . . . upon my word, I find trout harder to catch under water than on top. (J. W. Hills, *A Summer on the Test*)

Recommended reading: Kenneth Robson's *The Essential G. M. Skues.*

Smell Trout and salmon have a highly developed sense of smell. Experiments carried out in France in the early 1980s found that the trout's sense of smell was a million times more sensitive than that of a human, about the same as a tracker dog's, but nowhere near as keen as an eel's.

Throughout 1997 *The Field's* correspondence column contained letters from anglers praising the miraculous properties of female pubic hair. Much of it was of a light-hearted nature dwelling on the choice of name for a fly dressed

with such material. Suggestions ranged from Pub Grub, The Magic Merkin, Bush Baby, Frizzie Lizzy to *Nympha Pubis*.

Snipe and Purple Invaluable for fishing wet fly upstream. A traditional pattern probably dating back two hundred years or more, it was highly commended by Pritt in the nineteenth century and is very simple to dress:

> *Body:* purple floss silk
> *Hackle:* small dark feather from the outside of a snipe's wing
> *Hook:* 14 or 16

The Snipe and Purple is often fished as a middle fly in a team of three. Pritt also dressed it with a yellow silk body as a Snipe and Yellow, but purple seems to retain its popularity as the number one choice.

Soldier Palmer A palmer fly which takes its name from the scarlet and gold uniform of British soldiers of the line – Redcoats – of the eighteenth and nineteenth centuries. The body is a bright scarlet wool, the colour of a Guardsman's tunic, wrapped around with gold twist, allowing both the scarlet and gold to show through the brown hackle wound from head to bend.

Spencer, Sidney The Welsh lakes and the Scottish and Irish lochs were well covered by Sidney Spencer in a series of books, notably *The Art of Lake Fishing* (1934), in which the angler is urged never to fish the drift with a rod shorter than 12ft, as it will not work properly. Spencer must have been a fairly tough character, for he urged fishermen not to use boat cushions but to harden themselves to sitting on the wooden seats when fishing. The book has excellent diagrams about drift fishing and casting and much good practical advice.

Spey According to John Ashley-Cooper in *A Salmon Fisher's Odyssey:*

> The Spey is perhaps the most magnificent of Scottish rivers. It is not the largest, yielding place to both Tay and Tweed in this respect, but it is certainly the strongest and fastest, as anyone who has seen it in spate will confirm. It flows through a wonderful countryside of unforgettable surroundings and provides fishing for salmon and sea trout which is second to none.

It might be appropriate to add that it is among the most

expensive of rivers to fish – and yet at the same time it is also the cheapest, with many miles of association water at Grantown-on-Spey available for visitors. Private beats, often with lodges, are let by the Seafield Estate office at Grantown; the Tulchan Estate office at Adive; the Ballindalloch and Pitlochry Estates at Ballindalloch; the Gordon Castle Estate at Fochabers; and the Carron Estate at Carron. The Tulchan Lodge Hotel has good water for guests. Craigellachie Hotel water is now time-share, but rods are occasionally available. Other fishing hotels are The Boat Hotel, Boat of Garten; the Dowans Hotel, Aberlour; Blairfindy Lodge, Glenlivet; and Tulchan Lodge.

In recent years there have been petitions against over-netting in the estuary, and the best fishing is when the nets are off in the autumn, but there can be a good grilse run as well as a fine flush of big sea-trout in July.

The river is very broad and fast. Deep wading and long casting are essential.

In bright low water salmon will take quite small flies, (down to 10 or 12 doubles) such as Stoat's Tail and the Munro Killer, a local fly from Aberlour. When the water rises heavy tubes are needed, and at certain marks only spinning is possible.

Spey Casting   Salmon fishermen using a long double-handed rod have a special cast which is useful, sometimes essential, when there is a need for a long cast but a high bank or thick bushes and trees behind the angler make it impossible to use the ordinary overhead cast. The Spey cast is partly switch, partly roll, and when it is well done the swirling rhythm of the moving line around the head of the fisherman is beautiful to watch; when it is badly done it is dangerous. *See* page 228.

Spiders   Lightly dressed flies for upstream wet-fly fishing, generally in a team of three flies fished on a short line in true Border and Yorkshire style. They suggest drowned duns and spinners or, occasionally, nymphs. They are generally fished without movement so that the soft hackle in the water gives the impression of outspread wings. W. C. Stewart in *The Practical Angler* gave three dressings:

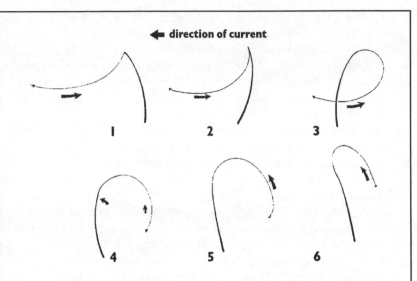

direction of current

1	2	3
4	5	6

The Spey Cast. When the fly is dangling downstream of the angler, he faces it, one foot pointing towards the fly, the other in the direction across the river where he intends the fly to go. Then these movements are made: *1.* The rod begins to move the fly upstream. *2.* The fly accelerates and . . . *3.* . . . passes in front of the angler. *4.* A forward stroke is made by the rod. *5.* The fly changes direction and . . . *6.* . . . follows the line as the power stroke ends.

Black Spider: body of brown silk, hackle made from the small feather of the cock starling
Red Spider: body of yellow silk, the hackle from the small feather taken from the outside wing of the landrail
Dun Spider: body of light brown or tawny silk, the hackle made from the small feather taken from the inside of the wing of a starling (the original dressing used a dotterel wing)
Hook sizes: 14–16

Stewart always dressed his flies very lightly. His Black Spider is now more frequently dressed with a black body and a black hen hackle and has been taken over by some reservoir fishermen as a better imitation of the midge than the standard reservoir patterns. The spider type of dressing is fairly common and applies to such well-known patterns as Partridge and Orange and Snipe and Purple.

STANIC The Salmon & Trout Association National Instructor's Certificate is administered solely by the Association and is recognised as the standard entry qualification to professional game angling instruction in the British Isles. It has the backing of the Sports Council and replaces the game angling qualification previously offered by the former National Anglers' Council. The Game Angling Instructors Association (GAIA) and the Register of Experienced Fly Fishing Instructors and Schools (REFFIS) require applicants to be holders of STANIC.

The certificate is awarded to candidates who are able to establish their proficiency to instruct game anglers and prospective game anglers of all ages and abilities. It is awarded at a single grade, and candidates may qualify as salmon and/or trout and/or fly dressing instructors. The qualification in fly dressing is awarded jointly by the Salmon & Trout Association and the Fly Dressers' Guild; candidates in fly dressing are expected to have a game angling background.

Further details are available from The Salmon & Trout Association STANIC Administrator, Fishmongers' Hall, London Bridge, London EC4R 9EL.

See also REFFIS *and* APGAI.

Still Water Fishing Thousands of years ago fishermen had discovered how to make rods, lines and hooks, even float tubes from inflated bladders which could be paddled out to where the fish were rising. When Britain was invaded by the Romans they brought their rods and tackle with them. They fished at Hadrian's Wall, on the Thames and on the Severn, using their standard fly known as a plume (a feathered lure of some kind, probably similar to what the Cornish call feathers when they take out visitors in a boat to fish for mackerel).

Still water fishing had probably been going on for many years, in the wild tarns in the mountainous countries of Scotland, Ireland and Wales by the local peasants and small farmers using nets, or rods with brandling worms (and when there were no worms because of the frost then a piece of red wool on a hook to give the impression of one).

After the Romans left the Normans arrived and began to organise the fishing, bringing in laws reserving the best of the fishing for the nobility and fashionable countrymen, the owners of large estates, and poor fishing was left to the common, or coarse, people (hence the expressions 'coarse fish'

and 'coarse fishing').

Later came the industrial revolution, and with it widespread pollution of the rivers, especially in the midlands of England. There are many records from the mid 1700s onwards of the 'dark satanic mills' of that time. We do not know exactly when it happened, but sometime around the 1850s to 1870s an enterprising water company in Manchester opened three of its reservoirs on the hills near the town 'for the relaxation of the working class'. The reservoirs were full of small wild trout, and the Manchester anglers had something to fish for at last. A day out cost the fishermen two shillings or two shillings and sixpence, depending on the number of fish taken. The idea caught on; Birmingham was among the first to open its reservoirs, which could be 'fished by all sporting methods'. Lake Vyrnwy opened for fly and minnow fishing for visitors to the local hotel. By the early 1900s over 150 reservoirs were open for fishing. However, the public was alarmed at the thought of maggots and worms being used as ground and hook bait in drinking water, and there were many protests and demonstrations, so eventually most of the water companies brought in a fly-only rule.

After World War II there was a sudden and overwhelming demand for reservoir fishing. Many people managed to buy or borrow small cars or motor bikes to take them to their favourite fishing. By 1983 there were more than 200 reservoirs offering day-ticket fishing at reasonable prices and records of three of the biggest show that during that one season anglers took 19,476 trout from Chew Valley Lake; 41,752 from Grafham Water and 60,358 from Rutland Water. Many private fisheries followed the reservoirs' example. Entrepreneurs moved in and bought up derelict quarries, creating lakes wherever they could; some of them wisely provided fishing huts, even snack bars. Some owners gave up the idea of day-ticket waters and offered rods on a seasonal basis, one of the pioneers of season-ticket water being Alex Behrendt at Two Lakes near Romsey in Hampshire.

Still water fishing can be said to have come of age with the publication in 1952 of T. C. Ivens' *Stillwater Fly Fishing* with the introduction of special patterns for lake fishing: the Brown and Green Brown Nymphs, the Black and Peacock Spider, the Jersey Herd and the Pretty Pretty lure. Several of these patterns are still widely fished today, after nearly fifty years – especially the Black and Peacock Spider which has been the winning fly in several national and international competitions.

Ivens' book was the first serious study of still water tactics and was devoted entirely to the reservoirs. Everything was studied: tackle, rods, lines, wading and boat fishing. Ivens improved upon the methods of Dr Bell of Blagdon and, like Bob Church and many others since, concentrated on the deeps:

> The trout's sporadic surface foraging has caused him to be widely regarded as a surface feeding fish, but you and I know better, and when we fish a lake or reservoir we concentrate on the things we cannot see and try to fish our flies at the depth most trout are feeding.

Ivens was followed by many fishermen, and we owe our subsequent progress notably to Peter Lapsley's *Trout From Stillwaters*, Bob Church's *Reservoir Trout Fishing* and many more.

Stoddart, Thomas Tod (1810–1880)   The poet-angler of Teviotdale, Stoddart was a friend of Sir Walter Scott and of James Hogg, the Ettrick Shepherd, another angler-poet. Famous in his time, a memoir by his daughter, Anna, was published with some of his poems as *Angling Songs* (1889):

> All joy be with our hearts' kin bold
> May care's nets ne'er entangle,
> Nor woe nor poverty depress
> A brother of the angle!

Stoddart was born in Argyle Square, Edinburgh, the son of a Royal Navy captain, Pringle Stoddart and his wife, Frances. He lived for a large part of his life at Bellevue Cottage, Kelso and is buried in Kelso churchyard. Teviot and Tweed were his loves:

> Let ither anglers chuse their ain,
> An'ither waters tak' te lead;
> O' Hielan' streams we covet nane,
> But gie to us the bonnie Tweed.

Stewart, W. C.   An Edinburgh lawyer who fished the Borders, W. C. Stewart wrote one of the most popular fly fishing books of the latter half of the nineteenth century. *The Practical Angler or the Art of Trout Fishing* was first published in 1857, with the second and third editions coming out the same year, followed by half a dozen reprints in subsequent years. A final revised

edition 62 years after the first, appeared in 1919, with notes and a foreword by W. Earl Hodgson. FCL published a facsimile edition in 1996 which has a new introduction by Richard Hunter and a foreword by Conrad Voss Bark. Only the works of Halford and Skues can equal that record.

See also Wet-fly Fishing, Spiders.

Stinchar An Ayrshire river with a good run of salmon in September and October, and probably one of the best of the Ayrshire rivers for the fly. The Bardrochat and Knockdolian Estates have occasional lettings.

Stoat's Tail One of the best hairwing salmon flies of this or any time. It was first tied by Wright of Sprouston on Tweed sometime in the 1870s and 1880s. There are a number of dressings but the best is Veniard's:

> *Body:* black floss
> *Rib:* silver or gold tinsel, preferably silver
> *Beard hackle:* black cock or hen
> *Wing:* the black tips from a stoat's tail, or squirrel dyed black
> *Hook:* with the stoat's tail wing, not much larger than 6 or 4, but larger if need be with black squirrel

The variations involve a tinsel tag, or dark claret floss, or blue or guinea-fowl beard hackle. Quite a few black flies – the Connemara and the Munro among them – make obeisance to the Stoat's Tail, which is also an excellent sea-trout fly.

Stone Flies (*Plecoptera*) These are flies of the uplands, the moorland streams, the becks and the spate rivers. In the north of England the big stonefly (*perla*) is called the mayfly and is just as important to a Yorkshireman as a true mayfly (*Ephemera danica*) is to the fishermen of Hampshire.

The nymphs of the big stone fly, about an inch long, are often used as bait. They creep to the shore and hatch out of the water; the adult flies return to the water to lay their eggs. The smaller stone flies are thin and narrow (needle fly, willow fly, yellow sally) and, because they have the same habits as the big flies, the trout feed mostly on the spent fly as it drifts downstream after egg-laying. Anglers generally find that it is not worthwhile to tie imitations of the small stone flies, and if there are any on the water the trout will most likely rise to a spider pattern, a Partridge and Orange, or a Grey Duster.

Stuart, Hamish Anyone who thinks that reservoir fishermen are sometimes a little unkind to the dry fly men of the chalk streams with their condemnation of purism had better read Hamish Stuart's *Lochs and Loch Fishing* (1899). Stuart was far more vindictive:

> Certain Purists have formed themselves into an exclusive society, in which mutual admiration, hypocrisy, sophistry, pharisaicism, and dispraise of the barbarian are strongly blended . . . .

He goes on like that for several pages, becoming, if possible even more vituperative. When Stuart does get round to loch fishing he is sound, though discursive, and the book is now a little difficult to read. There are, however, some interesting passages such as the one dealing with the hotel water at Loch Boisdale in South Uist.

Suir The River Suir, in Co. Tipperary, is one of Ireland's most famous brown trout fisheries. It is a limestone stream over a hundred miles long with many tributaries, such as Portlaw, Clodiagh, Clonmel, the Anner, Blackwater, Cahir and others. It is however, the main river, a pure limestone stream, which attracts visitors from overseas. It has a great attraction for dry fly men, and one of them is reputed to have remarked that the fishing was as good as a chalk stream and half the price. Fly hatches can be prolific at times, with all the usual olives, sedges, midges and hawthorns. The season is best from May to June for all-day fishing and in the evenings during the summer. Trout are from about one to two pounds. The main river has a strong current, and body waders and a wading staff are essential. Knocklofty House Hotel at Clonmel has excellent fishing reserved for guests and residents and fishing is also available through the Hayes Hotel, The Square, Thurles, Co. Tipperary; Ardmayle House, Cashel, Co. Tipperary; and Clonan Fly Fishing Centre, Ballymacarbry, Nire Valley, Co. Waterford.

Sutherland, Douglas A photograph of the 70lb salmon taken from the Tay is in *The Salmon Book* by Douglas Sutherland.

Sweeny Todd Named presumably because of a crimson throat, the Sweeny is an effective lure designed by Richard Walker and Peter Thomas:

Body: black floss silk, with a 'collar' of neon magenta fluorescent wool just behind the roots of the wing
Rib: fine silver wire
Beard hackle: crimson feather fibres
Wing: dyed black squirrel hair
Hook: down-eyed long-shank, 14 to 6

Without the neon magenta wool it is a variation of the Stoat's Tail (or Black Squirrel Tail), another effective still water pattern.

T

Tackle Collecting There is a strong collectors' market for vintage tackle and all the paraphernalia connected with angling, ranging from rods and reels to mounted specimen fish, paintings, catalogues, nets, gaffs, fly boxes and fly wallets, fly collections, fly tying kits, creels, memorabilia, etc. The annual *Miller's Antiques Price Guide* has a section devoted to angling. The standard guides to tackle collecting are: *Fishing Tackle of Yesterday* by Jamie Maxtone Graham; *Fishing Tackle* by Graham Turner; *To Catch a Fisherman* by Jamie Maxtone Graham. There are specialist guides devoted to a single manufacturer, such as John Drewett's *Hardy Brothers*, which must be the definitive book on Hardy reels. For American tackle: *Fishing Tackle Antiques and Collectables* by Karl T. White, and *The Collector's Guide to Antique Fishing Tackle* by Silvio Calabi. Some of the leading auction houses hold sales throughout the year, and there are several specialist dealers: a selection of both are given below.

Here are some highlights from auction sales held in 1998:

> The current British record wild brown trout mounted in a bow-fronted glazed case, caught by A. Finlay – Loch Awe, 7th April 1996. Wgt. 25lbs 5¾ozs. Donated by the captor with proceeds for the Loch Awe Improvement Association. £3,400. Bonhams, March 1998.
>
> Three oil paintings by John Russell made £4,400, £3,200, and £3,500. Bonhams, August 1998. Two others, also by John Russell, made £8,000 and £6,500. Bonhams, March 1998.
>
> A fine Edward Vom Hofe Restigouche 2/0 salmon fly reel, ebonite side plates and nickel silver fittings throughout with counter-balanced tapered handle on serpentine arm, rear knurled tension adjuster and optional check button to faceplate, in original black leather case, *c.* 1930. £1,350. Angling Auctions, April 1998.
>
> A Hardy 1896 pattern 'Perfect' salmon fly reel with shaded rod and hand trademark, enclosed oval and straightline logos, stapped

tension screw with turks head locking nut, dished alloy drum with large and small perforations. 14 cusps and central locking screw, ball bearings in open race, ivorine handle, 4¼". £500. Evans & Partridge, April 1998.

A rare 2⅜" all brass transitional 'Perfect' trout fly reel, *c.* 1894–5, with open ball race and brass bearings, brass bridged rim tensioner regulator screw, ivorine handle, faceplate stamped with 'Rod in Hand' logo, bordered oval logo and 'Hardy's' Pat'. (lacks drum retaining screw). £1,190. Bonhams, March 1998.

A scarce Ogden Smith 'The Test' angler's knife, nickel silver hinged shackle and side plates engraved with inch measure and hook gauge and fitted six Sheffield steel tools, *c.* 1940. £400. Angling Auctions, April 1998.

A scarce Hardy No. 3 angler's knife with nickel silver sideplates and hinged shackle and fitted seven various tools, *c.* 1940. £220. Angling Auctions, April 1998.

A 'Hardy-Zane Grey' 6ft 10in built cane boat rod, numbered E98212, 56lb test curve, two-piece, agate lined guides, complete with reel-locking spanner and wooden stopper in maker's bag, slight deterioration to whipping. £420. Bonhams, March 1998.

A scarce Hardy angler's pipe contained in the original pictorial trade box and with Hardy nickel silver pipe reamer, unused condition, *c.* 1950. £100. Angling Auctions, April 1998.

A superb P. D. Malloch plaster cast of a salmon, naturalistically painted and mounted into a barrel fronted glazed display case with graduated blue backboard painted maker's details to top left hand corner and legend below fish, 'Killed at Ballathie by Helen Orr-Lewis, August 10th 1920. Weight 34lb' and with gut-eyed salmon fly of capture. £2,800. Angling Auctions, April 1998.

A scarce 5" Allcock 'Aerial' casting reel with perforated drum flange, twin xylenite handles, the backplate having optional check and circular Allcock address enclosing 'The Allcock Aerial', brass foot (stamped 28). £1,200. Evans & Partridge, April 1998.

Auctioneers
Bonhams, 65-69 Lots Road, London SW10 0RN
Evans & Partridge, Agriculture House, High Street, Stockbridge, Hants SO20 6HF
Angling Auctions, PO Box 2905, London W12 8RU
Mullock-Madeley, Church Stretton, Shropshire SY6 7DS
Dealers
Timeless Tackle, 1 Blackwood Crescent, Edinburgh EH9 1QZ
Victor Bonutto, 11 Plymouth Road, Penarth, South Glamorgan CF64 3DA

The Tackle Exchange, Linden House (first floor), 95b Trentham Road, Dresden, Stoke-on-Trent ST3 4EG

See also Angling books.

Talyllyn   A natural 220-acre lake, in a truly beautiful setting, fed by the river Dysynni which rises on the southern slopes of Cader Idris in Snowdonia National Park. Talyllyn offers quality fly fishing for both wild and stocked brown trout. Float tube enthusiasts are welcome.

Except in rough weather conditions, a floating line, fished small, works best. Recommended flies: Harry Tom, Little Olive Palmer, Pheasant Tail nymph and Talyllyn Variant, with a local preference for anything black.

Fishing permits, mostly for residents but with some day tickets, from Tyncornel Hotel.

Tamar   This river, which separates Devon and Cornwall, rises in the north, near Bude, and flows right across the West Country peninsula before entering the sea at Plymouth in the south. The Tamar is one of the principal salmon rivers of the south-west and, together with its two main tributaries, the moorland Lyd and Inny, has sea-trout fishing. In the upper reaches and feeder streams – Ottery, Carey, Kensey, Lynher, Lyd, Wolf and Thrussel – there is also wild brown trout fishing. There are two good fishing hotels, The Arundell Arms at Lifton and Endsleigh House at Milton Abbot, both with their own private salmon and trout fishing for guests. The Tamar flows through rich agricultural land and generally has a touch of colour, so salmon flies must be slightly larger and more visible than on the clear waters of the Exe. The Yellow Torrish single on a 1 or 1/0 hook, or a 1-inch or 1½-inch Garry Dog tube are the most popular flies on the lower river, fished either with a sink-tip or sinking line, stripped fairly fast.

The Reverend Hartwell James, whose parish was near Bridgwater, used to fish the Tamar for trout in the 1920s, and his record catch was 152 trout in one day from 300 yards of river above the junction with the Lyd; all were taken on the fly. He would distribute his catch to the poor and needy of his parish.

Taw and Torridge   Two sister rivers in North Devon with good runs of salmon and sea-trout, at times better than those on many bigger rivers. Salmon and sea-trout run fairly early

on in the season, but you never know until your fly is in the water. Some large sea-trout are taken on quite small flies, a Peter Ross, for example, on a 12 hook. The salmon flies are on small hooks, compared to some rivers, such as 10, 8, and 6 with Stoat's Tail type of dressing (not many fishermen use tubes on these rivers). A change of fly is often the best way of producing a take.

There are several good hotels with private fishing for residents – the Rising Sun, Umberleigh; the Half Moon, Sheepwash; and the Woodford Bridge, Milton Damerel.

Tawe   The river Tawe rises high in the Black Mountains at Llyn-y-Fan Fawr. It is a wonderful example of a waterway that for a hundred years was heavily polluted and has now been reclaimed. Today it is a migratory river, with an extensive trout fishery, offering salmon, sea- and brown trout in an area not formerly noted for such angling. Virtually the whole of the river is controlled by just two angling clubs – from Pontardawe upstream, by the Tawe and Tributaries Angling Association; downstream to Swansea and the barrage by the Pontardawe and Swansea Angling Societies. Day tickets are available locally.

Tay   One of the three great salmon rivers of Scotland, the Tay has many fine salmon beats which at times and in the right conditions, can be highly productive. About 120 miles long, the Tay covers a huge catchment area and is fed by tributaries and lochs which in their own right are great salmon waters – Almond and Dochert, Faskally, Garry, Isla, Lochy, Lyon and Tummel.

The British record salmon was caught on the Tay – a 64-pounder taken in 1922 on a spinner from a boat by Miss G. W. Ballantyne, daughter of the gillie at Caputh. Ashley-Cooper records that two other fish over 60lb have been taken and many over 50lb, which makes it possible to compare the Tay with some of the big Norwegian rivers. If Miss Ballantyne's record is ever to be broken it is most likely to happen on these fast deep waters. On many beats, particularly below Dunkeld, the pools are so big and the river so wide that boat fishing is more or less essential to cover all the lies satisfactorily. In low water they should be waded deep and carefully, with breast waders and a wading staff.

There is good hotel water at Killin, Kenmore, Grandtully

and Dunkeld. John D. Wood and Strutt & Parker, London; J. D. D. Malloch and Renton Finlayson, Perth; Bell-Ingram, Edinburgh, and Country Pursuits, Bridge of Allan, have lettings. The best flies are in the range 6 to 10 with Hairy Mary, Blue Charm, Tosh, Stoat's Tail and Munro Killer the most popular, either singles or doubles. For deep pools, though, one needs a fast-sinking line and a big tube, a 2½ to 3-inch Garry Dog or Black and Silver. As for rods, a 14–16ft double-handed salmon fly rod with a 4¼" wide reel, a minimum of 200 yards of strong backing and 18lb leaders are recommended.

The Perthshire Tourist Board, Lower City Mills, West Mill Street, Perth PH1 5QP, publish a guide on fishing which includes details of hotel and club water on the Tay for salmon and trout.

Teal, Blue and Silver The most popular of teal-dressed trout and sea-trout flies, the standard dressing is:

Body: flat silver tinsel, ribbed fine oval
Whisks: a few strands of golden pheasant tippet
Beard hackle: bright blue feather fibres
Wings: two matching slips of teal breast (or failing teal, a light mallard)
Hook: from 14 upwards for brown trout; low-water salmon hooks 8, 6 or 4 for big sea-trout

The Teal, Blue and Silver is only one in a series. The Teal and Red is another and was the basis for the Peter Ross. The Teal and Green is always worth a try on the loch:

Body: apple green wool, ribbed oval gold
Beard hackle: red feather fibres

The whisks and wings are the same as the Teal, Blue and Silver.

Hook sizes depend where one is fishing. On the drift on a loch it can be as small as 14 for brown trout; for salmon and sea-trout a little larger, up to about 8 or 6.

Teifi A great Welsh river for sea trout with ample association water and permits for visitors. The sea-trout, or sewin in Wales, start to run from late June or early July, and there are some salmon about, but not as many as there were. As well as the usual olives and May duns you will find March browns

and mayflies on several stretches. In April the grannom sedge hatch is truly spectacular, making this an ideal dry fly river right from the start of the season and justly deserving its title 'Queen of Welsh rivers'. Around Newcastle Emlyn and Llandysul there is good association water and the several local hotels can arrange permits for visitors. The Porth Hotel, Llandysul, Dyfed, offers salmon and sea-trout fishing on 30 miles of association water. The Cawdor Estate at Broad Oak, Dyfed, has good fly water. Disabled anglers are catered for by several of the angling clubs: there are casting platforms suitable for those who fish from wheelchairs and a free transport service to and from the river.

Teign A Devon river of great charm, with small wild brown trout and a good run of sea-trout. The upper Teign between Chagford and Steps Bridge provides fine dry fly fishing. The well-named Angler's Rest Inn at Fingle Bridge, Drewsteignton, can supply permits for association water, but it is best to avoid holiday weekends.

Teme Rising in the Welsh hills and flowing down through Ludlow, Tenbury Wells before entering the Severn, the river Teme is noted for its grayling, wild brown trout and several species of coarse fish including chub. There is limited public fishing at Tenbury Wells and Boraston, and at Stanford Bridge the Bridge Inn has water, as does the Talbot Hotel at Knightwick. Both the Ludlow AC and the Birmingham AA have some stretches of the river, and day tickets are often available to visitors.

The Teme's major tributary is the river Onny which joins it in the area of Church Stretton and Craven Arms. This pretty little river also has trout and chub, though on many stretches eroding banks are noticeable. The wild brown trout average 1¼lb and there is some stocking. Midland Flyfishers Club control much of the fishing but day tickets are obtainable in some areas.

Terrestrials A fisherman's name for land-bred insects which at times fall on the water in sufficient numbers to provoke a rise. They include flying ants, mostly in August; crane flies (daddy-longlegs) in late August and September; the hawthorn fly in April-May; beetles at any time; and there can be an occasional odd drop of caterpillars and grasshoppers.

Whether it is worth tying patterns of all these must depend on the angler's inclination. It is possible that substitutions can be made – a Black Palmer for the hawthorn, a large mayfly trimmed with scissors can pass for a crane fly, and a Black and Peacock Spider or a Coachman for a beetle.

See also Ants.

Terry's Terror   A beetle-like pattern of a trout fly, generally fished dry or in the surface film. Designed by Dr Cecil Terry of Bath who fished the Hungerford Town water of the Kennet for many years from the 1920s to the 1950s.

> *Body:* one strand of bronze peacock herl, twisted with yellow tying silk
> *Rib:* a very fine flat copper tinsel
> *Tail:* stubby, consisting of equal parts of orange and yellow bucktail hair
> *Hackle:* medium red cock
> *Hook:* 12 - 16

Test   'A wonderful day truly. Five trout, the smallest 2lb exactly and the biggest 3lb 4oz. Was there ever such a sport as fishing, or a river as the Test?' Those who have not read J. W. Hills' book *A Summer on the Test* have a treat to come. In the 1983 edition (and there have been several since then) Anthony Atha's foreword rightly observes that Hills had a magic way with words as well as giving practical advice which was as good today as it was seventy years ago.

The Test is unique. Here were set standards for fly fishing that have spread world-wide, here fishermen come on pilgrimage.

It is also beautiful – broad in its lower reaches, fed by prolific springs from the chalk hills, and yet the river lies within one small county of Hampshire. Many famous men have fished the Test, and many famous men have cared for it, among them three generations of the Lunn family at the Houghton Club. This is Mick Lunn's description of his river:

> A spring bubbles from the chalk below the little village of Ashe, near Overton, and from this spring comes the Test. The infant stream makes its way to Laverstoke, where Portals make the banknote paper, and then, fed by many more springs, on to Whitchurch, Tufton, Longparish and Chilbolton.
>
> Before you get to Stockbridge the river is fed by three lovely

little tributaries – the Bourne, made famous by Plunket Greene in *Where the Bright Waters Meet*, the Dever and the Anton. Just above Stockbridge is the Leckford water, owned by the John Lewis Partnership, and below that is the Houghton Club water. This club was formed in 1822 and we have a continuous record of every fish caught on the club water from that date up to the present.

Past Stockbridge – under the bridge over the main A30 road – the river comes to the village of Houghton, from which the club takes its name. Then, at Barrington, it is joined by the wonderful little Wallop Brook, broadening the river even more; through now to Compton, Mottisfont and Kimbridge. Then the last real tributary comes in, the Dun, and on the river curves through the broad green valley to Timsbury and Romsey where, at Broadlands, it also becomes famous for the salmon fishing.

What a wonderful river it is – fed all the way by pure crystal clear spring water, filtered from the chalk, extremely alkaline, creating a prolific growth of weed and all the right food insects – olives, iron blues, pale wateries, blue-winged olives, the big mayfly and a host of sedges. The fish feed well on these and on a profusion of shrimps and snails and all those many creatures that fall by chance on the water, the beetles and hawthorn flies and ants.

River weed is all-important for the fishery, a sanctuary and feeding ground, and the river keeper by selective cutting can control the height of his water as well as creating lies for the trout. The weeds I call good are ranunculus, water celery and water carrot; the bad are starwort and Canadian pond weed which collect silt and are not easy to cut.

The upper Test is shallow and provides good breeding ground, and there is a fair survival rate from the spawning redds. I have always thought of the upper river as being upstream from Leckford, the middle from Leckford to and including Kimbridge, the lower downstream from Kimbridge. The upper probably has less fly than the middle or lower, and fly life is reasonably localised, the one exception being the mayfly (*E. danica*) for they have been known to fly miles upriver before egg-laying. These extraordinary migrations of the big mayfly probably only happen once or twice in a lifetime.

May brings the first olives and iron blues, then the fall of the hawthorn and of course the mayfly, in the so-called 'duffer's fortnight,' which is generally at its best between May 18 and June 8. June is less hectic, but towards the end of the month comes the evening fishing with the blue-winged olive, pale watery, and the

fall of the spinner. July and August see some of the best evening fishing but during the day there are black gnat and ants to bring the fish up; and I can remember some Augusts when the black ant had created more rise than the mayfly. September is a law unto itself, for by then the fish that survive are more accustomed to the sight of feathers on a hook and can recognise a clumsy cast. You will then need a finer nylon point, a smaller fly, and a greater attention paid to concealment. Fishing can be difficult in September but isn't that part of its charm?

Membership of clubs and syndicates on the Test is largely by invitation. Some rods are occasionally available for a day or a week through agencies, such as John D. Wood and Strutt & Parker Sporting in London. The Rod Box, a tackle shop at Winchester, also can arrange fishing. The Greyhound Inn at Stockbridge has water available for guests. The Leckford Estates and one or two other estates occasionally let rods for a short period.

See also Chalkstream Fishing; Hills, John Waller; Houghton Club

Test and Itchen Fishing Association Unique in several ways, the association has almost 100 per cent of the riparian owners and lessees of the Itchen and the Test amongst its membership. A high proportion of members also consist of those who fish the rivers as guests or paying rods. It is almost certainly the most powerful and influential angling organisation of its kind in the country, and has in its care two of our most beautiful and famous rivers. It is an organisation to preserve and if possible improve the fisheries on both these rivers and to maintain the scenery and amenities of the river valleys. Secretary: Mr J. G. Glasspool, West Haye, Itchen Abbas, Winchester SO21 1AX.

Thames The first salmon to be caught by an angler in the Thames for 150 years was taken in Chertsey Weir Pool in August 1983 – a symbol not so much of the renaissance of the Thames as a salmon river but of its freedom from pollution.

The return of salmon into the Thames is currently being aided by three bodies; the Environment Agency, Thames Water Utilities and the Thames Salmon Trust. The last is a registered charity involved in raising money to build fish passes over the major obstacles that exist between the tidal river and any

spawning and nursery habitat. Thames Water Utilities have responsibility for the water quality of the river, which is constantly reviewed and is generally improving. The Environment Agency is heavily involved through the Thames Rehabilitation Scheme and is responsible for: the design and implementation of fish passes built on the river; monitoring the return of adult fish through trapping and radio tracking; collecting of broodstock and rearing fry and smolts from Thames and other stocks; and liaison with Thames Water Utilities concerning improvements to water quality and abstraction points. A total of 37 fish passes is planned to allow the salmon to migrate from the tideway to spawning and nursery areas in the river Kennet, which has been identified as having the greatest potential for salmon production.

Some 200,000 juvenile salmon are introduced into the river each year: approximately 60,000 smolts and 140,000 fry. Returns of adults are very variable and, as with most river systems, heavily dependent on river flow, temperature and dissolved oxygen. The confirmed return in 1997 was a disappointingly low 29 adult salmon, but expectations for 1998 were considered to be better. Catches by anglers are generally less than ten fish per year.

There are not many trout in the Thames (though there are in its tributaries, such as the Kennet), but those there are haunt the weir pools and run big. The best places are said to be the weir pools at Bray, Marlow and Molesey, and upstream above Oxford. According to a letter in the *Flyfishers' Journal* (Winter number, 1975) a Mr Lowndes caught a brown trout on a mayfly at Sonning Lock around the year 1881 which weighed over 21lb. The Piscatorial Society has, or had, a 14lb specimen in a glass case. The legendary A. Edward Hobbs kept a meticulous record of his trout catches from 1890 until 1945, details of which appear in his book *Trout of the Thames*. In 55 years he caught 878 trout over 3lb each and in 1902–3, two in excess of 10lb. These and other specimen fish are on private display at Brakspear's Brewery, Henley-on-Thames.

Most Thames trout in past days were taken by spinning a dead bleak or dace. Today spinning a Rapala, or fishing a big salmon fly, especially in the pools at Chertsey or Teddington, might well do. Particular attention should be paid to fishing the white water below the sill and the eddy flows.

Thunder and Lightning Whether its name has anything to do with its longevity, this traditional salmon fly has survived from the late nineteenth century, when it was first dressed by James Wright of Sprouston on the Tweed:

Tag: two turns of flat gold tinsel followed by one of yellow floss
Tail: golden pheasant crest, up-turned
Butt: black ostrich herl
Body: black floss silk
Rib: flat gold tinsel
Hackle: orange feather fibre, tied beard, with blue jay or blue-guinea fowl in front
Wings: brown mallard topped by golden pheasant crest
Side wings (cheeks): jungle cock
Head: black

Thurso A salmon river in Caithness that is notable for the amount of water available to the public through Thurso Fishery estate office. There is a waiting list, and early application is advised. Fishermen have to stay at the Ulbster Arms Hotel at Halkirk. Summer and autumn fishing is best, with small dark flies on floating or sink-tip lines.

Till A small and picturesque stream which enters the Wylye near Great Wishford and is mostly private, but local enquiries may produce a rod. The water has a good head of wild brown trout which rise readily to the fly.

Torridge *See* Taw and Torridge.

Towy From its source in the Cambrian mountains, the Towy travels 60 miles through Llandovery, Llandeilo and Carmarthen. Above Llandovery the river is characterised by rocky gorges and tree-lined pools. On its middle and lower reaches this powerful river, with its broad racing glides and deep pools, is ideal for night fishing; the wading is mainly on gravel, and in many places fishing from the bank is possible. There is plenty of trout fishing for visitors, and salmon and sea-trout permits can generally be had at the Dyfed hotels. The Towy is one of the best sea-trout rivers in Britain, although catches are not what they were ten years ago.

The sea-trout (sewin) are best in May, June and July. Large flies, including tandems, are invaluable for night fishing, with hairwings and black, and silver dressings. Tube flies are

popular. Hamdden of Powys have nearly 15 miles of double bank-fishing on the prime Abercothi and Golden Grove beats.

Treacle Parkin   In Yorkshire a treacle parkin is a biscuit made of oatmeal and treacle, but why the name has been given to a trout fly which has the same dressing as the Red Tag we do not know. Courtney Williams has a long history of it as a grayling fly which emigrated from Wales to the north of England sometime in the mid-1800s. Anyway, here is the Red Tag/Treacle Parkin dressing:

> *Body:* bright green peacock herl
> *Hackle:* bright red cock
> *Tag:* a nice thick stub of bright red wool
> *Hook:* 14 or 16

Sometimes a turn of gold or silver tinsel is added between the tag and the herl.

Trout, Brook (*Salvelinus fontinali*)   The American brook trout, technically a member of the char family, has been imported into Britain for lake or reservoir fishing, and is sometimes crossed with brown or rainbow trout. The international record catch is 14lb 8oz caught in Ontario's Nipigon river in 1916. The British record is held by Ernest Holland, who took an 8lb 3oz cultivated brook trout at Fontburn Reservoir in 1998.

Trout, Brown (*Salmo trutta*)   The brown trout of the Test, the silver sea-trout of Devon, the gillaroo of Ireland, the sewin of Wales all belong to the same species, *Salmo trutta*. Although it was suspected as far back as 1860, it was not until the 1960s that scientists finally agreed that the differences in appearance were imposed by habit and environment.

S. trutta is native to Europe, parts of western Russia, Turkey and North Africa, and has been established artificially, from about 1863 onwards in many other countries, including New Zealand, Australia, North and South America, India and large parts of Africa.

The British record is held by Andrew Findlay, who landed a natural brown trout of 25lb 5oz 12dm from Loch Awe, Scotland in April 1996. Loch Awe was also responsible for the previous record catch of 19lb 10oz 6dm by A. Thorne in 1993. The record cultivated brown catch is 28lb 1oz in 1995 by David Taylor, from Dever Springs, Hampshire.

Trout, Rainbow (*Oncorhynchus mykiss*)   The scientific name covers two forms of rainbow, the steelhead, or migratory rainbow, and the non-migratory.   At one time the non-migratory form was given two names, *shasta* and *irideus;* these are not now accepted scientifically but are still sometimes used by fish breeders, who call spring spawners *irideus* and autumn spawners *shasta.*

Indigenous to North America, but now found throughout Europe, South America, Australia, New Zealand, Japan, Africa and India.   The first successful importation of rainbow eggs from the United States was in 1885, and fish were produced at the Delafield and Howietown hatcheries.

The record cultivated rainbow catch is 36lb 14oz 8dm in 1995 by Clive White, taken from Dever Springs, Hants.   The record resident rainbow catch is 24lb 10oz in 1995 by Kenneth Lynch, caught at Hanningfield, Essex.

Trout Fisherman   A magazine first published in 1978 under the editorship of John Wilshaw, originally intended to cater for the still water fisherman, but from 1981 coverage was extended to include angling on rivers and streams.   The first issue contained articles by Arthur Cove, Dick Walker and Bob Church and featured the impending opening of Rutland Water. The editor, since 1984, is Chris Dawn.   Published by EMAP Active Ltd, Bushfield House, Orton Centre, Peterborough PE2 5UW.

Trout & Salmon   Founded by Howard Marshall, Bernard Venables and R. P. Winfrey, then chairman of East Midland Allied Press, its publishers.   The first issue appeared in July 1955 and the editor was Scotsman, Ian Wood, who remained in the chair until retirement in 1969.   He was succeeded successively by Jack Thorndike (previously editor of *Angling Times*), Roy Eaton, John Wilshaw (who had helped launch *Trout Fisherman*) and, in 1986, Sandy Leventon. *Trout & Salmon* has risen in size and stature ever since its inception 43 years ago.   Published by EMAP Active Ltd, Bushfield House, Orton Centre, Peterborough   PE2 5UW.

Tup's Indispensable   R. S. Austin, tobacconist and fly dresser of Tiverton, tied a fly in the 1890s which was probably an imitation of the spinner of the pale watery.   Skues tried it out, sang its praises in *The Field,* and Austin and his daughter were

overwhelmed with orders. Skues gave it the name Tup's because part of the wool used in the dressing came from the genitals of a tup (ram) and indispensable because he could not be without it when trout were rising to pale watery spinners on the Itchen.

Body: a mixture of rams' wool, cream seal fur, lemon spaniel fur and a few pinches of crimson seal fur
Hackle: light blue cock freckled with gold
Tying silk: bright yellow, two turns exposed at the tail
Whisks: light blue cock spade feather, rather long
Hook: 16

Tweed The Tweed, queen of salmon rivers, rises high in the Southern Uplands and flows right through the heart of the Scottish Borders before finally discharging into the sea at Berwick. Its salmon pools attract anglers from all over the world. It is claimed that more salmon are taken with the fly on the Tweed than on any other river in Britain.

The Tweed has a long season, which runs from the beginning of February through to the end of November. The high season months of October and November for salmon and sea-trout are expensive but cheaper fishing can be had in the spring and summer. Some of the best summer sea-trout fishing is found on the Tweed's tributaries, the Till and the Whiteadder in particular, and later in the year throughout the main river itself.

In the past the Tweed has suffered from over-abstraction, pollution and heavy spates which fall away too fast, much to the annoyance of the salmon fisher. Concerted effort by the several interested parties has effected tremendous improvement of late, so much so that at the fifth International Salmon Symposium in Eire (September 1997) the Tweed Foundation, a charitable trust established in 1993 to promote the development of salmon and trout stocks in the river Tweed, was given the Atlantic Salmon Federation's award for outstanding achievement in the field of salmon conservation anywhere in the North Atlantic.

The Scottish Office has announced an Order to prohibit the use of worms as angling bait, and lures incorporating multiple hooks, in parts of the river Tweed. Lord Sewel, Scottish Fisheries Minister welcomed the initiative by the Tweed Commissioners in taking action to preserve spring salmon stocks, 'These measures will assist anglers in returning valuable spring fish to the river'. The Order came into force in February 1998.

The River Tweed Commissioners are charged under the Tweed Fisheries Acts (1857, 1859 and 1969) with the general preservation and increase of salmon, sea-trout, trout and other freshwater fish in the Tweed and its tributaries, the removal of nuisances and obstructions and the prevention of illegal fishing. The area of jurisdiction extends five miles out to sea and includes the coastline.

The 1997 run of spring fish was disappointing with rod catches of 1,050. In contrast catches in the second half of the year (July–November) were up on 1996 at almost 8,500 fish.

Waiting lists for the famous private beats are long but – a sign of the times – some have been advertised in recent years. Bell-Ingram of Edinburgh and Strutt & Parker of London handle lettings, including the famous Junction Pool.

There are fishing hotels at Cornhill, Melrose and Kelso.

An angling guide is issued by the Scottish Borders Tourist Board, Tourist Information Centre, Murray's Green, Jedburgh TD8 6BE.

UDN Ulcerative Dermal Necrosis, which in ordinary terms means the death of part of a living body. The first reported occurrence was in the early 1960s when gillies on an Irish river saw a salmon swimming about in an aimless fashion, its head covered with a white fungus. Eventually the disease occurred all over Ireland and spread to Wales, to Scotland and then England. Thousands of dead fish covered the banks of rivers everywhere.

The scientific explanation is that certain marine worms contain a substance known as porphyrin and, after a population explosion among these worms, salmon feeding on them absorb large quantities of porphyrin which causes their skin to become over-sensitive in strong sunlight. The lesions which this created are then attacked by fungus for which there was no cure.

Gradually, as with myxamatosis, the epidemic lessened and finally disappeared, and there have been no further outbreaks in recent years.

Uist *See* Western Isles.

Usk Skues was among the many visitors who have paid tribute to the fishing on the Usk. Well he might – it is one of the most charming of the Welsh rivers, and to fish the March Brown in spring when the naturals are hatching can be a great experience. It was there that such famous names as Bernard Venables, Lionel Sweet and Oliver Kite honed their skills with the dry fly and the nymph. Summer and autumn evenings on the Usk are filled with sherry spinners and numerous species of sedges interspersed, with a host of other flies.

Hamdden of Brecon, Powys, have fishing below Brecon. The salmon fishing is preserved but can be had at Gliffaes Hotel, Crickhowell, a country-house fishing hotel with 2½ miles of its own water. The Three Salmons Hotel, Usk, is conveniently situated between the Usk and the Wye.

Usk Grub   One of Lionel Sweet's salmon flies for the Usk water, and for many other salmon rivers too:

Body: rear half black floss; nearest the eye, yellow or orange seal fur
Tail: golden pheasant breast feather, wound as hackle
Tag: flat silver tinsel
Rib: round silver tinsel
Centre body hackle: light furnace or grizzle cock
Front hackle: same as centre body, but longer in the fibre
Wings: two long jungle-cock feathers
Head: black varnish
Hook: generally about 8 or 6, singles, but larger in heavy water

V

Venables, Bernard Painter, sculptor, author, journalist, Bernard Venables has fished in many countries for many kinds of fish but is convinced that fly fishing for trout is without rival. He began to write about fishing when working for the *Daily Express*. In 1946 he left to become angling correspondent of the *Daily Mirror*, creating the Mr Crabtree fishing strip. He left the *Mirror* to become, with Howard Marshall, co-founder of the *Angling Times* and later *Trout & Salmon*. He then founded *Creel* magazine which he edited for eighteen months. He was a regular broadcaster on television and radio, including *Angler's Corner* for BBC Television. His publications include *Mr Crabtree Goes Fishing, A Fisherman's Testament, Angling Waters, Fish and Fishing, The Gentle Art of Angling, Fishing Past and Present, The Angler's Companion, Fishing For Trout, The Piccolo Fishing Book* and *Bernard Venables: The Illustrated Memoirs of A Fisherman*.

Venables, Colonel Robert (1612/13–1687) One of Cromwell's commanders, Robert Venables took part in battles at Chester and in Ireland during the Civil War. An expedition which he led to the West Indies failed, and Venables was disgraced and for a time imprisoned in the Tower of London. He found time to write a useful and practical book on fishing, part of it on fly fishing. *The Experienced Angler* (1662), to which Walton wrote the foreword, is much sought after by the collector, and even the fifth edition (1683) can cost as much as £1,500. The book contains a soundly-based fly fishing philosophy:

> . . . the fish will sometimes take the fly much better at the top of the water, and at another time a little better under the superficies of the water; and in this your own observation must be your constant and daily instructor; for if they will not rise to the top try them under.

Sometimes it was right to fish upstream, sometimes down. On salmon fishing he wrote:

> The salmon takes the artificial fly very well, but you must use a troll, as for Pike, or he, being a strong fish, will hazzard your line, except you give him length; his flies must be much larger than you use for other fish, the wings very long, two or four, behind one another, with very long tails; his chiefest ground-bait is a great garden or lob worm.

By ground-bait he meant fishing the worm along the ground – the bottom of the river.

Veniard, John   John Veniard was a prolific, and a very successful author, and his *Fly Dressers' Guide* (1952) introduced a post-war generation to the art of fly-tying. *A Further Guide to Fly Dressing* appeared in 1964, followed by *Reservoir and Lake Flies* (1970) in response to the explosion of interest in reservoir and still water fishing. His regular column 'Fly-Tyers Forum' in *Trout & Salmon* magazine was the inspiration for *Fly Tying Problems and Their Answers* (1970).

Collaboration with the artist Donald Downs resulted in a number of books, unique at the time, which were a masterly combination of concise and knowledgeable texts with superb step-by-step drawings of tying sequences.

The firm of E. Veniard Ltd was formed by John's father and his older brother – the two Ernests – in 1925 and specialised in the supply of exotic feathers to the millinery trade, but after the Second World War fashions had changed and it was decided to concentrate on fly-tying materials. Veniard was the first company to select and pre-pack materials for the fly-tyer; John was responsible for the introduction of fluorescent materials to the UK in 1950 and later produced a specialist range of dyes for feather and fur.

John Veniard was the first president of the Fly Dressers' Guild formed in 1975 (Donald Downs was the second), and in 1973 was honoured by a request from HRH Prince Charles who wanted to learn how to tie flies, which he did with great competence after several lessons from 'the father of modern fly-tying'.

Viva A very successful lure devised by Victor Furse in the early 1970s. John Roberts says it is particularly useful during the early months, whilst Bob Church uses it throughout the season. The fluorescent green tag is a vital ingredient.

Body: black chenille
Wing: four black cock hackles; or black marabou
Tying silk: black
Tag: fluorescent green wool
Hook: long shank 6 - 10

Wading The deeper the wading in fast water, the stranger it feels – the more uncertain the balance, the more clumsy the legs and feet – until a point is reached where the water takes command, lifts the angler up and carries him downstream. Water is an alien element and no wading is safe.

Waders come with a variety of soles: the cheapest have rubber cleated soles but these are positively dangerous on slippery surfaces, and even the addition of studs does not give the grip provided by the synthetic felted sole. A combination sole of felt and metal studs is recommended for very fast, slippery water.

Safety fishing jackets are now available, ranging from the ordinary buoyancy aid to the rip-pull-operated or the automatic inflatable, which will turn you over and keep your head out of the water, even if you are unconscious. (One model is certified to inflate automatically within five seconds of water immersion). Essential for boat fishing.

Some basic rules to follow when wading:

Use a wading stick on a lanyard, and wade into the river with your back to the current. Put the wading stick at an angle in front of you and lean on it to make a tripod. Use it as a third leg.

Move out slowly, shuffling the feet, always with your back to the current. Never turn round to face the current, as you will lose the security – the tripod effect – of the third leg.

When you reach the place you want to be, place both feet carefully before giving up the tripod and putting the staff behind you.

When moving downstream to cover a pool, a step at a time, use the tripod and shuffle, keeping the feet well down, feeling the way with your feet, never hurrying or making uncontrolled steps.

When coming out of the water, shuffle out sideways, always

with the current coming from behind.

When using the staff as your third leg, always waggle it a little to make sure it has a firm grip, then shuffle one foot, then another. Remember that the normal walking balance of your body does not exist in water.

When a salmon takes and you are in deep water you must not move until the salmon is tiring and under some sort of control. Then – and only then – holding the rod lightly in one hand, the wading staff in the other, you can shuffle out towards the bank. If the salmon takes off, stand still until it is under control again.

Many big salmon rivers have hazards caused by gravel banks and sudden deep holes. Some gravel banks on the bend of a river are highly unstable; the gravel will slide away under the least pressure. 'Whalebacks' are another hazard – gravel is piled up facing downstream in a long ridge, shaped like the back of a whale – an angler wades down, but finds the current too strong to wade back again. Scours, shifting gravel, sudden potholes – all can cause accidents.

If you are carried away by the current and are not wearing a safety jacket:

As soon as possible, turn on your back.

Do not try to swim, keep floating. There will be enough air in your waders and clothes to allow you to float for a long time, providing you don't struggle or try to swim.

Let the current take you downstream, feet first. Sooner or later you will drift towards a bank; help yourself to do so by paddling with the hands.

Do not try and climb a high bank; pull yourself along until you come to a shallow flat.

Crawl out, lie on your back, and drain the water out of your waders. Then stand up and get home or to a fishing lodge as soon as possible. You will be shocked, bitterly cold, but alive. If you had panicked and shouted for help, struggled and tried to swim you might not be.

There are hazards for the trout angler on peaceful-looking rivers and lakes. On one stretch of the Itchen, for example, it is fatal to wade. A fisherman would sink quickly in soft mud. On one of the Hampshire lakes a man wearing boots waded in to net a fish and was quickly into mud over both ankles; he had to be pulled out, leaving his boots behind – which gradually sank out of sight.

Wales Wales has much to offer the game angler by way of
more than 200 salmon and trout rivers, hundreds of upland
lakes and numerous small still water fisheries. Add warm
Welsh hospitality and beautiful countryside and you have the
perfect ingredients for a memorable fishing excursion. The
Usk and the Taff provide excellent dry fly sport. The Towy
and the Dyfi are renowned for big sewin which will really put
your talents to the test. Dry fly fishing for the grayling, a
much underrated fish until comparatively recent times, is
nowhere better than on the Dee and the tributaries of the
Severn and Wye. For autumn salmon the Seiont, Teifi, Conwy
or the Tâf are hard to beat. (Gareth Edwards is reported as
saying he would rather catch a salmon on a Welsh river than
score a try at Cardiff Arms Park, so the angling must really be
something special.)

The Welsh mountain lakes, and there are well over a
hundred of them, offer truly wild trout – not of gigantic size,
but what they lack in weight is more than compensated for in
the exhilaration of the capture. The only problem about Wales
is that of choice, for the Principality has too many options for
the game angler.

You are required to check the local Environment Agency
Wales fishing by-laws before you begin fishing. These by-laws
are intended to protect fish stocks, and they cover a wide
range of subjects, including: the need to submit catch returns
for salmon and sea-trout (or sewin as they are called in Wales);
restrictions on fishing methods and baits at certain times of the
year (use of a gaff is prohibited at all times); requirements for
keep-nets, keep-sacks and landing nets; restrictions on fishing
near weirs and certain other obstructions; and close seasons for
salmon and trout.

In recent years the Environment Agency Wales has released
thousands of tagged salmon and sea-trout into rivers. The tag,
which is buried in the nose of the fish, is not visible, and so to
make these tagged fish identifiable the adipose fin (the small,
rubbery fin near the tail) is clipped off, (this does not harm the
fish in any way). If you catch a salmon or sea-trout with its
adipose fin missing, then dial 100 and ask the operator for
Freephone Fishwatch. Give your name and address and the
details of your catch – where, when, species and size. Keep the
fish (or just its head), frozen if necessary, and arrangements
will be made for it to be inspected. You will be paid a reward
if the fish carries a tag – and you may, of course, keep the fish.

If you see damage or danger to the natural environment – pollution, poaching, fish in distress, flooding incidents or illegal dumping – then report it by telephoning 0800 80 70 60. Lines are open all day, every day, and this emergency hotline may be used throughout the country and is not just confined to Wales. A comprehensive angling guide, edited by Pat O'Reilly, is available free of charge from the Wales Tourist Board, 2 Fitzalan Road, Cardiff CF2 1UY.

Recommended reading: *Moc Morgan's Trout and Salmon Flies of Wales*.

Walker, C. F. A chalk stream fisherman, C. F. Walker made an important contribution to the knowledge of lake fishing with the publication of *Lake Flies and Their Imitation*. Based on studies which he and Alex Behrendt carried out at Two Lakes, Hampshire, Walker designed a new series of flies for still water fishing, based on 26 patterns, of which the midge and sedge pupae are the best known. His midge pupa dressing has been widely copied and adapted:

> *Abdomen:* gut or nylon in various thicknesses and shades
> *Thorax:* ostrich, condor or peacock herl
> *Wings and legs:* a short hen hackle with the top fibres clipped off, or none
> *Hook:* 12–16

Walker's other works include *Fly Tying as an Art, Chalk Stream Flies, An Angler's Odyssey, The Angling Letters of G. E. M. Skues* and *Brown Trout and Dry Fly*.

Walker, Richard Angling correspondent of the *Angling Times* for more than 30 years, Richard Walker is probably best known for his capture in 1952 of the record British carp (44lb) which he presented to the London Aquarium. Walker wrote a number of books on coarse fishing and several on fly fishing, including *Modern Fly Dressings* and Dick Walker's *Trout Fishing*, edited by Peter Maskell and with a foreword by Peter Lapsley.

Walton, Izaak (1593–1683) No other fishing book anywhere or at any time has had the success of Walton's *Compleat Angler*. It was first published in 1653 and in Britain alone it has been reprinted more than a hundred times; worldwide there have been over 400 editions in some sixty languages. The second part of the book – on fly fishing and written by Charles Cotton – first appeared in the fifth edition of 1676.

Walton was born at Stafford and became an ironmonger in London ('on the north side of Fleet Street, two doors west of Chancery Lane') close to St Dunstan's Church. He cultivated literary men such as Michael Drayton, Henry Wotton, Ben Johnson and John Donne, and he wrote a number of books, including the lives of Donne and Wotton. In his later years he retired and lived with George Morley, Bishop of Winchester, at 7 The Close, Winchester, a house which still stands. He is buried in the cathedral's south aisle. There is a memorial window to him in the cathedral and a service to commemorate the tercentenary of his death was held there in July 1983.

Walton had a hazardous life – he was a Royalist, who managed to escape the purges carried out under Cromwell – and had more than his share of grief. When he wrote *The Compleat Angler* (which he always regarded as one of his less important books) he was nearing 60, had outlived two wives and seven of his eight children, and his two close friends and fishing companions were dead. It is more than likely that he wrote to escape from loneliness, for he had little to do, having retired from his business. Perhaps that is partly the reason for the charm of the book, its singing milkmaids and shepherds, friendly inns and good companions. Through it all moves Walton himself (Piscator), dispensing good advice, gossip and queer tales of distant parts and strange happenings.

To say, as some fishermen have, that a good deal of the fishing part of the book is nonsense is to miss the point: it is a picture of Arcady, of a world of romance, a world in which Piscator could escape from the drab and ugly and dangerous times in which he lived. Whether, as Walton said, pike are born from the pickerel weed or flies from drops of dew, is of no real consequence. What comes shining through all the pages of the book is the quality of the man himself:

> I will walk the meadows by some gliding stream, and there contemplate the lilies that take no care, and those very many other various little living creatures that are not only created, but fed, man knows not how, by the goodness of the god of nature, and therefore trust in him. This is my purpose; and so let everything that hath breath praise the Lord.

Walthamstow Complex   This Thames Water fishery, with three trout waters, in north London is just two minutes away from the nearest underground station and provides some of the best angling in the capital. (Fishing on the largest of the three reservoirs, East Warwick, is reserved for members of the Walthamstow Fly-Fisher's Club.) Stocked with rainbows throughout the year. Tackle shop on site and free car parking, with preferential parking for the disabled.

Waterlog The latest angling magazine, launched in December 1996, and published bi-monthly by Waterlog, The Grange, Ellesmere, Shropshire SY12 9DE. The co-editors are Chris Yates, of the BBC series *A Passion for Angling*, and Jon Ward-Allen.

Watson's Fancy A Scottish fly adopted by the Irish for fishing the drift, either at the tail or as the middle dropper. There are several variants but this is more or less the original pattern:

> *Body:* red fur on the rear, black fur on the front, both ribbed with silver tinsel
> *Tail:* golden pheasant crest
> *Wings:* crow with a tiny jungle-cock feather on each side of the wing
> *Tying:* black thread
> *Hook:* 12 - 8

Weaver, Mike MBE After a long career in publishing Mike joined the West Country Tourist Board in 1972 and retired as Deputy Director in 1995; in that year he was awarded the MBE for services to tourism. He is chairman of the Wild Trout Society, the River Teign Riparian Owners Association and the Upper Teign Fishing Association, and a member of the Regional Fisheries Advisory Committee, Devon Fisheries Forum, Devon Area Environment Group, Teign Catchment Steering Group, Dartmoor National Park Authority, National Trust Committee for Devon and Cornwall, South West Rivers Association Council and the South West Water Recreation and Conservation Forum.

Author of the much praised *The Pursuit of Wild Trout*, Mike has written for, and supplied photographs to, all the major angling magazines in this country, as well as the American journals *Flyfisher* and *Fly, Rod and Reel*. Contributor to the *Haig Guide to Trout Fishing in Britain*, *West Country Fly Fishing* and *The Complete Fly Fisher*.

Welshman's Button   Courtney Williams was quite right to say that the true Welshman's Button is a beetle (the word button being a distortion of 'butty', meaning friend). Applied, as it was by Halford to a sedge, a Welshman's Button is out of context. For the sedge, try Caperer. Williams gives Taverner's dressing for the friendly beetle:

Body: greenish-bronze peacock herl
Hackle: black cock
Wing cases: red feather from a partridge tail
Hook: 13

The wing cases should be a shining dark red (a beetle red) and if partridge tail is unavailable other red feather fibres, varnished, would be reasonable.

Welsh Partridge   A general-pattern trout fly recommended by Courtney Williams for limestone and spate rivers and still waters, fished wet or dry. One suspects it might be quite a good pattern to use during a hatch of March Brown.

Body: claret seal fur ribbed with fine gold wire
Head hackle: two – the back one a short, stiff claret hackle, the front one from a snipe's rump feather or the back of a partridge
Whisks: two strands from a partridge tail

West, Leonard   Author of *The Natural Trout Fly and Its Imitations*, which was privately printed in 1912, revised and enlarged in 1921. West was among the first fly dressers to call attention to the importance of midge patterns. His book gives drawings and coloured plates of something like 100 trout flies, side by side with the natural insects they represent, and of all the main hackle feathers used in fly dressing.

West Country Rivers Trust   Formed in 1994, the Trust works closely with farmers to improve the beauty and quality of West Country rivers. A pathfinder project, 'Tamar 2000', is already in progress to improve the quality of the Tamar. The director is Arlin Rickard, West Country Rivers Trust, Bradford Lodge, Blisland, Bodmin, Cornwall PL30 4LF.

Western Isles   There is game fishing to be had on all the main islands (Lewis, Harris, North Uist, Benbecula and South Uist, and Barra) of the Outer Hebrides – brown trout, sea-trout and salmon. None of the catches are likely to make the record

book, but what they lack in size is more than compensated for by the stunning settings and the fact all the fish are wild. Much of the brown trout fishing is free, but out of politeness do make enquiries locally before setting out for the day.

Here, as in the rest of Scotland, it is illegal to fish for salmon and sea-trout on Sundays, and although the taking of brown trout is not, out of courtesy, respect the local religious beliefs by refraining (an exception is Barra where Sunday brown trout fishing is acceptable).

A rod of between 9' 6" and 10', rated AFTM 5–6 with floating and intermediate lines and a leader of 3–6lb is all you will need for brown trout fishing. The local Clan Chief and Green French Glory are highly regarded and you need only supplement these with a few universals, such as Black Zulu, Soldier Palmer, Blae and Black, Alexandra and Golden Olive Bumbles.

The best months are May, June, early July and September, and the season runs from 15 March to 5 October.

The tackle used on most reservoirs will be satisfactory for sea-trout and salmon: a 10–11' rod rated AFTM 6–8 with floating and intermediate lines and two or three fly leaders of 6–12lb. A 10 Pearly Muddler on the bob is a local favourite. For the salmon fly proper, try Hairy Mary, Blue Charm, Thunder and Lightning and Garry Dog in sizes 10 and 8. Salmon begin to run here towards the end of June, and from then through to late September are the best months.

For accommodation write to The Western Isles Tourist Board, 26 Cromwell Street, Stornoway, Isle of Lewis HS1 2DD.

Recommended reading: *Trout Fishing in Lewis*, Norman Macleod, *70 Lochs: A Guide to Fishing in South Uist*, John Kennedy and *Fisher in the West*, Eddie Young.

Wet-fly Fishing

The whole art of the upstream wet fly is to give the flies as long a natural drift as possible, while covering as much water as possible. Just a little drag doesn't matter too much. It may even help to give the flies an extra bit of life. But a long pronounced drag just won't do (Reg Righyni, *Trout & Salmon*, October 1983).

Upstream wet-fly fishing for trout was developed to a peak of perfection in the Borders and North Country by the very early 1800s (it is difficult to give a precise date, and it may well have been earlier). By the mid-1850s it had reached a sophistication

which has never been surpassed, although modern rods and lines have made for easier presentation.

The Border and North Country streams are fairly fast, with a good deal of broken water and riffles. The fly patterns, sometimes one on the point, sometimes two or three (point, middle and bob) are cast upstream and float down without drag. They are hackle patterns which suggest drowned winged insects. The angler wades upstream, fishing the water or the rise, using a fairly long rod and casting a short line, delicately, so that the trout is unaware of his approach. That is the classic method of upstream wet-fly which Skues revived for the chalk streams in the form, ultimately, of fishing the inert unweighted nymph just below the surface.

For the Border and North Country upstream wet-fly fisherman it does not matter whether his flies float or sink, but he likes to prevent them sinking too deep and will frequently grease the upper part of his leader to prevent this.

A variation of this method involves working the fly. In most cases different patterns are used – types that suggest water beetles, larvae, pupae or nymphs, as with weighted nymph fishing. These are often used in pools between riffles, allowed to sink deep, and retrieved fast or slow or in jerks.

The great exponent of the upstream wet-fly in the classic style was an Edinburgh lawyer, W. C. Stewart, who fished the Border rivers from about 1800 until shortly before his death in 1872. His book, *The Practical Angler, or the Art of Trout Fishing*, published in 1857, had great influence and was reprinted many times in the next 80 years. He was the first to emphasise in print the importance of fishing upstream:

> The angler is less likely to be seen by the trout, is able to hook the fish better, does not disturb the water over which he has to fish, and is able to present his flies to the trout in a more natural manner.

Stewart, very much the practical angler, had no idea what his hackle flies represented; he called them spiders. He fished these with several droppers using a 12ft greenheart rod. The flies should 'fall first upon the water' and as little of the line as possible, so that the rod must be kept well up:

> After your flies alight, allow them to float gently downstream for a yard or two, taking care that neither they nor the lines ripple the surface. There is no occasion for keeping them on the surface, they will be quite as attractive a few inches under the water. As the

flies come downstream, raise the point of your rod so as to keep the line straight, and as little of it in the water as possible; and when they have traversed a few yards of water, throw them again about a yard or two higher up than where your flies alighted the previous cast, and so on.

Stewart's flies – the hackled or spider patterns – had been in use on Border rivers long before his time, and he pays tribute to a James Baillie, generally regarded as the most able fly fisherman in Scotland, who fished the Border rivers in the early 1800s (possibly the late 1700s). These were Baillie's and Stewart's patterns:

Black Spider: James Baillie's favourite, the hook covered with brown silk, the head hackle being 'the small feather of the cock starling'
Red Spider: a yellow silk body and the hackle from 'the small feather from the outside wing of the landrail'
Dun Spider: dun silk body and the hackle from 'the soft dun or ash-coloured feather from the outside wing of the dotterel', or the small feather from the inside of the starling

The main North Country methods of wet fly fishing were codified in 1885 by T. E. Pritt, angling editor of the *Yorkshire Post*. Pritt's *Yorkshire Trout Flies*, a valuable book costing £850 at 1998 prices, contained some 62 patterns which he had collected from anglers in the Dales; the second edition (1886) was entitled *North Country Flies*. Included were such classic flies as Orange Partridge, Poult Bloa and Dark Watchet. Perhaps the best book ever published on North Country fly fishing was *Brook and River Trouting* by Edmonds and Lee in 1916.

In Devon, a good account was given of upstream wet-fly fishing on the Mole and Bray in *The Art of Trout Fishing on Rapid Streams*, by H. C. Cutcliffe. He used hackle flies, with body dubbings of fur. *West Country Fly Fishing* has an informative article by David Pilkington on the upstream wet fly.

Variations of the classic method – the inert drift - were suggested in an article in *The Field* (25 August 1982). On fast streams like the Wharfe the olives hatch rapidly and do not ride the water as on the slower chalk streams.

The trout will often be seen rising, but are taking the ascending nymphs and not the surface fly. In such cases a traditional pattern – such as a winged Dark Watchet – cast above a rise and stripped back fast will often be effective.

The wet fly fished downstream (the lure) is the basic method of fishing for salmon and sea-trout where the lies are uncertain and the whole river has to be fished. The flies are cast towards the opposite bank and allowed to swing round in the current until well below the angler who then retrieves the fly, takes a step downstream, and casts again. The method is sometimes varied by drawing in the fly as it sweeps across the stream, giving it life.

Wharfe   The Wharfe is one of the finest, many would say *the* finest, of the Yorkshire trout streams, a lovely clear-water river flowing through some 50 or 60 miles of the Dales, past Bolton Abbey to join the Ouse near Cawood. A correspondent writes:

> Yorkshire anglers know how to fish the Wharfe as to the manner born, but the southerner who comes from the chalk streams has to learn. For one thing the river can be fast, and the wading over the gravel difficult. For another, the southerner will not find the duns riding the stream as they do on the Test or Itchen. There are plenty of nymphs about but they come up and hatch like lightning, no sooner getting their backs out of the water than the wings are up and away they go. Therefore, you will understand why your dry fly is pretty useless. Instead, fish the wet fly upstream, one if you like, but no more than three on a cast, and cast to and above any rise you may see. And if there is no take to a drifting sunk fly, strip it in fast, as though it was one of the river's fast- moving nymphs.

Most anglers seem to fish a point fly and a dropper, but there is no harm in using three flies if you like, or alternatively just one on the point. It is a prerequisite of fishing a Yorkshire river, especially the Wharfe, that you use the Yorkshire patterns that have been tried and tested for a couple of hundred years (and most likely far longer than that). They include Dark Watchet, Poult Bloa, Partridge and Orange, and Snipe and Purple.

The fly fishing is best in the middle and upper river – the closer to the Ouse the less interesting it becomes. Visitors can fish the Bolton Abbey Estate water (avoiding Bank holidays and hot summer weekends). The Devonshire Arms at Bolton Abbey has tickets. There are also good hotels at Burnsall, Ilkley and Grassington which issue permits for association water where there are some very good stretches and the occasional big trout.

Wheelyboats *See* Disabled, Angling for

Whipping A method of joining braided backing to the fly line – see diagram below.

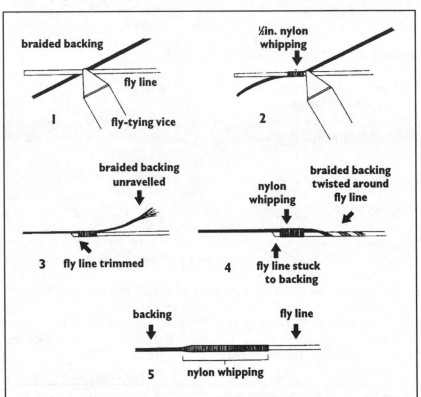

braided backing

fly line

I fly-tying vice

¼in. nylon whipping

2

braided backing unravelled

3 fly line trimmed

nylon whipping

braided backing twisted around fly line

4 fly line stuck to backing

backing

fly line

5 nylon whipping

Whipping. Joining braided backing to fly line. Needle knots can be used for joining nylon monofilament backing to a fly line but in the case of a braided backing the knot may be too bulky to pass through the top rod ring. In that case the backing must be whipped to the line. *1.* Place the ends of both lines in a fly vice. *2.* Using fine nylon, whip both lines togeher for about ½ inch. *3.* Trim the end of the fly line and unravel the braided backing. *4.* Use a strong adhesive to cover the joint, sticking the fly line to the backing, twisting and securing the braided ends round the line, making sure they are stuck fast. *5.* The whole joint is now whipped in the vice and varnished. Sometimes two coats of varnish are needed to make the whipping quite smooth.

Whisky Fly   A popular lure, designed in the 1970s by Albert Whillock for Hanningfield reservoir:

Body: silver tinsel
Tail: red or orange nylon fibres
Hackle: long red or orange fibres, well spread
Hook: long-shank 10, 8 or 6

As with most reservoir lures, this is a very useful fly for sea-trout fishing at night.

Wickham's Fancy   A trout fly designed well over a hundred years ago, by either a Captain Wickham or a Dr T. C. Wickham; Skues believes it was the latter. There is some confusion about the names; both fished the chalk streams of Hampshire.

The Wickham is often used during a sedge hatch, either wet or dry:

Body: flat gold tinsel, sometimes ribbed gold wire, palmer dressed from head to toe with ginger or ginger-red cock hackle
Whisks: red cock
Wings: starling primary, sometimes upright, but most commonly sloping back in sedge-fly style
Shoulder hackle: red cock, a few turns longer than the body hackle tied in front of the wings
Hook: 12, 14 or 16

On still waters it is best fished slowly in the surface film.

Wiggin, Maurice   *The Angler's Bedside Book*, edited by Maurice Wiggin, was one of the best anthologies about fishing for years. All the contributions were specially written by fishermen of the quality of Bernard Venables, Howard Marshall, Macdonald Hastings, Oliver Kite, Hugh Falkus, Fred Sawyer and others. It was excellently produced with many black and white photographs and line drawings.

Wild Trout Society   Formed in 1997 by Charles Rangeley-Wilson, together with Mike Weaver, Richard Slocock, Ronnie Butler, and Ron Holloway, to protect and enhance stocks of wild brown trout.

The Society, which is sponsored by Sage, already has a number of active projects in hand. These include the Dart (with the Duchy of Cornwall and the Environment Agency), the Avon (supporting a project by the Salisbury and District

Angling Club to restore a stretch of water below Amesbury) and the lower Don near Aberdeen (assisted by Famous Grouse Whisky, who are also sponsoring a new award for wild trout conservation, the publication of an annual yearbook and the preparation of a trout habitat management guidelines brochure).

Individual, club and commercial membership details are available from The Wild Trout Society, 92–104 Carnwath Road, London SW6 3HW

Williams, A. Courtney (1892–1951)   Williams introduced a classification of flies and their appropriate dressings in his *Dictionary of Trout Flies*, first published in 1949 and still in print. He wrote the book while he was with the well-established tackle firm of Allcock's of Redditch, where he was latterly a director in charge of advertising.

Williams' Favourite   A spider-type wet fly designed by Courtney Williams' father, often fished dry in small sizes, when it suggests a black gnat or midge. Midland reservoir fishermen with an identical pattern call it a Black Spider. This is Courtney Williams':

> *Body:* black silk, ribbed fine silver wire (or thin tinsel in the larger sizes)
> *Hackle:* black cock for the dry fly, black hen for the wet
> *Whisks:* none
> *Hook:* 12 to 18

Willie Ross   A gillie at the Altnaharra Hotel, Sutherland, from the early 1930s to his death in the 1950s, Willie Ross still has the record for the largest number of fish taken by his rods on Loch Hope and Loch Naver – one of them a 33½lb salmon from Loch Naver. He tied a variation of the Black Pennell (adding a scarlet hackle as a front hackle) which is excellent in small sizes for the wet fly and large, and bushy, for the dap.

> *Body:* black floss silk or black wool
> *Rib:* fine silver tinsel
> *Tail:* golden pheasant tippet
> *Hackle:* two – black behind and scarlet in front
> *Hook:* 6 or 8 long-shank low-water salmon hooks for the dap; 10 or 12 long-shank or standard for the wet fly

Wilson, Dermot MC   He started the first mail-order fishing tackle business in 1968, and ran it until 1981. Wilson was a former chairman of the ACA, a brilliant dry fly angler, Vice President of the Salmon & Trout Association and an honorary member of the Theodore Gordon Flyfishers' Club of America. His book *Dry Fly Beginnings* (1957) was revised and enlarged and reissued as *Fishing the Dry Fly* (1965). He died in 1996, aged 71.

Wiltshire Fishery Association   Formed in 1950 by two keen dry-fly fishermen, Colonel George Perkins, who became the first chairman, and Norman Rawlence, a partner in the well-known West Country estate agents Rawlence and Squarey, who became Treasurer.

Woodcock and Green   One of several (and probably the best) of the woodcock series – Woodcock and Red, Woodcock and Orange. Useful for rivers and lochs and lakes:

Body: green wool or fur
Rib: fine silver wire
Whisks: a few strands of golden pheasant tippet
Hackle: ginger or red hen
Wing: two slips from the inside feathers from a woodcock's wing
Hook: 14 to 8

Woolley, Roger   The author of *Modern Trout Fly Dressings* (1930). Roger was a professional fly-tier and hairdresser at Hatton in Derbyshire and was highly praised by many fishermen of his day. He used hackle points for the wings of his dry flies.

Wright, James (1829–1902)   A fishing-tackle-maker of Sprouston on the Tweed who tied the first Greenwell's Glory to the design of Canon Greenwell of Durham in 1854. Wright or his family created several well-known salmon flies, including the Garry Dog, Stoat's Tail, Durham Ranger and Thunder and Lightning (authentication is a little uncertain). Wright, who had three sons and four daughters, died at the age of 73 and is buried in Sprouston churchyard.

Wulff, Lee (1905–1991)   A remarkable man of many talents, and possibly the most influential angler of the twentieth-century. Wulff was born in Alaska, the son of a failed gold

prospector, and died age 86 at the controls of his light aircraft. Graduating as a civil engineer in 1926 he immediately changed direction to become an art student, working for a time in advertising, but the outdoors was his great love, and it was in that field that he became a writer, photographer, lecturer and film-maker.

Wulff's angling exploits are legendary, and his impact on every aspect of game fishing unparalleled. He is credited with the invention of the multi-pocketed anglers' waistcoat; his series of bushy flies – the famous Grey and White Wulffs date from 1929 whilst the Brown, Black and Grizzly came later – are some of the most widely used in the world and were the first to be made from animal hair; and the triangle-taper line, introduced in the mid-1980s, was his idea. But he would probably like to be remembered for his pioneering work as a conservationist and his early advocacy of catch and release. Never were Walton's words a more fitting epitaph, 'An excellent angler, and now with God'.

Wye (Derbyshire) The Wye, and its near neighbour, the Derwent, are small limestone streams with excellent-quality water and good weed growth which stand comparison with some of the chalk streams, though the fish are smaller and the banks less trimmed. The waters are clear, and the trout have to be stalked. Rainbow trout which breed in the Wye are generally fairly small fish of about a quarter to half a pound, though some are well over a pound. Chalk-stream patterns do well, but flies as small as 22, or even 24, are necessary in the height of summer. On many beats wading is prohibited. The fishing is dry fly only, and there is a bag limit of two brace. The Peacock Hotel at Rowsley and the Cavendish Hotel at Baslow on the Derwent can arrange fishing.

Wye (Herefordshire) A beautiful and powerful river that rises on the Welsh mountains of Plynlimon and winds through some spectacular scenery (Symond's Yat) to the Severn estuary near Chepstow. It has the reputation of being the finest salmon river in England and Wales and has produced some very big fish.

On 12 March 1923 Miss Doreen Davy, fishing the Cowpond Pool at Winforton, took a springer of 59½lb. Three years earlier a fly fisherman at Whitney was broken by a very large fish which a few days later was found decomposing on the bank;

one estimate suggested it might well have weighed nearly 80 lb when it was hooked. (In those days the average was around 12lb and a 30-pounder comparatively rare.)

The Wye is a lovely river to fish. On the lower reaches, boats are needed at times to cover the lies, but further up there is good bank fishing and wading. The most popular parts of the river are best avoided at holiday times and some weekends.

On the middle Wye a sink-tip-line is preferred for April and May but after that a floater. The flies are mostly doubles, from size 4 down to 10, especially yellow in coloured water. A middle-Wye angler, Mrs Nancy Whitlock, says:

> Tubes are not popular though I have some success with a lightly-dressed black hairwing tube, a half-inch long, in low water conditions. I personally prefer a single fly rather than a double. In a number of places it is necessary to 'work' the fly, a method frowned upon by many, including Scottish gillies, but assuredly more productive.

Working the fly, by bringing in line with the free hand as the fly swings round in the current has become popular in the south of England and in Wales. This may be because the rivers are not so fast as the Scottish rivers, or perhaps because they are more coloured or less disturbed by conflicting flows – whatever the reason, working the fly takes fish well. Possibly in most Scottish rivers the fly itself is adequately worked without a retrieve because of interlinking and diverging flows. All this is purely speculative, though.

Wylye   A beautiful little chalk stream rising at Maiden Bradley north of Mere, then running through Warminster, on to Heytesbury and Stapleford before joining the Nadder west of Salisbury. The Wylye is loved for its wild brown trout, though there is now a little stocking, and if ever rainbows escape from a fish farm, (as happens) they are hunted down by grimly determined men who are anxious to keep aliens from their cherished waters.

The native Wylye trout are cunning, and there is a good bit of weed for sanctuary, so that to take anything over a pound is regarded as skilful handling. Dry fly is pretty well universal but sometimes emerger patterns are used. There are mayfly (*E. danica*) and good hatches of olives and pale wateries. The black gnat abounds, and when spinners are on the water

Lunn's Particular seems to be in almost universal demand.

Anything over a pound is worth keeping, two pounders are rare, but *The Haig Guide to Trout Fishing in Britain* records that a trout of 7lb 2½oz was taken by Mr Carlton Cross at South Newton in May 1924. That would have been in the mayfly period, and if the ranunculus beds were thickening, as they would be, to land a 7lb fish was a remarkable achievement.

The Salisbury Anglers, the Piscatorial Society and the Wilton Club all have water.

Y & Z

Yellow Torrish   A splendid fully-dressed salmon fly for cloudy waters, originally with about nine feathers in the wing, now more like three or four:

Tag: silver tinsel and yellow silk
Tail: golden pheasant crest, up-turned
Butt: black ostrich herl
Lower body: black wool, ribbed silver, or sometimes just silver
Mid-body: black ostrich herl under a beard hackle of bright yellow feather fibres
Upper body: black wool, ribbed silver
Throat: beard hackle, fairly full, of yellow feather fibres
Wing: dark turkey tail or brown mallard, sided with grey drake with red, blue and yellow swan; or just red and yellow, topped with golden pheasant crest
Hook: almost any size

Yorkshire Trout Streams   No county in England can lay claim to such a variety of trout streams as Yorkshire. In the East Riding are the Costa, Driffield and Foston Becks (qq.v.) chalk streams comparable to the Hampshire rivers. In the North Riding are the big limestone rivers like the Wharfe (q.v.) and many others that hold large wild brown trout, like the Swale, Ure, Derwent, Aire and Nidd. The rivers of the Dales are great favourites for fishermen in the big northern industrial cities.

See also Wet-fly Fishing.

Zinger   An ingenious spring-loaded disc with a retractable cord (usually of about two feet in length); it clips onto the waistcoat or tackle bag. One may attach to it all manner of small tools – such as scissors, fly threader, disgorger, etc. – which are always to hand, yet conveniently out of the way when not needed. There are many different models on the market, including a variant (sometimes called a pin-on reel or

275

two-in-one retractor) which has two tightly wound cords, not unlike a telephone cable, which retracts into a tube when released.

Zulu   A black palmer trout fly, named after the head-dresses worn by warriors of Chief Cetawayo, the Zulu king who defeated the British during one of the South African wars of the 1870s.

Body: black wool, ribbed with fine flat silver tinsel
Tail: short stub of bright scarlet wool
Hackle: black cock, wound thinly from head to tail, held down by the silver ribbing
Hook: 14 –10, larger for sea-trout

The Blue Zulu is a variation, with a blue hackle in front of the black, or by itself, and sometimes with a blue wool body as well. An attractive looking fly sometimes used for dapping.

Select Bibliography

Adamson, W. A., *Lake and Loch Fishing for Salmon and Sea Trout*, A & C Black, 1961

Ade, Robin, *The Trout and Salmon Handbook*, Christopher Helm, 1989

Aldam, W. H., *A Quaint Treatyse on Flees and Artyfichall Flee-Making*, 1875

Andrews, Ted, *Basic Fly Tying in Pictures*, Stanley Paul, 1983, paperback 1992

Ashley-Cooper, John, *The Great Salmon Rivers of Scotland*, Gollancz, 1980, Witherby, 1987
 – *A Salmon Fisher's Odyssey*, Witherby, 1982, FCL, 1996
 – *A Ring of Wessex Waters*, Witherby, 1986

Bainbridge, G.C., *The Fly-fisher's Guide*, 1816

Bainbridge, W.G., *The Fly-fisher's Guide to Aquatic Flies and their Imitations*, A & C Black, 1936

Baird, R.D., *A Trout Rose*, *c.* 1948

Balfour Kinnear, G.P.R., *Flying Salmon*, Longman, 1937
 – *Spinning Salmon*, Longman,1938
 – *Catching Salmon and Sea Trout*, Nelson, 1958
 – *A Boy Goes Trouting*, Nelson, 1959

Barker, Thomas, *The Art of Angling*, 1651

Barr, David (ed), *Haig Guide to Salmon Fishing in Scotland*, Collins,1981
 – (ed) *Haig Guide to Trout Fishing in Britain*, Collins, 1983

Bates, J.D., *Streamer Fly Tying and Fishing*, Stackpole, USA, 1950
 – *Atlantic Salmon Flies and Fishing*, Stackpole, USA, 1970
 – *The Art of the Atlantic Salmon Fly*, Stackpole, USA, 1987, Swan Hill, 1990
 – and Pamela Bates Richards, *Fishing Atlantic Salmon: The Flies and the Patterns*, Stackpole, USA, 1996

Beever, John, *Practical Fly Fishing*, 1849

Behrendt, Alex, *The Management of Angling Waters*, Andre Deutsch, 1977

Bentley, H.T.B. *Loch Fishing for Trout: An Introduction*, Oliver & Boyd, 1963

Bernard, J., *Fly Dressing*, 1932

Berners, Dame Juliana, *The Treatyse of Fysshynge wyth an Angle*, 1496

Bickerdyke, John, *The Book of the All-Round Angler*, Bazaar, 1888, 1900, 1912, 1992
Bingham, Charles, *Salmon & Sea Trout Fishing*, Batsford, 1988
   – *The Game Fishing Year*, Batsford, 1989
   – *The River Test*, Witherby, 1990
   – *Chalk Stream Salmon & Sea Trout Fishing*, Swan Hill, 1993
   – *Trout, Salmon & Sea Trout Fishing*, Blandford, 1994
   – *Salmon Fishing on Small Rivers*, Blandford, 1994
   – *Sea Trout: how to catch them*, Swan Hill, 1998
   – (with Tony Allen), *Freshwater Fishing for Beginners*, Swan Hill, 1998
Blacker, William, *Catechism of Fly Making*, 1843
   – *The Art of Fly Making*, 1855
Bluett, J., *Sea Trout and Occasional Salmon*, Cassell, 1946
Bowlker, Richard, *The Art of Angling*, Birmingham, *c*.1746, ninth edition, Ludlow, 1826
Bridges, Antony, *Modern Salmon Fishing*, A & C Black, 1939
Bridgett, R. C., *Dry-fly Fishing*, Herbert Jenkins, 1922, 1929
   – *By Loch and Stream*, Herbert Jenkins, 1922
   – *Loch Fishing in Theory and Practice*, Herbert Jenkins, 1924
   – *Tight Lines*, Herbert Jenkins, 1926
   – *Sea Trout Fishing*, Herbert Jenkins, 1929
Briggs, E.E., *Angling and Art in Scotland*, Longman, 1908
Broughton, R. B., *Grayling: the Fourth Game Fish*, Crowood, 1989
Brookes, Richard, *The Art of Angling*, 1740
Buckland, John and Arthur Oglesby, *A Guide to Salmon Flies*, Crowood, 1990
Bucknall, Geoffrey, *Fly Fishing Tactics on Stillwater*, Muller, 1966
Buller, Fred, *Pike*, Macdonald, 1971
   – *Pike and the Pike Angler*, Stanley Paul, 1981
   – (and Hugh Falkus), *Freshwater Fishing*, Macdonald & Janes, 1975, paperback 1977, second edn Stanley Paul, 1988, 1989, paperback 1990, Cresset Press, 1992, 1993, Grange Books, 1994, 1998
   – (with Richard Walker, Fred J. Taylor and Hugh Falkus), *Successful Angling*, Stanley Paul, 1977,
Burrard, Major G., *Fly Tying Principles and Practice*, Herbert Jenkins, 1940
Carter Platts, W., *Trout Streams: Their Management and Improvement*, Field Press, 1927, 1934
   – *Modern Trout Fishing*, A & C Black, 1938
   – *Grayling Fishing*, A & C Black, 1939
Chaytor, A.H., *Letters to a Salmon Fisher's Sons*, 1910, 1919, 1925, 1936, 1948, 1992
Chetham, James, *The Angler's Vade Mecum*, 1681, second edn 1689, third edn 1700
Cholmondely-Pennell H., *The Angler-Naturalist: A Popular History of*

British Freshwater Fish, 1863
 – *The Modern Practical Angler*, 1870, fourth edn 1884
 – (ed) *Fishing: Salmon and Trout* (Badminton Library),
   1885, 1886, 1889, 1903
 – (ed) *Fishing: Pike and other Coarse Fish* (Badminton Library),
   1885, 1886, 1889, 1903
 – *The Sporting Fish of Great Britain*, 1886
 – *Modern Improvements in Fishing Tackle and Fish Hooks*, 1887
Church, Bob, *Reservoir Trout Fishing*, Cassell,1977, second edn A & C
 Black, 1983, 1984
 – *Bob Church's Guide to Trout Flies*, Crowood, 1987, 1997
 – *Bob Church's Guide to New Fly Patterns*, Crowood, 1993
Clarke, Brian, *The Pursuit of Stillwater Trout*, A & C Black, 1975
 – (and Goddard, John), *The Trout and the Fly*, Benn, 1988
Collyer, David J., *Fly-Dressing I*, David & Charles, 1975
 – *Fly-Dressing II*, David & Charles, 1981
Colquhoun, John, *The Moor and the Loch*, 1840, fourth edn 1878
Cotton, Charles, *The Compleat Angler*, 1676
Crossley, A., *The Floating Line for Salmon and Sea Trout*, Methuen, 1939
Cutcliffe, H. C., *The Art of Trout Fishing on Rapid Streams*, 1863.
 Facsimile of first edn, Porcupines, Barnstaple 1970, Limited edn,
 Chevington Press, 1982

Dawes, Mike, *The Fly Tier's Manual*, CollinsWillow 1985, 1992, 1995,
 1998
 – *The Fly Tier's Companion*, Swan Hill, 1989
Dewar, G.A.B., *The Book of the Dry Fly*, 1897
 – *In Pursuit of the Trout*, 1898
 – *The South Country Streams*, 1898
Drewett, John, *Hardy Brothers: The Masters, the Men and Their Reels*,
 privately published, 1998.
Dunne, J. W., *Sunshine and the Dry Fly*, A & C Black, 1924
Durnford, Rev. Richard, *The Fishing Diary: 1809-1819*, Simpkin, 1911
Edmonds, Harfield H. and Lee, Norman N., *Brook and River Trouting*,
 privately published, 1916, facsimile 1980, 1997
Edwards, Capt T.L. and Eric Horsfall Turner, *The Angler's Cast*,
 Herbert Jenkins, 1960
Elder, Frank, *The Book of the Hackle,* Scottish Academic Press, 1979
Ensom, Edward, *Dry-Fly Fishing for Chub, Dace, Roach and Rudd*, by
 'Faddist', 1946
Falkus, Hugh, *Sea Trout Fishing*, Witherby, 1962, 1971, 1975
 – *Salmon Fishing*, Witherby, 1984
 – *Spey Casting: A New Technique*, Excellent Press, 1994
 – (and Malcolm Greenhalgh), *The Salmon and Sea Trout Fisher's
   Handbook*, Excellent Press, 1998
 – (and Fred Buller), *Freshwater Fishing*, Macdonald, revised edn,
   Stanley Paul, 1998

Farson, Negley, *Going Fishing*, Country Life, 1942, 1943, second edn 1944, 1946, 1981, 1983, FCL, 1995, 1996

Fernie, F., *Dry-Fly Fishing in Border Waters*, A & C Black, 1912

Fisher, Major A.T., *Rod and River, or Fly Fishing for Salmon, Trout and Grayling*, 1892

Fitzgibbon, E., *Handbook of Angling*, by 'Ephemera', 1847

Fitzgibbon, E., *The Book of the Salmon*, by 'Ephemera', 1850

Fogg, W.S.Roger, *The Art of the Wet Fly*, A & C Black, 1979
　　– *A Handbook of North Country Flies*, Old Vicarage Publications, 1988

Foster, David, *The Scientific Angler*, 1882, 1883, fifth edn 1890

Francis, Francis, *A Book on Angling*, 1867, 1872, 1880, 1885, 1920, 1995, 1996 (*see also* Waltham, James)

Frodin, Mikael, *Classic Salmon Flies, History and Patterns*, Lochar, 1991

Frost, W.E and M.E.Brown, *New Naturalist Monograph: The Trout*, Collins, 1967

Gaidy, Charles, *Ephemeras, Mayflies, Naturals and Artificials*, 1986

Garrison, Everett and Hoagy B Carmichael, *A Master's Guide to Building a Bamboo Fly Rod*, 1977

Gathercole, Peter, *The Handbook of Fly Tying*, Crowood, 1989

Gierach, John, *Where the Trout are all as Long as Your Arm*, Robert Hale, 1999

Gilbert, H. A., *The Tale of a Wye Fisherman*, Methuen 1939, 1953

Gill, Emlyn M., *Practical Dry-Fly Fishing*, Scribners, New York, USA, 1912

Gingrich, Arnold, *The Fishing in Print: A Guided Tour Through Five Centuries of Angling Literature, English and American*, Winchester Press, USA, 1974

Goddard, John (ed), *Trout Fly Recognition*, A & C Black, 1966
　　– *Trout Flies of Stillwater*, A & C Black, 1969
　　– *Stillwater Flies, How and When to Fish Them*, Benn, 1982
　　– *John Goddard's Waterside Guide*, Unwin Hyman 1988, 1991, 1997
　　– *The Trout Flies of Britain and Europe*, A & C Black, 1991
　　– *John Goddard's Trout-fishing Techniques*, A & C Black, 1996
　　– (and Brian Clarke), *The Trout and the Fly*, Benn, 1988

Gordon, Theodore, *The Complete Fly Fisherman: The Notes and Letters of Theodore Gordon*, 1947

Granby, Marquess of, and others, *Fur, Feather and Fin Series: The Trout*, 1898

Gray, L. R, N., *Torridge Fishery*, Nicholas Kaye, 1957

Green, G. Garrow, *Trout Fishing in Brooks*, Routledge, 1920

Greene, Harry Plunkett, *Where the Bright Waters Meet*, 1924, 1946, 1969, 1972, 1983, FCL, 1992, 1998

Greenhalgh, Malcolm, *Trout Fishing in Rivers*, Witherby, 1987
　　– *Lake, Loch and Reservoir Fishing*, A & C Black, 1987
　　– *The Complete Salmon Fisher Volume I: The Life of the Salmon*, Cassell, 1995

    – *The Complete Salmon Fisher Volume II: Salmon on the Fly*, Cassell, 1996

    – *The Complete Flyfisher's Handbook*, Dorling Kindersley, 1998

Greer, Ron, *Ferox Trout and Arctic Charr*, Swan Hill Press, 1995

Grey, Sir Edward, *Fly Fishing*, Dent 1899, second edn 1899, third edn 1901, revised and enlarged edn, 1930, numerous reprints, 1990, FCL edn, 1992, 1997

Grimble, Augustus, *The Salmon Rivers of Scotland*, Kegan Paul, 1902, 1913

    – *The Salmon Rivers of Ireland*, Kegan Paul, 1903, 1913

    – *The Salmon and Sea Trout Rivers of England and Wales*, Kegan Paul, 1904, 1913

Haig-Brown, Roderick L., *A River Never Sleeps*, Collins, 1948

Hale, Capt J.H., *How to Tie Salmon Flies*, 1892, 1919, 1930

Halford, Frederic M., *Floating Flies and How to Dress Them*, 1886, 1974, FCL, 1993

    – *Dry Fly Fishing in Theory and Practice*, Sampson Low 1889, 1902, 1989, FCL, 1994

    – *Making a Fishery*, Horace Cox, 1895, 1902

    – *Dry Fly Entomology*, Vinton,1897, 1902

    – *An Angler's Autobiography*, Vinton, 1903, FCL, 1998

    – *The Modern Development of the Dry Fly*, Routledge, 1910

    – *The Dry Fly Man's Handbook*, Routledge, 1913

Hall, John Inglis, *Fishing a Highland Stream* [The Truim], Putnam, 1960, Viking, 1987

Hamilton, Edward, *Recollections of Fly Fishing for Salmon, Trout and Grayling*, 1884

Hampton, J. Fitzgerald, *Modern Angling Bibliography: Books Published on Angling, Fisheries, Fish Culture from 1881 to 1945*, Herbert Jenkins, 1947

Hancock, C.V., *Rod in Hand: An Angler's Moods and Memories*, 1958

Hanna, Thomas J., *Fly Fishing in Ireland*, Witherby, 1933

Harding, E. W., *The Flyfisher and the Trout's Point of View*, Seeley Service, 1931

Hardy, James Leighton, *The House the Hardy Brothers Built*, FCL, 1998

Harris, J. R., *An Angler's Entomology*, Collins New Naturalist series 1952, 1956, 1966, 1996

Hartley, J. R., *Fly Fishing*, Stanley Paul, 1991

    – *J. R. Hartley Casts Again*, Stanley Paul, 1992

Headley, Stan, *Trout and Salmon Flies of Scotland*, Merlin Unwin, 1998

    – *The New Trout Fishing Guide to Orkney*, privately published, 1998

Henzell, H, P., *The Art and Craft of Loch Fishing*, Philip Allan, 1937

Henzell, H, P., *Fishing for Sea Trout*, A & C Black, 1949

Hewitt, E. R., *Secrets of the Salmon*, Scribner, New York, 1922

    – *Telling on the Trout*, Scribner, New York 1926

    – *A Trout and Salmon Fisherman for Seventy-five Years*, Scribner, New York, 1948

Hill, F., *Salmon Fishing with Greased Line on Dee, Don and Earn*, Chapman & Hall, 1948

Hill, Raymond, *Wings and Hackle: A Pot-pourri of Fly Fishing for Trout and Grayling*, Hutchinson, 1933

Hills, John Waller, *A Summer on the Test*, Philip Allan, 1924, 1930, 1941, 1972, FCL, 1996
– *A History of Fly Fishing For Trout*, Philip Allan, 1921, 1973, FCL, 1995
– *River Keeper: The Life of William James Lunn*, Geoffrey Bles 1934, 1947, FCL 1998

Hobbs, A. Edward, *Trout of the Thames*, Herbert Jenkins, *c*. 1940

Hodgson, W. Earl., *Salmon Fishing*, A & C Black, 1906, 1927
– *Trout Fishing*, A & C Black, 1904, 1908, 1930

Holiday, F. W., *River Fishing For Sea Trout*, Herbert Jenkins, 1960

Hughes-Parry, *Fishing Fantasy: A Salmon Fisher's Notebook*, Eyre & Spottiswoode, 1949, second edn 1955

Ivens, T. C., *Still Water Fly Fishing*, Andre Deutsch, 1952, 1961, 1970

Jackson, John, *The Practical Fly-Fisher; More Particularly for Grayling or Umber*, 1854, 1880

Jacques, David, *Fisherman's Fly*, A & C Black, 1965
– *The Development of Modern Stillwater Fishing*, A & C Black, 1974

Jardine, Charles, *Dark Pools: The Dry Fly and the Nymph*, Crowood, 1991
– *The Sotheby's Guide to Fly Fishing for Trout*, Dorling Kindersley, 1991
– *Small Water Trout Fishing*, Batsford, 1994

Jones, J.W., *New Naturalist Monograph: The Salmon*, Collins, 1959

Kelson, George M., *The Salmon Fly*, 1895, 1979, FCL 1995

Kingsmill Moore, T. C., *A Man May Fish*, Herbert Jenkins, 1960, revised edn Colin Smythe, 1979

Kite, Oliver, *Nymph Fishing in Practice*, Herbert Jenkins, 1963
– *A Fisherman's Diary*, Andre Deutsch, 1969

Knowles, Derek, *Salmon on a Dry Fly*, Witherby, 1987

Kreh, Lefty, *Flyfishing in Saltwater*, Lyons & Burford, USA, 1974, 1998

La Branche, George M.L., *The Fly and Fast Water*, 1914
– *Salmon and the Dry Fly*, 1924

Lane, Joscelyn, *Lake and Loch Fishing For Trout*, Seeley Service, 1955

Lapsley, Peter, *The Bankside Book of Stillwater Trout Flies*, Benn, 1978, 1983
– *Stillwater Trout Flies*, A & C Black, 1978
– *Trout From Stillwaters*, A & C Black, 1981
– *River Trout Flyfishing*, Unwin Hyman, 1988
– (ed), *The Complete Flyfisher*, Stanley Paul, 1990
– *Fly Fishing for Trout*, Stanley Paul, 1992

Lawrie, W. H., *Border River Angling*, Oliver & Boyd, 1939, second edn 1946

    – *The Book of the Rough Stream Nymph*, Oliver and Boyd, 1947
    – *Scottish Trout Flies*, Muller, 1966
    – *A Reference Book of English Trout Flies*, Pelham,1967
    – *English and Welsh Trout Flies: Essays and Analysis*, Muller, 1967
    – *All Fur Flies and How to Dress Them*, Pelham, 1967
    – *International Trout Flies*, Muller, 1969
Lee, Art, *Fishing Dry Flies For Trout on Rivers and Streams*, Atheneum, New York,1983
Lunn, Mick with Graham-Ranger, Clive, *A Particular Lunn*, 1990, 1991

Mackie, Gordon, *Fly Leaves and Waterside Sketches*, Robert Hale, 1998
McCaskie, H. B., *The Guileless Trout*, 1950
McCaskie, Norman, *Fishing - My Life's Hobby*, Falcon Press, 1950
McClelland, H.G., *The Trout Fly-Dresser's Cabinet of Devices, or How to Tie Flies for Trout and Grayling*, Low 1899, 1905, 1919, 1927
McLaren, Charles, *Fishing For Salmon*, John Donald, Edinburgh, 1977
Magee, Leslie, *Fly Fishing: The North Country Tradition*, Smith Settle, 1994
Malone, E. J., *Irish Trout and Salmon Flies*, Colin Smythe 1981, FCL, 1993, 1998
Marinaro, Vincent, *A Modern Dry-Fly Code*, Putnam, New York, 1950, 1970, FCL 1996, 1998
    – *In the Ring of the Rise*, Lyons & Burford, New York, 1976, 1996, 1997, Robert Hale, 1999
Marshall, Howard, *Reflections on a River*, Witherby, 1967
Martin, The Rev James, *The Angler's Guide*, 1854
Mead, Tom, *Essentials of Fly Fishing*, Robert Hale, 1995
Merwin, John, (ed) *Stillwater Trout*, Nick Lyons, New York, 1980
Migel, J. Michael (ed), *The Masters on the Dry Fly*, Nick Lyons, New York, 1977, Robert Hale, 1994
    – *The Masters on the Nymph*, Nick Lyons, New York 1979, Robert Hale, 1994
Moore, John (ed), *Best Fishing Stories*, Faber, 1965
Morgan, Paul (ed), *Saltwater Flyfishing: Britain and Northern Europe*, Coch-y-Bonddu Books, 1998
Mottram, J. C., *Fly Fishing: Some New Arts and Mysteries*, Field & Queen, 1915,1921, FCL, 1994

Nelson, William, *Fishing in Eden*, 1922
Netboy, Anthony, *The Atlantic Salmon: A Vanishing Species*, Faber, 1968
    – *Salmon: The World's Most Harassed Fish*, Deutsch, 1980

Oatts, Col H.A., *Loch Trout*, Herbert Jenkins, 1958
Ogborne, Chris, *Competition Trout Fishing*, Crowood, 1988
    – *Advanced Stillwater Flyfishing*, David & Charles, 1993
Ogden, J., *Ogden on Fly Tying*, 1879, 1887

Oglesby, Arthur, *Salmon*, 1971, 1976, 1986
 – *Fly Fishing for Salmon and Sea Trout*, Crowood, 1986
O'Reilly, Pat, *Tactical Flyfishing for Trout and Sea Trout on River and Stream*, Crowood, 1990
 – (with Derek Hoskin) *An Introduction to Fly Fishing*, Crowood, 1992
 – *River Trout Fishing*, Crowood, 1993
 – *Matching the Hatch: Stillwater, River and Stream*, Swan Hill, 1997
O'Reilly, Peter, *Trout and Salmon Loughs of Ireland*, Unwin Hyman, 1987, Merlin Unwin, 1992, third edn *Loughs of Ireland: A Flyfisher's Guide*,1998
 – *Trout and Salmon Rivers of Ireland*, Merlin Unwin 1991, fourth edn *Rivers of Ireland: A Flyfisher's Guide*, 1998
 – *Trout and Salmon Flies of Ireland*, Merlin Unwin, 1995
Overfield, Donald, *Famous Flies and Their Originators*, A & C Black, 1972
 – G. E. M. Skues: *The Way of a Man With a Trout*, Benn, 1977

Parton, Steve, *Boatfishing for Trout*, Allen & Unwin, 1983
Patterson, Neil, *Chalk Stream Chronicle*, Merlin Unwin, 1995
Phillips, Ernest, *Trout in Lakes and Reservoirs*, Longmans Green, 1914
Price, Taff, *Lures For Game, Coarse and Sea Fishing*, A & C Black, 1972
 – *Rough Stream Trout Flies*, A & C Black, 1976
 – *Stillwater Flies*, volumes 1-3, Benn, 1979 - 1981
 – *Fly Patterns: An International Guide*, Ward Lock, 1986, 1992, 1997
 – *Angler's Sedge*, Blandford, 1989
 – *Tying & Fishing the Sedge*, Blandford, 1994
 – *Tying & Fishing the Nymph*, Blandford, 1995
Pritt, T. E., *Yorkshire Trout Flies*, Leeds 1885, second edn (as *North Country Trout Flies*) 1886, FCL, 1998
 – *The Book of the Grayling*, 1888
 – *An Angler's Basket*, 1896
Proper, Datus, *What the Trout Said*, Knopf, New York, 1982, 1989, 1993
Pryce-Tannatt, T.E., *How to Dress Salmon Flies*, 1914, 1948, 1977, 1991, 1997
Rabley, Charles, *Devonshire Trout Fishing*, privately published, *c.* 1910
Radcliffe, William, *Fishing From the Earliest Times*, John Murray, 1921, 1926
Ransome, Arthur, *Rod and Line*, Cape 1929, 1980, FCL, 1998
 – *Mainly About Fishing*, A & C Black, 1959, FCL, 1994
Restall, Eric (ed), *An Angler's Quotation Book*, Robert Hale, 1993
Righyni, R. V., *Salmon Taking Times*, Macdonald, 1965, 1996
 – *Grayling*, Macdonald, 1968, Swan Hill, 1996
 – *Advanced Salmon Fishing*, Macdonald, 1973, 1977
Ritz, Charles, *A Fly Fisher's Life*, Reinhardt, 1959, 1969, 1972, Robert

Hale,1996

Robb, James, *Notable Angling Literature*, Herbert Jenkins, *c.* 1947

Roberts, John, *The Grayling Angler*, Witherby 1982, 1999
 – *Illustrated Dictionary of Trout Flies*, Allen & Unwin, 1986,
   second edn Harper Collins, 1995
 – *To Rise a Trout: Dry Fly Fishing for Trout on Rivers and Streams*,
   Crowood, 1988, 1994
 – *A Guide to River Trout Flies*, Crowood, 1989, 1995
 – *Trout on a Nymph*, Crowood, 1991
 – *The World's Best Trout Flies*, Boxtree 1994

Robson, Kenneth, *Robson's Guide: Stillwater Trout Flies*, Beekay, 1985
 – *The Best of G. E. M. Skues*, A & C Black, 1998

Ronalds, Alfred *The Fly-Fisher's Entomology*, London, 1836, 1839,
 1844, 1849, 1862, 1883, tenth edn 1901, edn de luxe, Liverpool,
 1913, 1921, FCL, 1995

Samuel, William, *The Arte of Angling*, 1577, Princeton University
 Library 1958, FCL, 1999

Sandison, Bruce, *Tales of the Loch*, Mainstream, 1990

Sawyer, Frank, *Keeper of the Stream*, A & C Black 1952, 1954, 1985
 – *Nymphs and the Trout*, Stanley Paul, 1958, 1970, 1977, 1979,
   1981
 – *Keeper of the Stream* and *Nymphs and the Trout*, combined edn,
   FCL, 1997
 – and Sidney Vines, *Frank Sawyer: Man of the Riverside*, Allen &
   Unwin, 1984, 1987

Schwiebert, Ernest, *Nymphs: A Complete Guide to Naturals and
 Imitations*, Winchester, USA, 1973

Schwiebert, Ernest, *Trout*, Truman Tally, USA 1978, 1994
 – *Matching the Hatch*, Macmillan, 1955

'Scott, Jock', *The Art of Salmon Fishing*, Witherby, 1933
 – *Greased Line Fishing for Salmon: The Methods of
 A.H.E.Wood of Glassel*, Seeley Service, 1935, third edn
 1937
 – *Fine and Far Off: Salmon Fishing Methods in Practice*, Seeley
   Service, 1952
 – *Seatrout Fishing*, Lonsdale Library, 1969

Scrope, William, *Days and Nights of Salmon Fishing on the Tweed*, 1843,
 1885, 1898, 1921, FCL, 1991, 1995

Shipley, William, *The True Treatise on the Art of Fly Fishing*, 1838

Sheehan, Paul, *Irish Game Fishing*, Swan Hill, 1997

Sheringham, H. T., *Trout Fishing Memories and Morals*, Hodder &
 Stoughton, 1920
 – (and John Moore), *The Book of the Fly Rod*, 1931
 – (and G.E.Studdy), *Fishing: Its Cause, Treatment and Cure*, Philip
   Allan, 1925, FCL, 1996

Shipley, William, *The True Treatise on the Art of Fly Fishing*, 1838

Skues, G. E. M., *Minor Tactics of the Chalk Stream and Kindred Studies*, A & C Black 1910, 1914, third edn1924, 1950, FCL ,1995
- *The Way of a Trout With a Fly and Some Further Studies in Minor Tactics*, A & C Black, 1921, second edn 1928, third edn 1935, fourth edn 1949, 1967, 1973, 1977, FCL,1993
- *Side Lines, Sight Lines and Reflections: Fugitive Papers of a Chalk Stream Angler*, Seeley Service, 1932, FCL, 1996
- *Nymph Fishing For Chalk Stream Trout*, A & C Black, 1939, 1960, 1979, FCL, 1997
- *Itchen Memories*, Herbert Jenkins, 1951, second edn Robert Hale, 1999
- *Silk, Fur and Feather: The Trout-Fly Dresser's Year*, Fishing Gazette, 1950, FCL, 1993

Spencer, Sydney, *The Art of Lake Fishing*, Witherby, 1934
- *Salmon and Sea Trout in Wild Places*, Witherby, 1968
- *Newly from the Sea: Fishing for Salmon and Seatrout*, Witherby, 1969
- *Ways of Fishing: Trout, Salmon and Seatrout*, Witherby, 1972
- *Game Fishing Tactics*, Witherby, 1974

Stewart, Tom, *Fifty Popular Flies*, Ernest Benn, four volumes 1969–70

Stewart, W. C., *The Practical Angler*, Edinburgh 1857, second edn 1857, third edn 1857, seventh edn 1877, new edn 1907, new edn 1938, centenary edn 1958, FCL, 1996

Stuart, Hamish, *Lochs and Loch Fishing*, Chapman & Hall, 1899

Sutherland, Douglas, *The Salmon Book*, Collins, 1982

Tabory, Lou, *Inshore Fly Fishing*, Lyons & Burford, New York, USA, 1992

Taverner, Eric, *Trout Fishing from all Angles*, Lonsdale Library, 1929, 1933
- *Salmon Fishing*, Lonsdale Library, 1931, 1935, 1948,

Templeton, Robin G. (ed.) *Freshwater Fisheries Management*, Severn-Trent Water, 1984

Theakston, M., *British Angling Flies*, 1883, 1888

Traherne, Major John P., *Salmon Fishing with the Fly*, 1885, 1995

Venables, Robert, Col, *The Experienced Angler*, 1662, facsimile edn Antrobus,1969

Veniard, John, *Fly Dresser's Guide*, A & C Black 1952, 1953, 1960, 1964, second edn 1966, third edn 1968, fourth edn 1970, 1972, 1973, 1976, 1977
- *Further Guide to Fly Dressing*, A & C Black, 1964, second edn 1972, 1975, 1977, 1980, 1985
- *Reservoir and Lake Flies*, A & C Black, 1970, with addenda 1979
- *Fly Tying Problems and Their Answers* (and Donald Downs), A & C Black, 1970, 1973, 1975, 1977

    – (and Donald Downs) *Fly Tying Development and Progress*,
      A & C Black, 1973

    – (and Donald Downs) *Modern Fly Tying Techniques*, A & C
      Black, 1979, second edn, 1979

    – *Fly-Dressing Materials*, A & C Black, 1977, 1979

    – *500 Fly Dressings in Colour*, A & C Black, 1980, 1981, 1983, 1984,
      1985, 1986

Vickers, Ken, *A Review of Irish Salmon and Salmon Fisheries*, Atlantic
Salmon Trust, 1998

Voss Bark, Anne (ed), *West Country Fly Fishing*, Batsford, 1983,
second edn Robert Hale, 1998

Voss Bark, Conrad, *The Dry Fly: Progress Since Halford*, Merlin Unwin,
1996

    – *Fishing for Lake Trout with Fly and Nymph*, Witherby, 1972

    – *Encyclopaedia of Fly Fishing*, Batsford, 1986

    – *A History of Fly Fishing*, Merlin Unwin, 1992

    – *A Fly on the Water*, Allan & Unwin, 1986

    – *Fly Fishing with Conrad Voss Bark*, Unwin Hyman, 1989

Wakeford, Jacqueline, *Flytying Techniques*, Benn, 1980

    – *Flytying Tools and Materials*, A & C Black, 1991

Walker, C. F., *Trout Flies: A Discussion and a Dictionary*, A & C Black,
1932

    – *Chalk Stream Flies*, A & C Black, 1953

    – *Brown Trout and Dry Fly*, Seeley Service, 1955

    – *An Angler's Odyssey and Some Further Riverside Reflections*,
      1956

    – *Fly Tying as an Art*, Herbert Jenkins, 1957

    – *Lake Flies and their Imitation*, Herbert Jenkins, 1960

    – *The Complete Flyfisher*, Herbert Jenkins, 1968

Waltham, James, *Classic Salmon Flies: the Francis Francis Collection*,
1983

Walker, Richard, *Fly Dressing Innovations*, Benn, 1974

    – *Dick Walker's Trout Fishing*, edited by Peter Maskell, David &
      Charles, 1982

    – *Dick Walker's Trout Fishing: on Rivers and Stillwaters*, Swan Hill,
      1997

Walton, Izaak, *The Compleat Angler*, 1653, third edn 1661, fifth edn
(with Charles Cotton's contribution of fly fishing) 1676, Moses
Brown edn 1750, Hawkins edn 1760, Bagster edn 1808, Tegg edn
1824, William Pickering edn 1836, Washbourne edn 1842, Griggs
facsimile of first edn 1882, Rennie edn 1883, Nimmo edn 1885, Lea
and Dove edn, 1888, John Major edn 1889, Lowell (USA) edn
1889, Caradoc Press edn 1905, Hankey edn 1913, James Thorp
edn 1925, Rackham edn 1931, Penguin paperback 1939, Folio
Society edn 1949, Nottingham Court Press facsimile1983, FCL 1993

West, Leonard, *The Natural Trout Fly and Its Imitation*, privately pub, St Helens 1912, second edn 1921

Wiggin, Maurice, *The Angler's Bedside Book*, Batsford, 1965
    – *Teach Yourself Fly Fishing*, English Universities Press, 1958

Williams, Courtney, *A Dictionary of Trout Flies*, A & C Black 1949, 1950, 1961, 1965, 1978

Woolley, Roger, *Modern Trout Fly Dressings*, Fishing Gazette, 1932
    – *The Fly-Fisher's Flies*, Fishing Gazette, 1938

Wulff, Lee, *Lee Wulff on Trout Flies*, Stackpole, USA, 1980
    – *Trout on a Fly*, Lyons & Burford, New York, USA, 1986
    – *The Compleat Lee Wulff*, Truman Tally Books, USA, 1989
    – *Salmon on a Fly*, Simon & Schuster, USA, 1992

Young, Andrew, *Angler's Guide*, Edinburgh, 1857

Younger, John, *River Angling for Salmon and Trout*, 1840, 1995